REPORT OF THE TASK FORCE
ON THE
TRAVELLING COMMUNITY

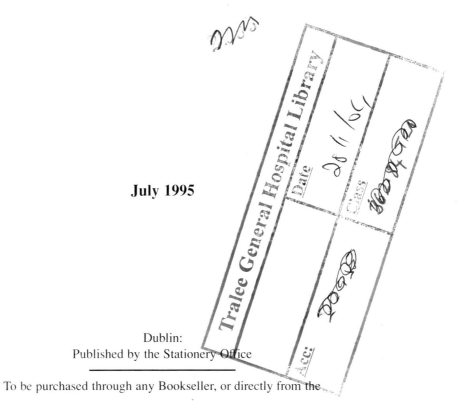

July 1995

Dublin:
Published by the Stationery Office

To be purchased through any Bookseller, or directly from the

Government Publications Sales Office
Sun Alliance House
Molesworth Street
Dublin 2.

£10.00

Pn. 1726

ISBN 0-7076-1630-1
© Government of Ireland 1995

P.42446 Gr.30–02 750 7/95 Brunswick Press Ltd.

CONTENTS

PREFACE

In June 1993, I was delighted to be appointed as a member of the Task Force on the Travelling Community. I also felt honoured when, in January, 1995, I replaced Deputy Liz McManus as Chairperson of the Task Force following her appointment as Minister of State at the Department of the Environment.

The two year period since the establishment of the Task Force has involved a substantial amount of work for the Task Force members, their substitutes and the Secretariat. In addition to the publication of an Interim Progress Report in January 1994, this work included the preparation of submissions to the Minister for Equality and Law Reform on the proposed Equal Status legislation and to the Minister for Education and the National Education Convention on education and training for Travellers.

During the course of its deliberations, the Task Force invited submissions from the general public and from interested organisations. A number of research papers were commissioned to assist the Task Force in its work and a large number of papers were also drafted by Task Force members and the Secretariat. I would like to express appreciation to all those who contributed to this process. These contributions were all studied in detail and greatly assisted the Task Force in arriving at its conclusions and recommendations.

By the time I assumed the Chair of the Task Force, most of the ground work had been completed. I would particularly like to compliment the former Chairperson on her hard work and dedication. Her tact and diplomacy were often tested, especially in the earlier meetings when positions were being established and points of view were forcefully being pressed. She encouraged a spirit of tolerance, understanding and compromise which runs through the Report. My job was to oversee the synthesis or bringing together of the text of the Report.

It was inevitable that given the diverse interests represented on the Task Force, such as Travellers, Traveller organisations, public representatives and representatives of statutory bodies, differing opinions were voiced at Task Force meetings. As members of the Task Force represent different strands in Irish society, so too, the differing opinions reflect the debate on Traveller issues within the wider community, a debate which was particularly strong during the time the Task Force was carrying out its work. Four members of the Task Force while endorsing the main thrust and recommendations of this Report felt that a comment was necessary on nomadism and the Traveller lifestyle.

However, there is universal agreement that the Traveller community in Ireland today should no longer be obliged to live in conditions which are reminiscent of refugee camps. What is proposed in the Report of the Task Force is an integrated package; without the provision of adequate accommodation, improvements in educational and health provision will be difficult to undertake. Likewise, it is hoped that with encouragement, Travellers will be able to participate more fully in our economic development both through the growth of the Traveller economy and by greater participation in the mainstream labour force and that the natural talent of Travellers to be self reliant and resourceful will be encouraged.

In our recommendations we propose a greater role for Travellers in decision making. This will bring with it challenges for the leaders among the Traveller community. For too long,

Travellers have been seen as passive victims of Irish society. The road towards being full participants in that society is not going to be either smooth or straight. It is very important therefore, that support is provided for the leaders who are emerging from within the Traveller community.

Rathkeale, County Limerick needs an in-depth study of its economy; inter-community relationships; accommodation and environmental problems. Consequently co-ordinated action is required to assist the town's development.

I would like to express my appreciation to Mervyn Taylor, T.D., Minister for Equality and Law Reform who appointed me. My sincere thanks also to all the members of the Task Force whose knowledge, co-operation and tolerance were important in the compilation of this Report.

Finally, thanks to the staff of the Task Force Secretariat from the Department of Equality and Law Reform, namely, David Costello, his predecessor Pat Wylie, May McCarthy, Irene O'Keeffe, but above all to Lucinda Mac Mahon whose patience and good humour never faltered.

Senator Mary Kelly
Chairperson

MESSAGE FROM FORMER CHAIRPERSON

It has been my privilege to serve as Chairperson of the Task Force on the Travelling Community until my appointment as Minister of State. I would like to express my gratitude firstly to Senator Mary Kelly for having filled the position of Chairperson with distinction. I would also like to record my respect and admiration for the members of the Task Force who worked diligently to fulfil their brief.

Their dedication, imagination and understanding offers great hope for the future and ensures that this Report will be of fundamental importance in meeting the needs of the Travelling Community.

Liz McManus, T.D.

Membership of Task Force

NOMINATING BODY	NOMINEE
Labour Party	Senator Mary Kelly (Chairperson)[1]
Dublin Travellers Education and Development Group (now known as Pavee Point)	Niall Crowley Martin Collins
Conference of the Major Religious Superiors of Ireland (now known as the Conference of Religious of Ireland)	Fr. Bill McKenna
National Federation of Irish Travelling People	Mary Moriarty
Irish Travellers Movement	Chrissie O'Sullivan
National Association of Traveller Training Centres	John McGee
Minister for Equality and Law Reform	Liam Keane, Social Worker, Kilkenny County Council
South Dublin County Council (formerly Dublin County Council)	Dan O'Sullivan
Department of Education	Matt Ryan[2]
Department of the Environment	Peter Greene[3]
Department of Health	Brian Mullen
Department of Social Welfare	Mary Mallon[4]
Fine Gael	Councillor Joan Maher
Progressive Democrats	Councillor Catherine Quinn
Fianna Fáil	Councillor Gabriel Cribben Councillor Ita Green
Democratic Left	Councillor Seamus Rodgers[5]

---

[1] Senator Mary Kelly was appointed Chairperson on 9th January, 1995 following the appointment of the former Chairperson Deputy Liz McManus as Minister of State.

[2] replaced Liam Hughes, with effect from 14th December, 1994.

[3] replaced Brian Breathnach, with effect from 2nd December, 1993.

[4] replaced Sylda Langford, with effect from 5th November, 1993.

[5] Councillor Rodgers was appointed to the Task Force on 16th February, 1995 to replace Deputy Liz McManus as the representative of the Democratic Left.

The Task Force also wishes to acknowledge the contribution of the following people, who on occasion substituted for members:

> Michael Galvin for Dan O'Sullivan
> David Joyce for John McGee
> John O'Connell, Ronnie Fay for Niall Crowley
> Jack Killane for Brian Breathnach, Peter Greene
> Tony Fallon for Mary Mallon
> Catherine Joyce for Martin Collins
> Ann Doherty for Chrissie O'Sullivan

Secretariat

The Secretariat of the Task Force, which comprised three officials, was provided by the Department of Equality and Law Reform. These were David Costello, Secretary to the Task Force who replaced Pat Wylie with effect from October, 1994, Lucinda Mac Mahon, May McCarthy and Irene O'Keeffe (Job-Sharing). The Task Force Secretariat also had the assistance of Ann Casey, Betty Ann Carroll and Colette Deely at various points during its work.

TERMS OF REFERENCE

1. To advise and report on the needs of travellers and on Government policy generally in relation to travellers, with specific reference to the co-ordination in policy approaches by Government Departments and local authorities.

2. To make recommendations, for consideration by relevant Ministers, to ensure that appropriate and co-ordinated planning is undertaken at national and local level in the areas of Housing, Health, Education, Equality, Employment, Cultural and anti-discrimination areas.

3. To draw up a strategy for consideration by relevant Ministers, to define and delineate the respective roles and functions of relevant statutory bodies which cater for the needs of travellers, including recommendations for ensuring that services are provided for travellers in all local authority areas, and likewise throughout the functional area of each local authority.

4. To report on implementation of measures to meet the Government target of providing permanent serviced caravan site accommodation for all traveller families who require it by the year 2000. Pending the realisation of that target, to report on arrangements whereby temporary serviced caravan sites should be provided by local authorities for traveller families who require them; and to examine and report on the costings of such sites and to advise and report on the most efficient use of resources in the provision of such sites.

5. To explore the possibilities for developing mechanisms including statutory mechanisms to enable travellers to participate and contribute to decisions affecting their lifestyle and environment.

6. To analyse nomadism in modern Irish society and to explore ways whereby mutual understanding and respect can be developed between the travelling community and the settled community.

7. To report and make recommendations to the Minister on any other matters affecting the general welfare of travellers.

Recommendations

Section A: Relationships between Traveller and 'Settled' Communities

AR.1   The improvement of relationships between the Traveller and the 'Settled' communities through the development of mutual understanding and respect requires an adjustment in attitudes towards one another and an acceptance of each other's culture. In order to achieve this key goal, the Task Force recommends that every opportunity must be taken to increase levels of contact between the Traveller and 'Settled' communities at national level and more particularly at local community level. It is the view of the Task Force that improved levels of contact will :

–   result in a better understanding on the part of the 'Settled' population of the general needs of Travellers, their culture and aspirations and also of the contribution which cultural diversity makes to society;

–   enable Travellers to understand more about the anxieties of the 'Settled' population;

–   contribute to the reduction in the present levels of conflict and tension which exist between both communities by helping to eradicate misconceptions, intolerance and hostility.

AR.2   In widening the focus of their activities, Traveller organisations should have access to additional resources.

AR.3   The statutory sector has a contribution to make in terms of providing institutional support and resources for the proposed initiatives and also, through its activities, in conveying a more positive attitude to the Traveller community and to issues affecting the well being of Travellers. In particular, the Government should make these issues the focus of a sustained and committed media campaign.

AR.4   The Task Force recommends that the social partners, in drawing up future National Agreements, should take account of the needs of disadvantaged groups such as Travellers and should involve Traveller organisations where the needs of Travellers are being discussed.

AR.5   The Task Force recommends that the Department of Equality and Law Reform, in conjunction with other relevant Departments and Non-Governmental Organisations taking account of previous work in this field, should play a role in exploring and devising a framework for mediation.

AR.6   The media should adopt a more pro-active approach on issues of concern to and relating to the Traveller community, in consultation, where necessary, with Traveller organisations. This could include the provision of more programming time on television and on radio (both at national and local levels) and more print features on such issues as Traveller culture, lifestyles and achievements.

AR.7   The National Union of Journalists' "Guidelines on Race Reporting" if followed more consistently, could make an important contribution to the development of better relations between Travellers and the 'Settled' population. It is recommended that these Guidelines be developed into a Code of Practice to be adopted by the various media institutions.

AR.8   The proposed White Paper on Broadcasting Policy offers another important opportunity to develop the media's contribution to better relationships between Travellers and the 'Settled' community. The White Paper should give a firm commitment to the following:

–   Highlight the role and responsibility of public broadcasting in the development of interculturalism and anti-racism.

–   Point to the need for programmes which promote respect for cultural diversity, and the rights of minorities including Travellers.

— Emphasise the importance of a code of practice and guidelines which encourage broadcasters to avoid sensationalism and negative stereotypical images of Travellers and other minority groups.

— Encourage education programmes which challenge intolerance, racism, xenophobia and discrimination and which provide a voice for communities experiencing exclusion such as Travellers.

— Broaden the concept of 'Equal Opportunities' to include Travellers.

— Encourage and support Traveller groups and other organisations representing communities experiencing exclusion, to have access to the production and delivery of public broadcasting.

AR.9   Anti-racist modules have a particular relevance to the professional training of people who will have contact with Travellers in their work situation. They should be an obligatory component of all courses in professional training where this contact is likely. Traveller groups should be involved in the design and delivery of such modules.

AR.10   Modules dealing with Traveller issues should be extended, as far as is practicable, to courses other than Social Policy/Social Science, for example, Political Science and Business Studies, which are pursued by many of the policy makers of the future.

AR.11   Guidelines should be developed in relation to the collection and use of academic research relating to Travellers by education institutions. These guidelines could be modelled on the code of ethics for Aboriginal health research in the Australian National Aboriginal Health Strategy.

AR.12   The Task Force recommends that every opportunity be taken by the IPA to include specific modules on Traveller issues and anti-racism in its courses of professional training for public servants and that Travellers and Traveller support groups should be involved in the design and delivery of such modules.

Section B: Culture

BR.1   That the distinct culture and identity of the Traveller community be recognised and taken into account.

Section C: Discrimination

CR.1   That the Equal Status legislation would define Travellers in a manner that acknowledges their distinct culture and identity.

CR.2.1   That the Equal Status legislation would define indirect discrimination in a manner that incorporates not only terms and conditions set for the provision of goods, services and facilities but also policies or practices governing or relevant to these.

CR.2.2   That the Equal Status legislation would identify a twenty per cent differential between communities in their access to goods, services and facilities as the point beyond which indirect discrimination requires to be investigated. The experience of British Race Relations legislation indicates that this figure would be appropriate.

CR.3.1   That the Equal Status legislation would prohibit:

— policies and procedures that discriminate against Travellers' culture and identity;

— the exclusion of Travellers, just because they are Travellers, from the normal benefit of goods, services and facilities;

— the segregation of Travellers in the general provision of goods, services and facilities unless this is for reasons of positive action.

CR.3.2 That the Equal Status legislation would specifically name the statutory sector as being bound by its provisions, as this sector is the predominant provider of goods, services and facilities to the Traveller community and experience in Britain has demonstrated that it is necessary to specifically name this sector. Any exemption in this area should be strictly necessary and subject to regular review by the Equality Authority/Commission.

CR.3.3 That the Equal Status legislation would ensure equality of treatment for all citizens in the areas of law enforcement and the judicial process.

CR.3.4 That the Equal Status legislation would ensure protection from victimisation for those making a complaint of discrimination under the legislation, supporting such a complaint, giving evidence in relation to a complaint, or intending t do any of these things.

CR.3.5 That the Equal Status legislation would ensure that Travellers can continue to benefit from affirmative action to prevent discrimination, promote equality, and redress past discrimination.

CR.3.6 That the Equal Status legislation would ensure protection from victimisation for those who support, work with or resource the Traveller community.

CR.3.7 That the Equal Status legislation would provide a legislative basis for the Equality Authority/ Commission's Codes of Practice and for Equal Status policy programmes so that these can be taken into account in the deliberations around any complaint.

CR.4.1 That Equal Status legislation would specifically identify its intention to protect cultural identity.

CR.4.2 That Equal Status legislation would ensure that Travellers are protected from indirect discrimination where they are unable to comply with requirements, conditions, policies or practices consistent with the maintenance of their cultural norms.

CR.5.1 That Equal Status legislation would clearly identify that neither direct nor indirect discrimination against Travellers could be justified on the grounds of potential financial disadvantage to the provider.

CR.6.1 That an Equality Authority/Commission be established based on a re-structured Employment Equality Agency. The Equality Authority/Commission is to be comprised of an Employment Board and a Non-Employment Board.

CR.6.2 That the Employment Board of the Equality Authority/Commission would include representation from Traveller organisations.

CR.6.3 That the Non-Employment Board would include Travellers and Traveller organisations along with representation from the appropriate Government Department with responsibility for co-ordinating services to the Traveller community.

CR.6.4 That an executive committee would be drawn from both the Employment and Non-Employment Boards to co-ordinate policy and to control resources and administration.

CR.7 That the Equality Authority/Commission would have legal powers and necessary resources to:

CR.7.1 Initiate and pursue investigations into instances and patterns of discrimination.

CR.7.2 Receive complaints and provide advice and support to those taking a case under the legislation.

CR.7.3 Take cases on its own initiative.

CR.7.4 Develop codes of practice to set standards in relation to Equal Status policy programmes to be implemented in private, voluntary and public sector institutions and organisations.

CR.7.5 Monitor and evaluate the quality and impact of Equal Status policy programmes put in place by institutions or organisations, to ensure consistency and minimum standards for these Equal Status policy programmes, and to provide support and advice to institutions or organisations designing, implementing or reviewing such programmes.

CR.7.6 Require an institution or organisation to develop and implement an Equal Status policy programme.

CR.7.7 Secure affirmative action where discrimination has been identified, to correct this discrimination and to redress its past impact.

CR.7.8 Proof legislation, existing and new, to ensure that it takes account of its impact on Travellers.

CR.7.9 Develop an information service on relevant international instruments, and taking into account needs of Travellers and Traveller organisations.

CR.7.10 Form consultative groups to assist it in its work.

CR.7.11 Develop educational projects on equality issues and rights under equality legislation.

CR.7.12 Review on a regular basis all equality legislation and any exemptions therein.

CR.8.1 That the Non-Employment Board of the Equality Authority/Commission would establish a distinct Traveller unit which would ensure cohesive action on Traveller issues, which would encompass officers in the following areas; legal, enforcement, information, legislation, positive action and research, and which would have adequate clerical and financial support. The research officer would initiate in-house research, co-ordinate with research commissioned in other sections of the Equality Authority/Commission and make an input into such research.

CR.8.2 That the staff training programme for all officers of the Equality Authority/Commission would include intercultural methods, anti-discriminatory practices, and an appreciation of the importance of identity and cultural difference.

CR.8.3 That the Non-Employment Board would operate through sub-committees dealing with legislation, positive action, enforcement, information and research to facilitate decision making between Board meetings and to ensure a consistent and co-ordinated approach. The officers assigned to these functions in the Traveller unit would participate in the relevant sub-committees.

CR.8.4 That the Equality Authority/Commission would be able to recruit outside the Civil Service.

CR.8.5 That the Non-Employment Board would put in place a programme to create the conditions for the recruitment of staff from the Traveller community. This programme would include a form of Apprenticeship Scheme as a step towards this goal.

CR.8.6 That the nomadic element of the Traveller way of life would be accommodated in the delivery of information and case support through initiatives such as a free phone service and regular outreach clinics, and that all relevant materials developed by the Equality Authority/Commission would be in a format and medium appropriate to the Traveller community.

CR.9.1 That an Equality court would be established, similar to, but separate from, the Labour Court, to deal with cases of discrimination in the non-employment area.

CR.9.2 That the right to redress throughout the court system would not be precluded by the establishment of an Equality Court.

CR.9.3 That the Free Legal Aid Scheme would be expanded to cover those taking action on the grounds of discrimination in both employment and non-employment areas.

CR.9.4   That respondents to a case before the Equality Court would be required to show that their action was necessary on grounds other than those prohibited by Equal Status Legislation once differential treatment is established.

CR.10.1   That each government department, semi-state body, State agency, local authority private sector and voluntary sector organisation would adopt, implement and monitor an Equal Status Policy appropriate to the nature of its function and, that public and voluntary sector organisations and institutions would be adequately resourced to meet their obligations in this regard.

CR.10.2   That, while an Equal Status Policy is the responsibility of management, it would be designed in co-operation with employees and their trade unions, and that the Equal Status Policy would be clearly communicated to all staff within the institution or organisation and to the general public served by the institution or organisation.

CR.10.3   That individual employees would be encouraged to draw the attention of management and their trade union to areas and incidents of suspected discrimination - a staff suggestion scheme with incentives could be developed similar to the present Input Scheme operating in the Civil Service.

CR.10.4   That an Equal Status Policy would include the following commitments as appropriate to the size and nature of the institution or organisation:

–   a member of senior management to be given responsibility for implementation and monitoring of the Equal Status Policy. (In the public sector this could be an extension of the present functions of Equality Officers. However, it is preferable that this role be established outside of the personnel department.);

–   goods, services and facilities to be provided in a manner that respects and is appropriate to the distinct culture and identity of the Traveller community;

–   materials to be developed that are appropriate to the Traveller culture and identity, within services and facilities availed of by this community;

–   communications with the general public to be couched in a language and imagery that reflect the commitments in the Equal Status Policy and that is accessible to the Traveller community;

–   training to be provided for all staff to ensure an understanding of the Equal Status Policy;

–   training to be provided for staff with responsibility for Traveller issues and services to ensure an understanding of the Traveller culture and identity and a knowledge of intercultural and anti-discrimination work methods;

–   Travellers and appropriate Traveller organisations to participate at the relevant level within the institution in decision-making processes that impact on the Traveller community and on the implementation of the Equal Status Policy;

–   where the institution or organisation is involved in the creation of policy fora or task forces, any Traveller dimension be recognised and Traveller and Traveller organisation representation ensured;

–   positive action programmes to be developed for Travellers, including programmes for the recruitment of Travellers into the institution or organisation, and creating the conditions for this to happen;

–   existing policies and procedures, including the Equal Status Policy, to be reviewed on a regular basis and changed wherever the potential for discrimination is discovered or where scope for further or alternative positive action is identified;

– annual reports, or other appropriate reporting mechanisms engaged in by the institution or organisation, to include details of equality issues arising during the year, including implementation of work done, complaints of discrimination dealt with and positive action taken.

CR.11.1   That the Department of Equality and Law Reform, or its successor, in its work of co-ordination in relation to services to Travellers, would promote and support the introduction of an Equal Status Policy, based on the above recommendations, within the various public sector institutions that provide services of an essential nature to the Traveller community, as a matter of priority.

CR.12.1   That the Irish Government in responding to the first report of the U.N. Human Rights Committee as it relates to cultural minorities, would take particular cognisance of Article 27 of the International Covenant on Civil and Political Rights, 1966 and that future reports from the Irish Government to the Human Rights Committee on this Covenant would make specific references to the application of Article 27 to the Traveller community.

CR.13.1   That the Irish Government would ratify the U.N. Covenant on the Elimination of all Forms of Racial Discrimination.

and

CR.13.2   That in ratifying this Covenant the Irish Government should accept the right of individual petition under Article 14.

CR.14.1   That the Irish Government, in preparing its report on the International Covenant on Economic, Social and Cultural Rights, and those reports required by other international instruments, would pay due regard to the involvement of Traveller organisations.

CR.15.1   In contributing to reports being made under International Instruments by the Irish Government and in making direct petitions and submissions to the relevant United Nations Committees Travellers' organisations should be assisted appropriately by the Government.

CR.15.2   The Government, through the appropriate statutory bodies, should, in partnership with Traveller organisations, develop appropriate actions in response to the requirements of this declaration to "encourage conditions for the promotion" of the Traveller identity.

CR.16.1   That the Irish Government would press for the specific inclusion of the cultural rights of nomadic groups including Irish Travellers within a proposed new Protocol on Minority Cultural Rights to be drafted for the European Convention on Human Rights and that this would be done in consultation with Traveller organisations.

CR.17.1   That the Irish Government would continue to participate in CSCE Human Dimension conferences and similar conferences and would involve Traveller organisations.

CR.18   The Electoral Act, 1992 makes residence within a constituency a pre-requisite for registration and as such, nomadism can disenfranchise Travellers as the legislation stands. The Department of the Environment should introduce procedures and any necessary amendments to legislation to ensure that this situation does not continue. They should also satisfy the requirements of the Human Rights Committee of the United Nations as referred to in para. 5.2(a) of the Report of the Task Force.

Section D: Accommodation

DR.1   The Task Force recommends the provision of 3,100 units of additional Traveller accommodation. The investment in Traveller accommodation should therefore be substantially increased to meet the Government target of accommodating all Traveller families in need of accommodation.

DR.2   The location of Traveller specific accommodation will depend on a number of variables. These will include land availability and technical and planning considerations. Consideration should also be given to the preferences and needs of the prospective Traveller tenants. Equally, it should include good access to services, schools and shops.

DR.3   The design of particular accommodation schemes will vary from locality to locality. However, a number of principles can be identified as usefully informing the final design of all schemes. The accommodation provided should:

  (i)   acknowledge the distinct needs and identity of Travellers;

  (ii)   cater for the work patterns of Travellers in accordance with the recommendations of Section G on the Traveller Economy and take account of technical and planning considerations;

  (iii)   take cognizance of the needs and compatibility of extended family groupings, and of the different population structure of the Traveller community with over fifty per cent under the age of fifteen;

  (iv)   contribute to improving relations between Travellers and 'Settled' people;

  (v)   include proper landscaping to ensure the site is not only functional but also pleasant to live on and aesthetically pleasing to look at. This should include not only the site itself but also the outer boundary;

  (vi)   have adequate public lighting for security and safety purposes;

  (vii)   ensure an appropriate balance between personal privacy and communal needs compatible with the requirements of the Fire Officer;

  (viii)   allow for the integration of the family caravan with the accommodation facilities provided for each family as well as adequate parking space for vehicles used by the family;

  (ix)   include facilities for play space, caretaker's office, communal meeting rooms, and public telephone;

  (x)   where possible cater for changing family structures;

  (xi)   be accessible and appropriate for Traveller tenants with a disability.

DR.4   Traveller tenants and Traveller organisations should be involved at an early stage in the design of Traveller accommodation.

DR.5   The Traveller Accommodation Agency should stimulate dialogue on the design concepts of Traveller accommodation as exemplified in "The President Robinson Awards for the Design of Travellers Accommodation". This dialogue should include the Department of the Environment and local authorities, Travellers and Traveller organisations, private sector architects and architectural students.

DR.6.1   A network of permanent sites is required across the country. The final parameters of this network should be defined by the Traveller Accommodation Agency based on local authority programmes approved by the Agency.

DR.6.2   The bay should allow for safe fuel storage with electricity, sewerage services and water supply provided.

DR.6.3   Accommodation provided should include kitchen, toilets, bathroom, washing and drying facilities, and family room.

DR.6.4   While the size may vary with the requirements of particular areas, it is recommended that the focus should be on moderately sized sites, having regard to the compatibility of families and size of extended family.

DR.7   **(a)** A network of transient halting sites is required across the country. These sites should be provided simultaneously with the other types of accommodation facilities as an integral part of a National Programme.

The final parameters of this network should be defined by the Traveller Accommodation Agency based on the following:

(i)   A network of transient sites should be provided in each local authority administrative area.

(ii)   The specific locations of these sites should include:

(a) cities, towns, villages and other centres of population;

(b) other areas where there is a tradition of Traveller transient camping.

The Agency should be informed by the advice/information from the local authority and should take account of appropriate linkages between the provision of transient and permanent accommodation. These linkages should ensure that visiting families can be accommodated on a transient site within a reasonable distance.

(b) Bays on transient sites should provide access to electricity, running water, sewage disposal and refuse collection. A suitable hard surface should be provided. While the size may vary with the requirements of particular areas, it is recommended that the focus should be on small sites.

(c) Guidelines should be developed for transient sites covering design features, management issues and appropriate size by the Traveller Accommodation Agency.

DR.8   It is recognised that caravans are not designed for long term living. The Traveller Accommodation Agency should develop a research project to develop a caravan design that continues to allow mobility while improving its capacity for long term occupation as well as increasing its fire safety features.

DR.9   A specific capital allocation, separate from the general housing construction allocation should continue to be provided annually for the construction of Traveller specific accommodation. This allocation should therefore cover group housing, single housing, permanent sites and transient sites.

DR.10   Given the importance of this investment, local authorities should be provided with seventy-five per cent funding from central government to cover the cost of managing and maintaining existing and new Traveller specific accommodation, including costs of a caretaker service where this is provided.

DR.11   In addition to direct provision of accommodation by local authorities, the Traveller Accommodation Agency should investigate the possibility of direct provision of accommodation by Travellers themselves or by Traveller organisations. Such schemes could include low interest rate house purchase loans, the provision of houses and/or serviced caravan parks by approved bodies under Section 6 of the Housing (Miscellaneous Provisions) Act, 1992, use of Capital Assistance and Rental Subsidy Schemes.

DR.12   In the context of the National Strategy, where each local authority is playing its part, local authority approaches should be flexible and should avoid determining specific numbers of Travellers to be accommodated within particular areas. This does not in any way preclude the need for all areas to be included in the local authority's plan for Traveller specific accommodation.

DR.13   It is recognised that local authorities must be allowed to exercise control over unauthorised Traveller encampments. However, in the absence of adequate provision local authorities should be required to deal sensitively with such cases and use the option of eviction only as a last resort.

DR.14   Traveller families who are provided with accommodation in the functional area of one local authority cannot expect duplicate provision to be made by other local authorities, save where they avail of transient halting sites, for stays of short duration.

DR.15   Where private firms are used in a caretaker role, they should operate to clear guidelines and should not be employed in contradictory roles, including evictions.

DR.16   Existing temporary sites should be replaced with permanent sites and housing as appropriate or should be adapted as permanent or transient sites.

DR.17   In view of the absence of open land in the city area, Dublin Corporation, should pursue a policy of identifying and developing a range of infill sites for Traveller specific accommodation.

DR.18   Co-ordinated strategies for the accommodation of Travellers over the Greater Dublin area are required between the four local authorities. A Strategic Planning Unit should be established drawing together relevant officials from the four councils chaired by a representative from the Traveller Accommodation Agency to ensure co-ordination and best use of resources. This Unit should also meet on a regular basis with relevant Traveller organisations.

DR.19   The Traveller Accommodation Agency should ensure even progress in the development of Traveller accommodation facilities across the country. This should be done in a manner to ensure that any drift towards Dublin due to lack of facilities in other areas would be eliminated.

DR.20   The Traveller Accommodation Agency should ensure that provision in other local authority areas should include any Traveller families that might now choose to relocate from Dublin. This should be done on the basis of a survey carried out independently by the Agency.

DR.21   Existing official temporary sites should be upgraded where appropriate, to the standard of permanent halting sites or transient sites, on the basis of consultation. These sites should be phased out as permanent accommodation is provided, with a view to temporary sites not being required after the year 2000.

DR.22   An independent statutory body, to be known as the Traveller Accommodation Agency[6], should be established to draw up, in consultation with local authorities, a National Programme for the provision of Traveller specific accommodation in order to achieve the Government's objective of provision of such accommodation by the year 2000.

(a) Structure

The Agency to be established by the Minister for the Environment should consist of a Chairperson to be appointed by the Minister for the Environment and nine directors to be drawn from the following three categories with balanced representation:

(i)   direct appointments of the Minister for the Environment, including elected local representatives;

(ii)   direct appointments of the Minister for Equality & Law Reform or his/her successor, with a specific expertise on equality issues; and

(iii) nominations made by relevant National Traveller Organisations.

The right of Travellers to a presence on the Board should be recognised. The Ministers concerned should ensure appropriate balances on the Board in terms of gender and of Travellers/'Settled' people.

The Agency's Chairperson and directors should be part-time and appointed for a five year period. The Agency should have a Chief Executive Officer, appointed following public advertisement and sufficient staff as required by the Board of the Agency. The Agency should be designated a prescribed body for the purpose of Section 21 of the Local Government (Planning and Development) Act, 1963 and Article 5 of the Local Government (Planning and Development) Regulations, 1994.

---

[6] **Reservation by Mr P Greene**

I disagree with this recommendation. It would, in my view, delay the provision of urgently needed accommodation for traveller people by creating uncertainty in the responsiblity and role of local authorities and by providing a further focus for opposition to halting site locations. The establishment of a further statutory body in the Local Government sector is not compatible with a programme of devolution and a widening of the role of Local Government. Other recommendations in this section, when implemented, will remove obstacles to the provision of halting sites except local community opposition which can only be addressed at local level - see Section A (Strategy for Reconciliation).

(b) Functions

The functions of the Agency should be as follows:

– draw up a National Programme for the provision of Traveller specific accommodation on the basis of programmes submitted by the local authorities;

– monitor, assess, advise on and secure the implementation of the annual building and refurbishment programmes of local authorities for Traveller specific accommodation;

– monitor and review local development plans under the Planning Acts to ensure they provide for the provision of Traveller specific accommodation;

– develop guidelines for Planning Authorities for the appropriate inclusion of Traveller specific accommodation in development plans;

– advise the Minister for the Environment on the information sought and the manner in which it is sought for the Assessment of Housing Needs under Section 9 of the Housing Act, 1988;

– carry out research as necessary into and advise on matters relating to the provision and refurbishment of accommodation of Travellers including the participation of Travellers in the management of same;

– organise and promote, where necessary, appropriate training in intercultural skills and similar issues relevant to work in this area for staff involved in the provision, refurbishment and management of Traveller specific accommodation;

– advise the Minister for the Environment on all legislation relevant to Traveller accommodation;

– advise Regional Authorities on the individual local authorities' proposals for Traveller accommodation to ensure a co-ordinated and integrated approach in each region;

– liaise as necessary with the other bodies which the Task Force proposes should be established, namely the Traveller Education Service, Traveller Health Advisory Committee and the Equality Authority/Commission;

– analyse patterns of movement of Travellers within the State.

(c) Powers

The Agency should have the following powers:

– where a local authority fails to draw up an annual programme for the provision and refurbishment of Traveller specific accommodation, or where the Agency finds the local authority's annual programme is inadequate the Agency should issue a directive to the local authority to rectify the identified problem;

– where the Agency is of the opinion that a local authority fails to meet the annual targets agreed with the Agency without reasonable cause, it should direct the authority to carry out the necessary works within a time specified by the Agency;

– where the Agency is of the opinion that a planning authority fails to include appropriate provision for Traveller specific accommodation in its development plan or a revision of the plan, the Agency shall direct the authority to make such provision within a time specified by the Agency;

– in the event of a local authority or planning authority failing to carry out a directive by the Agency without reasonable cause, it shall apply to the High Court for an appropriate Court order to compel compliance;

– other powers appropriate to statutory bodies such as employing staff, and having a seal.

DR.23 In relation to Statements of Policy on Housing Management, local authorities should ensure:

(a) the involvement of Traveller tenants in the development of a participation programme;

(b) the statements contain an anti-discrimination commitment to ensure that tenant participation strategies cannot contribute to the exclusion of Travellers, purely because they are Travellers.

DR.24 Each local authority should establish a Traveller Tenant Accommodation Committee.

DR.25 The provisions of the Department of the Environment Memorandum relating to tenant involvement should be applied to Travellers in Traveller specific accommodation. The Task Force supports the piloting and promotion of tenant participation strategies.

DR.26 Letting agreements with Traveller tenants should show flexibility to ensure they are appropriate to the use of Traveller Specific Accommodation.

DR.27 It is recommended that the formal duties of the local authority social worker for Travellers be revised at national level by a Committee representing the social workers, local authorities, health boards, Department of the Environment, Department of Health, Travellers and relevant Traveller organisations. The Committee should take account of the need to shift the social workers' role from a rehabilitative focus to one of intercultural respect, and consider and make recommendations in relation to, inter alia, the following issues:

– job description and selection criteria;
– career structure;
– in-service training;
– management/reporting structure;
– liaison with other relevant agencies;
– harassment;
– case load size.

DR.28 To amend Sub-Section (9) of Section (2) of the City and County Management (Amendment) Act 1955, which reads:

"Nothing in the foregoing provisions of this section shall prevent the manager from dealing forthwith with any situation which he considers is an emergency situation calling for immediate action without regard to those provisions."

by the insertion of the following words at the end of the Sub-Section:

"or in the case of the provision of Traveller specific accommodation, where the members fail to agree with the Manager's proposals or with amended proposals within six months of being first presented by the Manager".

DR.29 To amend Section (27) of the Housing Act 1988, which reads:

"The City and County Management (Amendment) Act, 1955, is hereby amended by the insertion in Section 2 of the following sub-section after sub-section (9):

"(10) An emergency situation for the purpose of sub-section (9) of this Section shall be deemed to exist where, in the opinion of the manager, the works concerned are urgent and necessary (having regard to personal health, public health and safety considerations) in order to provide a reasonable standard of accommodation for any person".

by the insertion of the following words at the end of the Section:

"including Travellers who are parked in unserviced and unofficial locations without access to basic facilities which exist on a serviced site".

DR.30   That Section 8 of the 1988 Housing Act be amended:

– to have group housing and halting sites, permanent and transient requirements named as being included within the general estimate of requirements carried out by the local authority, including Traveller families likely to move into the functional area of the authority within the time period of the estimate;

– to require the local authority to have regard to consultation with and submissions from Travellers and local Traveller organisations in making this estimate.

DR.31   That Section 9 of the Housing Act, 1988 be amended to require a local authority to give one month's notice of its intention to carry out a housing assessment to local Traveller organisations and to make this assessment available to these organisations upon completion.

DR.32   To facilitate the implementation of Section 10, Housing (Miscellaneous Provisions) Act, 1992 and Section 69, Roads Act, 1993, priority needs to be given to the implementation of the Task Force's recommendations concerning the network of transient sites. Each of these Sections should be amended to provide that Travellers whose temporary dwelling is removed to storage cannot be deemed to be deliberately homeless.

DR.33   It is recommended that a statutory requirement be placed on public bodies including Government Departments that lands in their possession which are not clearly identified as being required for their statutory purposes within five years and which are deemed to be suitable by the local authority for the provision of accommodation for Traveller people be made available to the local authority for that purpose.

DR.34   It is recommended that the necessary legislative changes be put in place to confirm that the term "necessary works of public utility" as used in Article 44.2.6 of Bunreacht na hÉireann, includes the provision of Traveller-specific accommodation.

DR.35   It is recommended that the Third Schedule of the Local Government (Planning and Development) Act, 1963 be amended to include a reference to the provision of Traveller specific accommodation as an objective.

DR.36   Planning authorities should review and where necessary, amend their Development Plans immediately in order to allow the provision of Traveller specific accommodation in all land zones[7].

DR.37   It is recommended that Section 39 of the Local Government (Planning and Development) Act, 1963, be amended to provide that the provision of Traveller specific accommodation would not be regarded as a material contravention of the Development Plan.

(This is a temporary measure pending revision of existing plans following enactment of amendment of the Third Schedule as recommended at DR.35 above).

DR.38   Where a system of land use zoning is not specified in a Development Plan to cover all land in the administrative area, the written statement of the Plan should clearly indicate that the provision of Traveller Specific Accommodation is permissible in all land whether zoned or unzoned[8].

DR.39   The Minister should issue a general directive under Section 7 of the Local Government (Planning and Development) Act, 1982 in relation to the inclusion in Development Plans for the provision of Traveller accommodation on the basis of Task Force Recommendations DR.35 and DR.36 above.

DR.40   Legislation should be amended to provide for the acquisition of land for the provision of accommodation for the Traveller community on the same model as set out in the Roads Act, 1993

---

[7] Councillor Joan Maher does not agree that amenities/B & G zoning should permit Traveller specific accommodation.

[8] Councillor Joan Maher does not agree that amenities/B & G zoning should permit Traveller specific accommodation.

(Section 47). The legislative procedures set out in the Roads Act, 1993 (Section 47) for the making of a Motorway, Busway and Protected Road Scheme represents the most expeditious procedures for compulsory acquisition of land for public purposes. It is recommended that this model should be applied to the acquisition of land for the provision of Traveller Specific Accommodation by appropriate amending legislation. The procedure envisaged would require each local authority to adopt a Traveller Specific Accommodation Scheme at specific times which would set out its programme of accommodation for Travellers for the following appropriate period.

DR.41 The provisions of the proposed Freedom of Information Act should apply to requests from Travellers and relevant Traveller organisations to local authorities, seeking relevant information in relation to the provision of Traveller accommodation.

DR.42 Legislation should be introduced to control wandering horses as promised in "A Government of Renewal".

DR.43 Legislation should be enacted to prevent parking of caravans and other temporary dwellings within one mile of Traveller specific accommodation. The local authority should be given powers to keep these areas clear of such parking. This legislation should not apply to existing families on long term unofficial sites, without prejudice to the provisions of Section 10, Housing (Miscellaneous Provisions) Act, 1992.

DR.44 Local authorities should be provided with powers of immediate access to the High Court to remove those who break into Traveller specific accommodation, or who park adjacent to such facilities, or who come in to use these facilities continually, without the permission of the local authority. One method to achieve this would be specific legislative procedures for short service of an interlocutory application to the High Court in these cases. The provision of a network of transient sites, which is dealt with elsewhere, is an essential element in dealing with this issue. These powers are not intended to be availed of by local authorities to cause Travellers, who are in their functional area, to move to an adjoining area, thus evading their obligations.

DR.45 In the case of existing tenants identified by the local authority as responsible for vandalising a facility or interfering with other tenants or residents of that facility, a speedy and effective response is required. A process incorporating the following elements is proposed:

(a) warning notice;
(b) interview;
(c) rehabilitation programme, where appropriate;
(d) if (a), (b) and (c) do not produce the desired result, then the ultimate sanction of eviction would be pursued.

Persistent anti-social behaviour should constitute a breach of the tenancy agreement and, following the procedure outlined above, the ultimate sanction should be eviction. Priority should be given to seeking court orders for this purpose. Given the difficulty of obtaining primary evidence in these cases, secondary evidence should be admissible.

DR.46 Local authorities should develop responses to the specific experience of intimidation against Travellers moving into standard housing. This protection should be reflected in the general tenancy agreement.

DR.47 The Traveller Accommodation Agency should review the necessity for an Annual Count and if found to be necessary, should take responsibility for its compilation and publication. Pending this review, the Annual Count should continue to take place.

DR.48 The 1995 Annual Count should be carried out on the basis of a partnership between the local authorities and local Traveller groups.

DR.49 The Task Force recommends that the Central Statistics Office include the Traveller community as a separate heading in its classification of households in all future Censuses of Population.

Section E: Health

ER.1 Equity has been defined as a fundamental principle of Irish health policy. Increased funding, commensurate with the scale of the issue, should be allocated to tackling the unacceptable health status of the Traveller community and the widespread obstacles to Traveller access to health services.

ER.2 The immediate improvement of the accommodation situation of Travellers is a pre-requisite to the general improvement of the health status of Travellers. Health boards should periodically inspect all halting sites so as to report on health and safety matters. The resulting reports should be publicly available.

ER.3 The Task Force notes the Minister for Health's commitment, as stated in the National Health Strategy (1994), to addressing the particular health needs of the Traveller community. It recommends that a Traveller Health Advisory Committee should be appointed by the Minister for Health. Its brief should include:

- drawing up a national policy for a health strategy to improve the health status of the Traveller community;

- ensuring that Traveller health is a priority area within the Department of Health and setting targets against which performance can be measured;

- ensuring co-ordination and liaison in the implementation of national strategies of relevance to the health status of Travellers;

- ensuring the co-ordination, collection and collation of data on Travellers' health;

- supporting health boards in developing strategies to improve Traveller access to health services;

- providing a forum for the discussion of health initiatives for Travellers and for ongoing consultation with Travellers and Traveller organisations on health service delivery to Travellers.

The Traveller Health Advisory Committee should be drawn from the various divisions in the Department of Health, representatives of the Traveller community, from Health Boards and national Traveller organisations. It should have a small staff attached to it and be provided with an adequate budget. It should have a direct reporting relationship to the Minister.

ER.4 Each health board should establish a Traveller Health Unit. The brief of such a unit would include:

- monitoring the delivery of health services to Travellers and setting regional targets against which performance can be measured;

- ensuring that Traveller health is given prominence on the agenda of the health board;

- ensuring co-ordination and liaison within the health board, and between the health board and other statutory and voluntary bodies, in relation to the health situation of Travellers;

- collection of data on Traveller health and utilisation of health services;

- ensuring appropriate training of health service providers in terms of their understanding of and relationship with Travellers.

- supporting the development of Traveller specific services, either directly by the health board or, indirectly through funding appropriate voluntary organisations.

The health board Traveller Health Unit should have a committee drawn from the various sectors in the health board and from local Travellers and Traveller organisations. It should have a small staff attached to it. It should have a reporting relationship to each of the Programme Managers and to the new Directors of Public Health. These units should incorporate existing inter-sectoral structures focusing on Traveller health issues at health board level.

ER.5   An improved health record keeping system should be introduced by the Department of Health and the health boards to collect more detailed socio-economic data and make provision for the identification of Travellers. Provision should be made for the identification of Travellers on notification of births, deaths, hospital morbidity and maternal and perinatal statistical collections. A strict code of practice should be designed to govern this. This code should be based on the code of ethics for Aboriginal health research in the Australian National Aboriginal Health Strategy. It should ensure that identification is voluntary and should guarantee confidentiality and sensitivity. The code of practice should be approved by the Data Protection Commissioner.

ER.6   A system of patient held records should be introduced nationwide. These records should provide information on a patient's medical history, in addition to all hospital and general practice consultations, and details of prescribed medicines. This should operate on a voluntary basis. It is envisaged that it would make a particular contribution to improving continuity of care for Travellers who are nomadic.

ER.7   An improved system of transferring records, both within and between health board regions, should be introduced. The application of information technology systems, such as those used in the field of banking, should be explored to establish data bases of Traveller health records that would ensure this transfer of records between community care, hospital services and pharmacies within and between health board regions. The process should be approved by the Data Protection Commissioner.

ER.8   Given the various difficulties, identified in the research, of communication between Traveller patients and the health service, a system, whereby correspondence from health services is provided through personal communications, should be offered to Traveller patients. Where requested, an appropriate channel should be identified in consultation with the patient. The patient should make the nominated person aware of any change of address.

ER.9   Traveller specific services should be designed to complement mainstream services and to improve Traveller access to these. Travellers should have the right to opt out of any Traveller specific service and to choose to use mainstream services. In the implementation and provision of these services, there should be no segregation of Travellers.

ER.10   Traveller participation in health service delivery at all levels should be supported. This is especially important in the area of primary health care. In particular:

–   Peer led services (such as Traveller paramedics) such as that piloted in the Eastern Health Board, should be expanded. This expansion should be based on an independent evaluation of the initiative with the participation of Travellers and Traveller organisations.

–   Support should be provided to encourage and resource Travellers to gain qualifications as health professionals and to take up careers in the health field.

ER.11   Primary health care services for the Traveller community should be delivered on an out-reach basis. It is important to stress that these out-reach initiatives should complement, improve, and encourage access to mainstream provision and not replace such provision. On-site clinics in Traveller specific accommodation facilities should be established and serviced by various members of the Community Care teams, including Public Health Nurses, Dental Nurses, Speech Therapists and Social Workers. Priority should be given to child health, the care of the elderly, and to ante-natal and post-natal services. The facilities provided should be of a high standard and should guarantee confidentiality.

Traveller specific services in the primary health care area, requiring equipment that is not easily transportable, should be provided on an outreach basis through the designation of special Traveller clinics at an existing health centre. This approach would be particularly important in areas such as dental care. It would also ensure high standards in Traveller specific services.

The practice of designating particular Public Health Nurses to have a Traveller specific brief should be expanded. Recruitment for this brief should be by way of interview to ensure suitability. Training should be provided to successful candidates in intercultural methods.

ER.12   In general hospital services, provision should be made for out-reach paediatric and obstetric clinics for Travellers. Special provision should also be made for improved liaison between general hospital and general practitioner services where, for example, after care could be provided increasingly by general practitioners rather than by out-patient clinics.

ER.13   In special hospital services, provision should be made for community psychiatric out-reach services to deal with issues of mental health in the Traveller community.

ER.14   (a)   The Department of Health should commission an in-depth analysis by independent experts of issues related to consanguinity in the Irish context, taking account of WHO work in this area.

           (b)   Given that Travellers predominantly marry within their own community, marriage of close relatives is common. Accordingly, a specific genetic counselling service to Travellers is required to address any risks associated with this.

ER.15   The provision of Traveller specific services recommended in the preceding recommendations should be subject to ongoing evaluation. This evaluation should measure the impact of the particular service, assess the continuing need for the particular service and ensure that the service is complementary to mainstream provision and has not resulted in any segregation.

ER.16   A regular conference of service providers and Traveller organisations should be organised by the Department of Health to facilitate the transfer of experiences of Traveller specific services between health boards.

ER.17   Traveller support groups have an important contribution to make in the targeting and in the appropriate delivery of health services to the Traveller community. This role can be considerably enhanced through support from the health boards. In particular, health boards should:

–   make funding available for Traveller support groups to employ community workers;

–   make resources available to enable Traveller support groups and Senior Traveller Training Centres to include health modules and activities in their training and education initiatives;

–   provide information to Traveller support groups and Senior Traveller Training Centres on Traveller uptake of services, the local conditions and other factors impacting on Traveller health and on the general health status of Travellers safeguarding confidentiality in respect of such information.

ER.18   The terms of the GMS for General Practitioners should prohibit the refusal to accept people as registered patients solely on the basis that they are Travellers.

ER.19   Where specific practices have a large proportion of Travellers on their lists, an audit and evaluation of drug utilisation by such practices should be conducted with the regional General Practitioner Unit to establish if there is an impact on their drugs bill and to analyse any high prescription rates. If it is found that this has an impact on the drugs costs of such practices, a special allowance should be introduced in the drugs payment scheme.

ER.20   For the additional out-reach services recommended in Recommendation ER.12, special fees and allowances should be drawn up under the terms of the GMS.

ER.21   A simplified system of renewing and amending Traveller medical cards, in an expeditious manner that does not require detailed form filling on the part of the Traveller, should be introduced. The validity of medical cards held by Travellers should be extended to a minimum of three years. Simplified procedures should be put in place for General Practitioners to receive payment for Traveller patients who move into their area or who are in temporary residence there.

ER.22   The Health Promotion Unit in the Department of Health, in partnership with relevant Traveller organisations, should draw up a policy for health promotion and education for Travellers. This should be provided in all health board regions and should:

–   aim to restore Travellers' confidence in their ability to distinguish and to cope with minor illnesses;

–   prioritise child health, breast feeding, the role of preventative and after-care services and the care of the aged;

–   be based around personal skills development in order to support Travellers in appropriately meeting the many challenges in their lives and should not merely focus on lifestyle behaviour.

Lifestyle health education should give due recognition to the constraints on Travellers' circumstances, should resource the community to make informed choices and also provide access to the findings of relevant research including that recommended in ER.14 above.

ER.23   Health promotion work, with the general public, should inform people of the impact which the living circumstances and discrimination against Travellers have on Traveller health status. This should be done through a number of approaches such as:

–   use of materials on these issues in school health education and lifeskills courses;

–   use of mass media campaigns by the Health Promotion Unit.

Travellers and Traveller organisations should be involved in the preparation of materials for this work.

ER.24   All health professionals should receive training on the circumstances, culture of, and discrimination practised against Travellers, as part of their training. Service providers in frequent contact with Travellers should receive more in-depth training in intercultural and anti-discrimination practices. This training should also include a focus on Travellers' perspectives on health and illness. Travellers and Traveller organisations should be resourced to play an active role in this training and education.

ER.25   The Department of Social Welfare should address the difficulties that arise in respect of access to the carer's allowance that arise from Traveller families in multiple dwellings.

ER.26   Adequate support facilities, including day care centres for children involved in begging, should be provided by the relevant statutory authorities.

ER.27   Where the problem of child begging exists, an Outreach Worker should be appointed in major urban areas by the relevant statutory authorities, to work with vulnerable Traveller children and their families, in conjunction with the social work teams already in place. Adequate resources should be provided by the relevant statutory authorities for this purpose.

ER.28   In order to deter begging by unaccompanied children, Section 14 of the Childrens' Act 1908, which makes it an offence on the part of parents to cause or procure their children to beg or to be involved in petty theft, should be updated to a level where the penalties are an effective deterrent, including the power to confiscate any monies proven to be procured from such activity.

ER.29   The relevant provisions of the Child Care Act 1991 should be implemented to assist the relevant statutory authorities in removing children involved in begging to a suitable place.

ER.30   Social Workers in health boards who may have responsibility for Traveller children, should receive in-service training both in understanding the Traveller culture and in developing skills to interculturally assess children's needs and neglect where it exists.

ER.31   Traveller mobility means that families may move out of the remit of a particular health board social work team. As Traveller mobility is common, it is recommended that effective formal co-ordination is put in place to trace families with children at risk within health boards and between health boards.

ER.32   Health board social workers whose Traveller case moves away, should be obliged to trace the family's whereabouts through the local authority social worker service and then fully inform the appropriate health board social worker in the new area of residence. Similar procedures should also be applied to families who move out of the jurisdiction.

ER.33   Where a Traveller family comes to the attention of a health board social work team and subsequently moves away before the case is closed, regardless of its significance, that case should not be deemed closed without notifying the appropriate social worker in the new area where the Traveller family locates.

Section F: Education and Training

FR.1   The Visiting Teacher Service has an important role to play in encouraging Traveller parents to ensure that their children participate in the education system, particularly at pre-school, primary and second levels. This role should be supported and, where necessary, adequately resourced by the relevant statutory authorities.

FR.2   The Task Force endorses the recommendations contained in the Department of Education Working Group Report entitled "School Attendance/Truancy Report" (1994). It is, however, important in applying these recommendations to Travellers that they are placed firmly and sensitively in the context of the human rights of the child.

FR.3   As a model of good practice, the Task Force strongly supports the integrated effort being adopted between the visiting teacher, the Gardaí and others at community level in Galway, to encourage school attendance and recommends that this approach be adopted as a model elsewhere.

FR.4   Present legislation needs to be reinforced to enable the integrated approach referred to in FR.3 above to have general application. Arrangements should be made by the relevant statutory authorities to have the necessary legislative changes introduced as a matter of urgency.

FR.5   Traveller parents should be facilitated to enrol their own children in schools rather than this being done by the visiting teacher. The lack of this initial contact can set the scene for poor future involvement.

FR.6   Attention needs to be given to developing a range of ways which would permit ongoing direct contact between teachers and Traveller parents. There can be direct contact when problems arise, but in some instances, these problems can end up being dealt with through the Visiting Teacher. Traveller parents should be particularly targeted so as to encourage their involvement in open days or similar events before problems arise.

FR.7   The lack of direct communication is evident in the low level of knowledge that can be displayed by Traveller parents as to what is happening to or being done for their children in school. The method of communication between parent and school must, however, be accessible. The note sent home in the child's school bag is not sufficient for various reasons, including where literacy is a problem or where the terminology is not understood. The visiting teacher should also be informed where problems arise in the education of a Traveller child so as to encourage the parents to communicate with the Teacher. Other appropriate channels through which this communication might be encouraged, could also be explored, where necessary.

FR.8   Levels of literacy and lack of experience or knowledge in some school subjects on the part of Traveller parents can be a source of embarassment and a barrier to communication with teachers. Access to adult education has an important contribution to make to Traveller parental involvement.

FR.9   Homework programmes have an important contribution to make to parental involvement, but can, in some instances, involve a further removal of Traveller parents. There should be some linked follow up with parents of children on these programmes. Where possible, people on these programmes should be from the Traveller community; the supervisors of the programmes should encourage parents to become involved; adequate training of those who deliver the programmes should be a prerequisite to ensure sensitivity to Travellers' culture.

FR.10   There is a lack of information among Traveller parents on how schools are administered and there is an absence of Traveller parents playing roles within the school. Travellers playing roles within the school as committee members or being employed as childcare assistants and classroom assistants would contribute to addressing this information gap.

FR.11   Traveller parents should be encouraged to join Boards of Management and other parent bodies. The National Parents Council should also include Traveller representatives among its membership. In addition, Boards of Management should formulate policies on issues related to Traveller children only after consultation with Traveller interests.

FR.12   Creative ways of bringing Travellers into the planning and administration of the education system should be explored.

FR.13   The use of different books in different schools is a barrier to Traveller mobility. Movement from one area to another requires the purchase of a new set of books. Some form of book exchange system needs to be put in place to reduce the financial burden on the parents of children who change schools.

FR.14   It should be recognised that strict enrolment cut-off dates have a particularly negative impact on Traveller children moving from one area to another. This can also result in Traveller children missing out on school when they first move into an area as the family is required to prove its intention to stay before the child is admitted. Whether a child is in a mainstream or a special class, flexibility in enrolment dates for children who are moving from one area to another needs to be introduced and should be resourced and supported by the Department of Education.

FR.15   Visiting teacher support has an important contribution to make in facilitating entry into the new school from the child's perspective and the school's perspective. However, this should be done in a manner that supports direct contact between the Traveller parents and the school teachers.

FR.16   The children of occupational Travellers in other European countries are benefiting from the development of resources to facilitate distance learning. There is a need to explore this in order to find out how Irish Travellers could benefit from this approach. This task could be undertaken by the proposed Traveller Education Service.

FR.17   In order to implement a curriculum along the lines suggested in this report, there is need for a comprehensive Traveller Education Service in the Department of Education as recommended by the INTO, the ITM, the EC Intercultural Education Project, the ATTP and in this Report under Traveller Education Service. Such a service would have responsibility not only for monitoring the curriculum but also for ensuring greater integration and coherence between all the key personnel and organisations involved in Traveller education and training such as: the National Education Officer, the inspectorate, the visiting teachers, the ATTP, Traveller parents, National Traveller organisations, NATC and other relevant bodies.

FR.18   The Department of Education should commission the design of an intercultural/ anti-racist programme (with videos, tapes, materials and games) to be used in national schools and second level schools, at both junior and senior levels in each case. This would require the setting up of a steering committee involving school psychologists, special teachers, inspectorate and visiting teachers for Travellers, and the involvement of the National Parents Council, teacher unions, representatives from national Traveller organisations and other minority group organisations, on the lines of that used to form the Child Abuse Prevention Programme in 1991. Funding for such an initiative could be shared between the Department of Equality and Law Reform, the Department of Education and the National Lottery.

FR.19   Resources and materials are needed to implement an intercultural, anti-racist curriculum and these should be developed for all pupils. However, such resources are ineffective in the hands of teachers or trainers who have limited understanding and, in some instances, negative attitudes towards Travellers and other minorities. Staff development programmes are necessary therefore and should include administrators, counsellors and other ancillary members involved in education and training schemes.

FR.20   A pilot action programme should be initiated in a number of National Schools to implement such a curriculum and to develop a programme for general use in national schools.

FR.21   Changes in text books and teaching materials designed to promote interculturalism and anti-racism should be supported by school organisation and administration procedures and in the drawing up of school plans. There is a need for policies for combating prejudice and anti-Traveller incidents in schools and other education and training institutions.

FR.22   The Department of Education should ensure that Regulations for Publishers should contain guidelines in relation to promoting such a curriculum and only books that comply with the Regulations should be recommended for use in schools.

FR.23   An information pack which could be made available to schools, parents' associations and other relevant bodies should be produced in order to increase awareness of interculturalism in the curriculum.

FR.24   Training courses should assist teachers to acquire:

- a reflective and clearer understanding of their own cultural heritage and social status, how these relate to others and fit with the professional responsibility for the educational and social development of pupils;

- a critical knowledge of multicultural society, and an understanding of the causes and effects of prejudice, racism and xenophobia and other negative attitudes which contribute to discrimination;

- a positive attitude towards cultural diversity;

- pedagogical skills to counteract prejudice, racism and xenophobia to devise teaching strategies and activities which will facilitate academic achievement in the context of cultural diversity;

- democratic values and attitudes towards minority ethnic groups;

- an ability to see and understand the other's point of view;

- knowledge of the curricular and teaching implications of cultural diversity;

- an awareness of equality and anti-discrimination laws and regulations in the State.

FR.25   In-service training, in order to be effective, should be participative, involving not just lectures, but the presentation of diverse experiences, visits, exposure trips, guest speakers, multimedia materials, combined with inputs, analysis and fresh information.

FR.26   Intercultural education should be included in the training programmes of all student teachers, such as higher diploma courses in all universities, teacher training colleges and regional technical colleges.

FR.27   Travellers and Traveller organisations should be resourced to ensure that they can have a significant role in the pre-service and in-service training process.

FR.28   In order to facilitate a more co-ordinated, structured and comprehensive approach to Traveller education, the Task Force recommends the establishment without delay of a Traveller Education Service under the aegis of the Department of Education.

FR.29   The TES should comprise

   (i)   A Traveller Education Unit in the Department of Education under the direction of an Assistant Secretary with necessary support staff drawn from both general service and departmental grades (such as Inspectors and representatives of the Psychological service). This Unit should also comprise the National Education Officer for Travellers and the National Co-ordinator for Traveller Training Centres.

   (ii) An Advisory Committee to advise the Traveller Education Unit in its work. This Committee should be appointed by the Minister for Education and include staff and management representatives from the pre-school, primary, second-level, adult education and third level areas, Traveller parents, Traveller organisations, ATTP, NATC and others with relevant expertise or experience in Traveller education.

FR.30   The work of the Special Education Section of the Department of Education in relation to pre-school and primary education provision for Travellers should continue but a similar section should be established to deal with second-level education provision for Travellers.

FR.31   An examination needs to be carried out by the Department of Education with a view to establishing new Departmental structures for dealing with adult and third-level education for Travellers.

FR.32   The National Education Officer for Travellers should report on a regular basis to the TES. The National Education Officer will continue to have an important role to play within the framework set out for the Traveller Education Service. In view of the major changes which the Task Force is recommending in the area of Traveller Education, it is also recommended that the National Education Officer for Travellers, should be supported by two assistants to deal with education services for Traveller children at primary and post-primary levels, respectively.

FR.33   Within the Department of Education, the primary focus of the Traveller Education Service should be on policy and strategy development in respect of education provision for Travellers and monitoring their implementation to ensure that policy/strategy is accomplished. The delivery of services should be the responsibility of other existing agencies.

   With a view to achieving a co-ordinated and comprehensive approach to Traveller education, the TES should:

   (i)   Have overall responsibility for the development of Traveller education and co-ordinate the activities of the various sections within the Department of Education dealing with the education needs of Travellers including the Special Education Section at primary level and the proposed new section to deal with second-level education.

   (ii)   Draw up, within one year of its formation, a statement of policy in relation to Traveller education which would include medium term plans for all areas of educational provision for Travellers and the staff involved, including special classes, special schools and the Visiting Teacher Service.

   (iii) Oversee the implementation of the various recommendations in the Report of the Task Force dealing with education provision for members of the Traveller community.

   (iv)   Ensure coherence and consistency in the delivery of educational services for Travellers at all levels.

   (v)   Establish a consultation process with all interested groups and particularly with Travellers and relevant Traveller organisations.

   (vi)   Draw up a comprehensive operational strategy for the education of Travellers based on the statement of policy referred to previously. Without neglecting any other aspect of this policy, special urgency should be given in this strategy to resourcing a major increase in the participation rate of Traveller children in mainstream second-level education.

(vii)   Facilitate and monitor the execution of this strategy, including the establishment of clear targets to ensure that it is executed with maximum efficiency and speed from pre-school to third-level. Review the policy and strategy on an annual basis in the light of experience and of the need to develop further resources for Traveller education.

(viii)   Ensure the allocation of the resources necessary to implement the policy on Traveller education set out by the Task Force.

(ix)   Promote a major in-service development programme for teachers at primary and post-primary levels on the scale of the Child Abuse Prevention Programme in 1991, which consisted of one in-service day for every teacher in the country.

(x)   Commission the training colleges and University education institutions to design and include Intercultural Education modules in all courses for trainee teachers on a compulsory basis.

(xi)   Turn into practice the principles in relation to intercultural education, outlined elsewhere in this report, in relation to education provision and promote an intercultural approach and positive learning environment for Travellers at all levels of education and training.

(xii)   Promote curriculum development in intercultural education and the development of appropriate intercultural text books and teaching aids, all of which should be inclusive of Traveller culture. The achievement of this recommendation may require the setting up of a steering committee.

(xiii)   Publish guidelines on second level education for Travellers in accordance with the policy set out by the Task Force.

(xiv)   Review the activities of special schools and seek to apply experiences learnt by them to the mainstream education sector.

(xv)   Undertake, as a matter of priority, an in-depth analysis (including a qualitative evaluation of attainment) into the reasons for the failure of the present primary education system for many Traveller children (See FR.50).

(xvi)   Undertake a liaison function between Visiting Teachers to keep them up to date on educational practices and to ensure that they are adequately resourced.

(xvii)   Ensure that adequate liaison arrangements and back-up resources exist for those Traveller children whose families are mobile so that such mobility does not interfere with their educational provision.

(xviii) Ensure that there is transparency and accountability in relation to the expenditure of monies on all aspects of Traveller education.

(xix)   Develop a comprehensive management structure for all Traveller pre-schools (See FR.46).

(xx)   Carry out a review of the use by second level schools of standardised intelligence tests for Traveller children prior to or following admission to such schools.

(xxi)   Monitor the development and size of the Visiting Teacher Service to ensure that it has sufficient resources and draw up guidelines for use by the managers of that Service.

FR.34   It is widely acknowledged that Traveller children who attend pre-schools are better prepared for primary school. The Task Force considers, therefore, that a comprehensive pre-school service

32

should be provided for all Traveller children. This service should be available to each Traveller child for a period of up to two years before entering primary school and should be staffed by personnel qualified for this age group and be supported by local management structures. Prior to this extension taking place, however, an external evaluation of existing pre-school provision should be undertaken to see what improvements in the system are required.

FR.35   At the present time, there is no standard programme or national policy on pre-school education in Ireland. Such a national policy and programme needs to be developed and co-ordinated by the Department of Education throughout the country. The Department of Education should also provide guidelines on such issues as enrolment procedures, hours of class contact/parent contact, transport, health and safety, ratios, curriculum, procedures for dealing with children at risk, general programmes for early childhood education, children with special needs, parental involvement, minimum requirements for accommodation and in-service training. All of these would form an essential element in the future development of the pre-school education service.

FR.36   The Department of Education should take over responsibility for pre-school provision for Traveller children. In addition, within the pre-school area, there is need for the development of a co-ordinated inter-departmental and inter-agency approach (including: voluntary and statutory bodies including teachers, social workers, childcare workers, youth workers, community workers, public health nurses, speech therapists and psychologists).

FR.37   The existing provision of pre-schools for Traveller children should be maintained and expanded in line with demand. The Task Force notes the Government's commitment to develop a system of pre-schools in disadvantaged areas and considers that the range of supports currently provided for Traveller children should be reviewed in this context.

FR.38   Travellers should be trained and employed in pre-schools as teachers and child care assistants. In section G on the Traveller Economy, the Task Force identifies strategies by which this can be effectively achieved.

FR.39   Child care assistants should be appointed to all pre-schools for Travellers.

FR.40   The Department of Education, through the Visiting Teacher Service, should promote the development and maintenance of close links between pre-schools for Travellers and local primary schools to ensure more effective Traveller pupil participation.

FR.41   Consultation with and involvement of parents, and Traveller organisations should be encouraged and developed.

FR.42   Personnel working in pre-schools should have early education/childcare training and have a child centred approach and training to ensure an understanding of Traveller culture and the specific needs of Traveller children.

FR.43   School transport has had a major impact on attendance levels at schools for Traveller children. Increased funding needs to be provided by the relevant statutory bodies in the area of school transport and, in particular, grants should be provided to voluntary groups for the purchase of buses.

FR.44   The mobile Pre-School Service for Travellers provided by Barnardos is commended. The Traveller Education Service should be requested to examine the need for and feasibility of extending this service.

FR.45   Where necessary, the attendance of Traveller children at local community play groups and pre-schools should be resourced by the Department of Health where there is no Traveller pre-school in the area concerned.

FR.46   At present a variety of management/administrative arrangements are in place in existing pre-schools. It is recommended that the Department of Education through the Traveller Education Service develop a comprehensive management structure for all Traveller pre-schools.

FR.47   The full salaries and PRSI contributions, as appropriate, of teaching staff in pre-schools should be resourced on the same basis as teachers in the primary education sector.

FR.48   Capitation grants should be provided on the same basis as the Department of Education Pre-School Pilot Project to cover accommodation, maintenance costs and rent.

FR.49   The provision of Traveller specific pre-schools should not preclude Traveller parents from choosing to send their children to integrated pre-schools.

FR.50   While it is recognised by the Task Force that problems associated with the underachievement of children who have undertaken primary education are not unique to children from the Traveller community, the problem of poor performance of many Traveller children is of concern especially considering the level of resources invested in the education of such children. Accordingly, while it is the view of the Task Force that many of our recommendations in relation to primary level schooling will assist in addressing the problem of underachievement, the Task Force recommends that an in-depth analysis be carried out (including a qualitative evaluation of attainment) into the reasons for the failure of the present primary education system for many Traveller children. The Task Force further recommends that this survey should be carried out, as a matter of priority, by the proposed Traveller Education Service.

FR.51   Agreed procedures should be established, as a matter of urgency, to ensure that Traveller children have equal access to the education provision best suited to their individual needs, taking parents' wishes into account. Every School Plan should include a statement of policy on access and equality of opportunity to Traveller children.

FR.52   Where Traveller children are at present in a particular location, enrolment arrangements in the local school should not be restricted to any particular date.

FR.53   Following enrolment, Traveller children who need them, should have immediate access to all the necessary support services, including resource teachers, (either on a full-time or part time-basis), visiting teacher service, social and psychological services and essential ancillary staff, particularly classroom assistants or child care workers.

FR.54   School authorities and, in particular, principal teachers, should have the authority to demand the provision of all the necessary resources, support services and ancillary staff to cater for the individual needs of Traveller children. Appropriate levels of provision should be available, irrespective of the number of Traveller children enroled in individual schools.

FR.55   Substantial additional resources should be invested in supporting Traveller children at primary level, to ensure a level of attainment and personal development which would enable them to gain truly equal access to second level education.

FR.56   As an essential pre-requisite for successful integrated education, realistic grants should be made towards cost of transport, books, uniforms, and material expenses.

FR.57   The higher rate of capitation grant should be paid in respect of all Traveller children enroled in national schools regardless of the type of educational provision being made for them.

FR.58   In recognising the transient lifestyle of many nomadic Traveller families, the Department of Education should ensure that flexible arrangements are in place to enable schools to receive additional capitation funding in respect of Traveller children who are enrolled after September 30.

FR.59   On the first appointment of special class or Traveller resource teachers, once off grants should be paid to the schools concerned to cover the purchase of items such as books, equipment and art materials.

FR.60   In order to address the problems faced by those Traveller children who change schools because of the nomadic way of life of their families, a Traveller book exchange system needs to be put in place and resources also need to be provided to primary schools to enable them to purchase new text books for these children. Every effort should be made to ensure that such children are fully integrated in their new schools as quickly as possible.

FR.61 The Department of Education has issued a copy of its document "The Education of Traveller Children in National Schools - Guidelines" to all primary level schools. The Task Force recommends that the Department should now issue a Circular:

  (i) instructing teachers to implement their provisions in day to day teaching practice;

  (ii) clearly stating that, as a matter of policy, Boards of Management are obliged to guarantee similar rights of enrolment to Traveller children as those which apply to children of the 'Settled' community.

FR.62 The school timetable (both daily arrival and departure times) should be the same for   all children including those of Traveller families.

FR.63 The pupil teacher ratio in special schools - except where additional special needs justify a lower ratio - should immediately be set at that applying to special classes.

FR.64 Except in special circumstances, integration of Traveller children at primary level should be mandatory within an intercultural and anti-racist framework. This would enhance participation and educational achievement and would contribute to greater access to second level education.

FR.65 It is recommended that a regular review be carried out of Traveller children in special classes to ensure that their educational needs are being met and that they are not retained in such classes if they are ready for integration into mainstream classes. This review should be carried out by the school principal and class teachers in consultation with the parents and the visiting teacher.

FR.66 Where problems in relation to individual Traveller children are identified, initial education provision for those children should take account of reports from pre-schools, psychological assessments, where carried out, and recommendations from the visiting teachers and parents.

FR.67 Only in cases of special educational need which have been identified in consultation with the visiting teachers or parents, should there be a requirement for provision in special classes. Even in such cases, placement should be regarded as temporary and subject to review by the Department of Education Inspectorate on an annual basis. The objective should be to have all Traveller children integrated by sixth standard so as to facilitate their progression to second-level.

FR.68 Special classes for Traveller children should be seen as a transitional resource in the process towards integration. Cultural, social, emotional and academic support should be offered to Traveller children on a withdrawal basis where necessary.

FR.69 The assessment of a child's attainment level, particularly that relating to language competency, should be based on tests which are clear of cultural bias.

FR.70 Traveller children, on enrolment, should be assigned to the classes which more closely relate to their chronological age irrespective of the short term provision being made for them within the school. Due regard should be taken, however, of the level of attainment and educational disadvantage of the children. While special provision should be made for such children in the circumstances outlined previously, and for the main core subjects (for example Maths and English), Traveller children should be fully integrated with other children for school activities such as sport.

FR.71 Only in exceptional circumstances should Traveller children be retained in primary school after their twelfth/thirteenth year.

FR.72 The pupil/teacher ratio in special classes for Travellers or, for the appointment of Traveller resource teachers, should be reduced from its current level of 15:1 to 10:1.

FR.73   Special Additional Assistants who are appointed to work with Travellers in schools, should be designated Traveller resource teachers.

FR.74   All schools should plan a programme of action designed to ensure that Traveller and 'Settled' pupils are integrated.

FR.75   The Task Force supports the recommendation of the Special Education Review Committee that:

"Schools should adopt an inclusive, intercultural approach to curriculum development so as to ensure that their School Plan, class programmes and teaching materials reflect a positive attitude towards the special customs, traditions and lifestyle of minority groups, including the children of travellers."

The Department of Education, in consultation with the National Council for Curriculum Assessment, should ensure that Travellers and their lifestyle are reflected in an integrated way in all aspects of the primary level curriculum. The way of life and culture of Travellers and other minorities should be reflected in materials in an intercultural way.

FR.76   Flexible structures and curriculum options should be explored in the curriculum for all pupils, Travellers should be included as a group with a distinct culture within and integral to Irish society.

Resources and materials needed to implement an intercultural, anti-racist curriculum (which include Travellers) should be developed for all children.

FR.77   The Department of Education should commission the NCCA to ensure that in developing the primary curriculum, Travellers are explicitly targeted. This is particularly important in designing "Education for Life" and equality measures.

FR.78   Training for all primary level teachers and allied professionals such as speech therapists, psychologists and welfare staff should be informed by and transmit intercultural and anti-racist principles and practice, and should present Travellers as a group with a distinct culture.

Teacher Training Colleges should also include modules on Traveller issues in their core curriculum and further training should be provided for those who have responsibility for the education of Travellers.

FR.79   As earlier recommended in this Report, the Department of Education should provide a comprehensive teacher in-service programme on Traveller education for all teachers. The Task Force supports the recommendation of the Special Education Review Committee that:

"to raise the level of awareness among teachers of the attitudes, values, customs and lifestyle of minority groups, including Travellers, both pre-service and in-service teacher training courses should incorporate modules on intercultural education".

FR.80   Based on teacher vigilance and the concerns of parents, any Traveller children who are experiencing learning difficulties should have access to a psychological service at primary level. A standard psychological test, appropriate to Traveller children, should be designed and used for this purpose.

FR.81   Where required, Traveller children, including children from transient families, should have access to speech therapists.

FR.82   The Task Force welcomes the sample "Family Record Card" and "School Record Card" contained in the Department of Education document "The Education of Traveller Children in National Schools - Guidelines". A comprehensive school record system needs to be developed in recognition of the nomadic lifestyle of Travellers. This record system should ensure the speedy transfer of information on individual pupil attainment between schools. Whenever a "School Record Card" is issued in respect of a Traveller child, a copy should be given to the child's parents.

FR.83   The school record card should be designed to enable the educational progress of children of transient families to be documented. A suitable network should be established to ensure that the transfer of information to schools on the enrolment of pupils is carried out. In view of Traveller mobility across the border with Northern Ireland, such a network should have a North/South dimension; a data base should be provided in the proposed Traveller Education Service to facilitate the transfer of information between schools.

FR.84   The Department of Education currently pays ninety-eight per cent of the running costs of approved special transport systems. Full transport costs (including capital costs) should be borne by the Department of Education.

FR.85   Traveller children, who are fully integrated in mainstream schools, do not always have access to an appropriate school transport system. Traveller children, irrespective of whether they are placed in mainstream classes or in special classes, should have access to a school transport system, when necessary.

FR.86   In relation to Primary education provision for Travellers in Special Education Centres (such as detention centres and centres for people with disabilities), the general recommendations in this report would also apply in relation to such issues as access, equipment, teachers training, intercultural education and literacy.

FR.87   All Travellers should have access to properly resourced homework projects. Where necessary, the Traveller resource teacher should play a role in organising these. The Department of Education should grant aid the provision of teachers for these homework projects.

FR.88   The Task Force considered the Report of the Department of Education Working Group on Post-Primary Education for Traveller Children (1992), and endorses the implementation of the following recommendations from that Report:

> ***14.2** There should be continuous evaluation of the provision being made for Traveller children at primary level.*
>
> ***14.3** The Visiting Teacher Service for Traveller children should be extended to the post-primary sector.*
>
> ***14.5** The making of arrangements for the transfer of Traveller children to post-primary schools should be commenced at the beginning of the school year in which they are due to finish their primary education.*
>
> ***14.9** Schools should exercise a particular sensitivity in relation to the use of standardised tests for Traveller children.*
>
> ***14.11** The receiving post-primary school should make a special effort to acknowledge and respect the Travellers' distinctive culture and identity.*
>
> ***14.13** Traveller children should be integrated with the remainder of the pupils in so far as this is possible.*
>
> ***14.25** The question of certification and assessment for pupils who would not attempt or achieve success in the Junior Certificate Examination should be referred to the Assessment Committee of the NCCA.*
>
> ***14.27** Teachers directly involved with Traveller children will require an extensive programme of in-service education. All practising teachers should be provided with in-service training relating to the general area of Traveller education.*
>
> ***14.28** Co-operation with the United Kingdom on Traveller education should be pursued in certain specified areas.*

14.32 A formal system of co-ordination between the different sections of the Department dealing with Travellers should be set up."

The Task Force has varying degrees of disagreement with the other recommendations in the 1992 Working Group Report chiefly for the following reasons:

– In several recommendations there appears to be an assumption that every Traveller student has remedial needs. The Task Force is aware of the harm which can result from personnel in the education services having low expectations of Traveller children.

– Some of the recommendations, and points made in the body of the Report, might result in a segregationist policy towards Travellers. Travellers in general, abhor the experience and the negative results of segregationist policies in former and in some current, primary school provision for Travellers. Care must be taken not to repeat these at second level.

– Some recommendations, especially those relating to the curriculum, fail in some instances to note that the measures proposed should be culturally appropriate or, in other instances, to acknowledge the importance of adopting an intercultural approach.

– The Task Force has endeavoured to incorporate what it considered valuable in these recommendations in its own recommendations.

FR.89   At the beginning of the final year in primary schools, arrangements for the transfer of Traveller children to second-level schools should commence. It is recommended that the Visiting Teacher should meet with teenage Travellers themselves, have discussions with Traveller parents over a significant length of time and create links (i) between Travellers and post-primary schools, and (ii) between national schools and post-primary schools.

FR.90   Through a comprehensive intercultural approach, the school ethos, curriculum and teaching materials should reflect respect for cultural difference, particularly those cultures relevant to the pupils, including Traveller culture, and enable students to appreciate the richness of cultural diversity.

FR.91   Second-level schools should draw up a School Plan which should include a policy on Traveller education and measures to overcome prejudice. The Department of Education should facilitate this process by issuing guidelines on the preparation of the School Plan. The formulation, implementation and review of the Plan should be the responsibility of the school principal on behalf of the Board of Management. The day-to-day implementation of the plan in relation to Travellers should be the responsibility of the resource teacher, where such a post has been allocated. (see FR.92 below)

FR.92   As a matter of urgency, the Department of Education should allocate ex-quota resource teachers to second-level schools which enrol Travellers. Where the number of Travellers enrolled in a group of neighbouring schools is sufficient to justify the allocation of a resource teacher, a resource teacher should be shared between those schools. A pupil teacher ratio of 8:1 is suggested.

FR.93   The resource teacher for Travellers should be responsible for facilitating the full social and educational integration of Traveller pupils into the school system.

FR.94   The resource teacher for Travellers in liaison with the Visiting Teacher Service should advise the teaching staff on Traveller resource materials relevant to the curriculum and on in-service courses on Traveller education.

FR.95   All Travellers do not share the same education needs and, while special provisions may be required to meet the varied education needs, access to mainstream provision must be regarded as the norm for Travellers. Traveller pupils must not be segregated.

FR.96   Traveller children should not be stereotyped as low academic achievers. Only when special education needs have been identified should more information than is normal be transferred from primary to second-level schools in the case of individual Travellers. Schools should exercise particular caution in the use for Traveller children of tests of intellectual functioning which have not been refined to take account of the specific culture of Travellers.

FR.97   All Travellers should have access to properly resourced homework projects. Where necessary, the Traveller resource teacher should play a role in organising these. The Department of Education should grant aid the provision of teachers for these homework projects.

FR.98   The Department of Education should publish guidelines on second-level education for Travellers based on the principles set out in this Report.

FR.99   In relation to second-level education provision for Travellers in Special Education Centres, the general recommendations in this section should apply in relation to such issues as access, equipment, teacher training, intercultural education and literacy.

Many Traveller children suffer from the same financial difficulties as children from disadvantaged backgrounds, but the degree of disadvantage while not insurmountable, is often greater due to the absence of a school-going network. A general example of possible costs to be faced by families at second level is included at Appendix F(I) of the Task Force's Report.

FR.100   In order to assist in reducing the financial burden imposed on Traveller families at second level, the Task Force recommends that:

(i)   Child benefit levels should reflect and respond to times of particular financial difficulty in school life.

(ii)   A realistic school clothing and footwear grant and school books allowance be provided for Traveller pupils.

(iii)   Greater communication between School Principals, Community Welfare Officers and voluntary groups should take place in order to co-ordinate help for families with full respect for the privacy of these families.

(iv)   Families should be fully informed of schooling costs and their rights fully explained to them.

FR.101   The Department of Education should commission the NCCA to develop the Junior Certificate School Programme to cater for the needs of Travellers. In particular the civic, social, political, environmental education dimension of the Junior Cycle opens up new possibilities which should be availed of in the context of the preparation of young people for their roles as citizens.

FR.102   The Department of Education should commission the NCCA to develop the curriculum at Senior Cycle level in continuity and progression from the Junior Certificate in ways which are relevant and appropriate for Travellers.

FR.103   The Task Force recommends that no further Junior Training Centres should be established, and that the existing JTCs, with the exception of those at primary level, should be taken over by the Vocational Education Committees on the basis of the agreement which the CEO's in the areas where these Centres are located have established with the Department of Education, regarding management structures, staffing, capital provision and non-pay and pay provision. (See Appendix F(2) in the Task Force's Report). These VEC's should be given responsibility for the ultimate phasing out of Junior Training Centres at the most appropriate speed. The speed of this transition will be determined by the successful application of the Task Force recommendations in relation to second level education. Capital costs associated with this transition period should be additional to the existing budget of the VEC's. Immediate measures should be taken by the VEC's to ensure improvement in the quality of the curriculum and of teaching where this may be required. The Traveller Education Service of the Department of Education should monitor the policy set out here for Junior Training Centres.

FR.104   This does not exempt other schools from improving their provision for Traveller education. All Travellers must have equality of access to all mainstream second level schools.

FR.105   The resourcing of the Task Force policy for the improvement of mainstream second level education provision, particularly in relation to visiting teachers, resource teachers and the creation of an intercultural education environment for Traveller education, must be urgently addressed.

FR.106   In view of the positive impact which the Visiting Teacher Service has had in areas where visiting teachers have been appointed, it is recommended that the number of such teachers should be immediately increased by the Department of Education in line with the ratio of one visiting teacher to every one hundred Traveller families as proposed by the INTO in its Report entitled "Travellers in Education".

Based on this ratio and subject to other factors influencing the allocation of visiting teachers being taken into account, such as: distances to be travelled, the number of schools involved, and the size of Traveller families in each area of a teacher's responsibility, it is recommended that the number of visiting teachers be increased to thirty-nine. We note the commitment of the Minister for Education to increase the size of the Visiting Teacher Service to thirty-two and, with due regard to the recommendations on the VTS contained in this Report, request that this be implemented as a matter of urgency.

FR.107   Traveller families should have to deal with one visiting teacher only whether their children are attending primary or second-level schools. This would enable a bond of trust to develop as the basis for a good constructive working relationship between the visiting teacher and individual families.

Accordingly, as proposed in Recommendation 14.3 of the Report of the Department of Education Working Group on Post Primary Education for Traveller Children it is recommended that the Visiting Teacher Service for Traveller pupils should be extended to the post-primary sector. Individual visiting teachers should be responsible for pupils of both primary and post-primary school age in their area and operate in an integrated service embracing both sectors. Qualified primary and second-level teachers should be eligible to apply for positions in the service and a suitable balance between teachers from both sectors should be maintained in recruitment to the VTS.

FR.108   As indicated in recommendation FR.106 above, the resources allocated to each VTS area should reflect its geographical size, the total number of Traveller families and the number of schools in that area.

FR.109   Due to the isolated nature of the VTS, provision should also be made to enable the teachers concerned to meet, on a more regular basis, with the National Education Officer for Travellers, with VTS management and with the proposed Traveller Education Service in the Department of Education to discuss issues of common concern.

FR.110   In situations where large numbers of Traveller families move into a particular area, a visiting teacher, or an additional visiting teacher, should be appointed on a temporary basis without delay to arrange education provision and support for the children.

FR.111   A number of 'supply' teachers should be appointed in order to provide substitute cover for all recognised absences of existing visiting teachers, such as sick leave and maternity leave. The pilot Supply Panel Project operating in a number of national schools in Ballymun/Finglas, North Mayo and Limerick City provides a useful model of substitute cover.

FR.112   The managers of the Visiting Teacher Service should be given clear guidelines, which should be drawn up by the proposed Traveller Education Service, regarding the question of equal access for visiting teachers, including the responsibility and authority to ensure that such guidelines are being implemented. This should apply at both primary and post-primary levels with a suitable mechanism being put in place to ensure that any problems are resolved with particular reference to difficulties arising in the area of cross-sector (primary and second-level) access by visiting teachers.

FR.113   The Task Force endorses the role of the Visiting Teacher Service as set out in the Department of Education Guidelines entitled "The Education of Traveller Children in National Schools". The Task Force, however, recommends that the current Visiting Teacher Service should be expanded into an education service which can meet, in a co-ordinated way, all the education needs of Traveller families in any given area. Central to the visiting teachers' role should be ensuring that each school catchment area has an explicit policy and mechanism formulated to ensure that all schools in the catchment make provision for the special educational needs of Travellers and seek to accommodate them. As recommended in 'Issues of Concern to All Education Sectors' elsewhere in the Task Force's Report, the role of the Visiting Teacher Service should not be seen as a substitute for parental involvement in the education of their children.

FR.114   The visiting teacher in co-operation with the parents should ensure that Traveller children are enrolled in adequate time to commence their second-level education in the school of their choice.

FR.115   In the case of Traveller children who are perceived to be apprehensive about entry to a second-level school, the visiting teacher should ensure that appropriate measures are implemented to facilitate the successful transfer of these children to second level education. This process requires identification of the inhibiting factors and development of measures to overcome these in consultation with the children concerned, their parents and the relevant teachers in primary and second-level schools.

FR.116   The Task Force recommends that appropriate measures be put in place to ensure that teachers in the Visiting Teacher Service do not suffer from 'burnout'.

FR.117   In the long-term, it is essential that more Travellers progress through the mainstream system and gain access to third level education in the normal way. In the short term, it is possible for more Travellers to benefit from third level education. Universities and other third level and post second level institutes should be encouraged to take positive action in this regard.

FR.118   The Department of Education should encourage Traveller participation in third level education by targeting Travellers through the Higher Education Grants Scheme and by ensuring that grants are adequate to cover the costs involved.

FR.119   A national trust should be established, with Government support and private sector sponsorship, to facilitate and encourage Travellers to avail of third level education.

FR.120   The Traveller Education Service should identify where Travellers have gained access to and successfully completed third level courses in order to derive lessons for the future.

FR.121   The importance of adult education should be reflected in the status attributed to adult education within the whole system and in the allocation of resources. The Traveller Education Service should examine current adult education provision in order to ensure that it addresses inequality issues and has the capacity to address the educational needs of Travellers.

FR.122   The values and ideals associated with progressive forms of adult education should be cultivated and the richness of the varied provision should be encouraged. There is need for long-term planning and greater co-operation between statutory and voluntary sectors in order to arrive at a more coherent national policy and a statement of practice on adult education. Such a policy should draw on the experience and insights of Traveller organisations involved in the provision of adult education.

FR.123   There is a need to tackle the many disincentives and barriers which prevent Travellers from participating in adult education. A pro-active approach is needed and adequate information and guidance should be designed for and targeted at Travellers. Entry requirements and structures should be sufficiently flexible to facilitate access and there is a need for resources to cover materials and expenses as well as child care facilities.

FR.124   As well as making adult education courses more accessible for Travellers there is also a need to resource courses specifically designed for and targeted at adult Travellers in order to address their education needs. Such resourcing should also be transparent so as to clearly benefit adult Travellers.

FR.125   Accreditation of adult education courses, including prior learning, should be given careful consideration so that established accrediting bodies are involved and progression is possible, but also to ensure that educational credentials do not become another obstacle to Traveller involvement.

FR.126   Illiteracy is still a major issue in the adult Traveller population and a key factor contributing to their social exclusion. The Department of Education and the VEC's should allocate more resources and personnel to tackle this issue in a comprehensive way and to build on the existing initiatives of voluntary organisations. Special literacy programmes for Travellers should be developed by each VEC with full-time organisers to enable Travellers to access existing literacy schemes. Courses should be specifically designed for Travellers and should include one-to-one as well as group tuition as provided under the Adult Literacy and Community Education Scheme.

FR.127   As indicated in 'Issues of Concern to All Education Sectors' contained in the Task Force's Report, the involvement of Traveller parents in the education of their children is essential for progress. Specific education should be available for Traveller parents to enable them to provide the best support for their children. In this regard, the Task Force endorses the recommendation of the Department of Education Working Group on Post-Primary Education for Traveller Children which states:

"The Adult Education Section of the Department distributes about £1,000,000 each year to Vocational Education Committees for Adult Literacy and Community Education. Sports Section distributes £225,000 per year to Vocational Education Committees under the Special Projects for the Less Advantaged Grant Scheme. We recommend that, in the local allocation of these funds, VEC's give top priority to the financing of courses/activities aimed at Traveller parents. The objective of these courses/activities would be to facilitate Traveller parents in appreciating the benefits of education for their children and to encourage them to give full support to their children's attendance at school up to the compulsory school leaving age and beyond".

FR.128   The Task Force welcomes the commitment in the Green Paper on Education to:

–   develop a comprehensive integrated youth work service across the country;
–   target resources for disadvantaged people;
–   improve mechanisms for grant-aiding;
–   agree mechanisms for monitoring and evaluating youth work;
–   identify criteria of excellence.

It is important, however, that Traveller youth are given explicit mention in youth service provision and not just assume that the "disadvantaged" category will automatically ensure that the needs of Travellers are adequately and appropriately addressed. This means explicit targeting of resources for appropriate Traveller projects, and appropriate inclusion of Travellers. It also involves clear monitoring and evaluation mechanisms.

FR.129   The Department of Education should:

–   ensure that youth work with Travellers is based on an analysis of the needs of Travellers. In order to achieve this the Department should commission a review of existing provision, identify gaps in the service, and formulate guidelines for policy and standardisation of support services;

–   promote the development of a clearer understanding of youth work with Travellers based on a set of values and principles which have been identified as pre-requisites for good practice;

–   ensure that youth work projects should be required to operate from within a written Code of Practice which reflects the principles and values of youth work including respect for Traveller identity and a recognition of the special needs of Travellers.

Organisations involved in the delivery of youth services to Travellers should be funded on the basis of their capacity to deliver a good quality service in accordance with the process and values outlined in this section.

FR.130   The Department of Education should consolidate youth work practice by providing grants for a three year period, subject to fulfilment of annual contractual requirements including evidence of satisfactory progress and financial accountability. Funding should be provided to cover salaries of youth workers and programme activities. Under the present system it is very difficult or impossible for voluntary organisations to pay wage increases because insurance premiums and programme funding have to be taken from the same grant allocation.

FR.131   The European Youth Campaign against racism, xenophobia, intolerance and anti-semitism organised by the Council of Europe, the UNESCO International Year of Tolerance, and the EU Year of Racial Harmony make 1995 an opportune year for ensuring that youth work addresses the issue of discrimination, and in particular racism. This opportunity should be grasped to ensure that young Travellers are accepted, included and treated as equal citizens in Irish society and that youth organisations are aware of the implications for youth work practice.

FR.132   There is need to give recognition to the value and contribution of youth work. The Task Force welcomes therefore the commitment in the Government programme "A Government of Renewal" to provide a statutory basis for youth work in Ireland. The primary role of youth work as informal education would thereby be reinforced in this process. However, it is especially important for Travellers that the priority role of youth work as informal education is reinforced in this process. The Education Act which is expected to follow the White Paper should link the youth service to the relevant education authorities.

FR.133   The Department of Education with the other relevant Departments should ensure that an integrated inter-departmental approach is achieved between youth work, child care, sports and recreation, home/school links, the Juvenile Liaison Scheme, literacy and other adult education schemes. This integrated approach should be reflected in structures at national and local level.

FR.134   An effective and appropriate youth service with Travellers should be based on a social education model containing such values as: respect, co-operation, participation, consultation, responsibility, empowerment and equality. Youth work with Travellers should avoid any connotations of a rescue mission for the deprived or a top down social control approach.

FR.135   Funding should be provided to cover salaries of youth workers and also programme activities.

FR.136   (a) It is essential that training for youth workers is provided and adequately resourced. Such training to include pre-service and in-service, would ensure a professional approach whether workers are unpaid volunteers or paid workers.

(b) In order to sensitise and develop a better understanding of Travellers' needs and concerns, in-service training programmes should be a requirement of all youth projects and organisations. Such programmes should be designed to assist youth workers and youth organisations to develop an inter-cultural approach and to promote good relations with Travellers.

FR.137   Special efforts on the basis of positive action should be made to resource Travellers to acquire the training necessary to become youth workers. It should be noted that in Section G on the Traveller Economy, Youth workers are included among the identified posts for public service employment for Travellers.

FR.138   There is an ongoing danger that young Travellers may be targeted in disadvantaged youth projects but in practice not included or very marginally present in mainstream youth organisations. Therefore, integrated youth projects in receipt of funding for work with young Travellers should specify actions and objectives in their proposed programmes and provide explicit information about results in order to ensure accountability.

FR.139   The special youth work needs of Travellers should be met by a community based service supported and managed by a local voluntary committee in partnership with the Vocational

Education Committees. Such local committees should foster a community youth work approach as recommended in the various reports referred to in this section.

FR.140   Young Travellers are not a homogenous group and it is important that the different needs of young men and young women are acknowledged. It is also important that youth work as informal education challenges sex-stereotyping and promotes respect and responsibility between the sexes.

FR.141   **(a)** The Department of Education should be assigned responsibility for the full administration of Senior Traveller Training Centres in accordance with the policy for these Centres set out by this Task Force. This recommendation is made on the basis that it will have no negative implications in relation to the funding of the Centres and of training allowances, including the provision of EU funding.

(b) It is important that FÁS continue to accept responsibility for promoting and resourcing the development of the employment and enterprise needs of the Traveller community at regional level. This should include the appointment of FÁS representatives to local Traveller Training Centre Management Committees. Such representatives should advise the Centres on resources available through FÁS for promoting this development and promote the progression of trainees from Traveller Training Centres to mainline training courses in FÁS Training Centres, whenever this is the desired option of such trainees.

FR.142   The Department of Education should appoint a National Co-Ordinator to promote the development and monitor the performance of Senior Traveller Training Centres. The person appointed should have a clear commitment to Travellers' development, and knowledge of the development of Traveller Training Centres and proven management and facilitation skills.

FR.143   The National Association of Traveller Training Centres should have the authority to advise the Department of Education and FÁS on the running of Senior Traveller Training Centres. This should include representation on the Advisory Group of the Traveller Education Service.

FR.144   The Code of Practice for Senior Traveller Training Centres should be revised in accordance with the policy set out by the Task Force through consultation between the Department of Education, FÁS and NATC.

FR.145   A determined effort should be made to develop full Traveller participation in the Management Committees of Senior Traveller Training Centres.

FR.146   The training programme in every Centre must be based on a clear analysis of Travellers' interests and needs and it must be culturally appropriate to them.

FR.147   A minimum of three years' training should be available to Travellers in Senior Training Centres and teaching resources should be increased appropriately.

FR.148   There should not be an upper age limit on Travellers attending Traveller Training Centres. Older Travellers should be encouraged and facilitated to attend.

FR.149   Mechanisms should be developed to promote progression of trainees from Senior Traveller Training Centres into a range of mainstream and other options.

FR.150   Where mixed Traveller Training Centres are in operation:

(a) priority should be given to the recruitment of Traveller trainees which should be ensured through range of flexibilities including:

(i) holding places for Travellers who are temporarily absent from an area;

(ii) varying the maximum enrolment numbers.

(b) Priority should be given to cultural needs of Traveller trainees.

(c) It should be recognised that these Centres are not geared to the specific needs of young offenders.

FR.151   Allowances for Trainees in Traveller Training Centres need to be increased to reflect the true costs of participation and to provide adequate incentives over and above Social Welfare entitlements.

FR.152   An appropriate training methodology for Senior Traveller Training Centres should be developed.

FR.153   Training programmes offered in Traveller Centres should be to nationally recognised standards which should be externally monitored by an approved certification agency.

FR.154   All teaching staff in Traveller Centres should have a proven ability to empathise and work with Travellers and have recognised professional qualifications.

FR.155   Resources should be available to all Centres for ongoing staff development.

FR.156   There should be a determined pro-active effort to train and recruit Traveller teachers to the staff of Training Centres.

FR.157   Measures should be put in place without delay to bring all Traveller Training Centre premises up to mainstream national standards and to make available an adequate level of other resources, such as teaching equipment, in all these centres.

FR.158   A culturally appropriate enterprise training and development programme should be developed for Senior Traveller Training Centres.

FR.159   All members of staff in the Senior Training Centres should receive in-service training in an understanding of Traveller culture and its implications for their work, if they have not already received such training.

FR.160   Traveller Training Centre Directors should have at least a third level qualification, or equivalent, and should have competency in education management.

FR.161   The conditions of pay and employment of staff in Senior Traveller Training Centres should be reviewed immediately so as to provide permanent pensionable employment and a pay structure and other conditions of employment which are on parity with staff in other mainstream training and education centres under FÁS and the Departments of Health and Education.

FR.162   Incubator enterprise development units should be provided adjacent to Training Centres, where appropriate.

FR.163   The name of Senior Traveller Training Centres should be changed to Traveller Development Centres.

FR.164   Management Committees should be organised in the Senior Traveller Training Centres in accordance with the policy set out in the Task Force's Report.

FR.165   In order to monitor the progress of Traveller participation in the education system, the Task Force recommends that a detailed examination should be carried out of the systems at present in place in the Department of Education at all education levels, for the collection and collation of statistics on Traveller participation rates. It is particularly essential that this review be carried out at pre-school, primary and second levels of the education system and take cognisance of the gender make up of Traveller pupils. This examination should be undertaken by an expert statistician who should recommend changes which need to be put in place in the statisical collection system in the Department of Education so as to ensure that detailed statistics on Travellers participation rates are available at all education levels and are updated on an annual basis.

FR.166   When the Report of the expert statistician is available, the necessary resources should be allocated by the Department of Education to ensure that any changes which are required in relation to statistical collection arrangements are implemented.

FR.167   The Task Force notes that Vocational Education Committees continue to be excluded from the ambit of the Ombudsman Act 1980 and recommends that the second schedule of that Act be amended to remove the exemptions to Vocational Education Committees.

Section G: Traveller Economy

GR.1   Local authorities, in being authorised to licence traders, should provide casual trading space based on a full assessment of requirements and impact on existing consumer services.

GR.2   Where Transient Trading groups require living accommodation, local authorities should allow them to park on transient sites where available for an agreed period.

GR.3   Larger groups, beyond the capacity of a transient site, should be required to secure adequate space to accommodate their own needs, and deemed to have adequate resources. It is envisaged that the local authority would advise on orderly movement and parking.

GR.4   Transient Traders should be required to maintain contact with local authorities so that orderly movement and parking can be achieved through co-operation.

GR.5   Travellers should be identified as one target group in the licensing of casual trading given their tradition in this area and given the appropriateness of this activity to the way in which their economy is organised. Licences and pitches should be available in a manner accessible to Travellers.

GR.6   The design and construction of Traveller specific accommodation should include limited storage/workspace. Such space is seen as the first step in the development of trading activity under planned conditions. Where the trading activity develops to the level that the storage space provided is inadequate and therefore unacceptable in a residential environment, the Traveller should be required to relocate the activity to an appropriate location.

GR.7   A range of strategies should be developed by the Department of Enterprise and Employment to support Travellers and others in Market Trading. These strategies should be based on the proposals in the EU White Paper in relation to supporting the social economy.

GR.8   Waste management policy and legislation in Ireland should recognise and encourage Traveller recycling activities and the distinct manner in which they are organised.

GR.9   With the implementation of the packaging directive and the Department of the Environment's "Recycling for Ireland" strategy there will be a broad new range of opportunities for recycling in Ireland. These should be promoted within the social economy sector with a range of strategies put in place to secure their viability in line with the proposals in the EU White Paper on "Growth, Competitiveness, Employment". These would include:

–   tax exemptions;
–   public/private partnerships;
–   part work and part income support models;
–   public expenditure associated with EU environment programmes.

Travellers should be one priority target group for these strategies.

GR.10   The Department of the Environment, with the participation of relevant Traveller organisations, should design and develop strategies to support social economy recycling initiatives targetted on the Traveller community.

GR.11 Should a general consultative process be deemed necessary prior to implementation of EU Directives relevant to recycling, relevant Traveller organisations should be included.

GR.12 The implementation of the landfill Directive will require an upgrading of Irish landfill sites and their management structures and procedures. This should be used as an opportunity to develop site designs and procedures that will allow safe access to recyclable materials. The development of baling stations should allow similar access to recyclable materials. This is the approach that is outlined in the "Recycling for Ireland" strategy. This process should not disadvantage Travellers currently involved in recycling.

GR.13 The approach adopted under Recommendation GR.4 above for storage of trading materials should also apply in relation to recycling.

GR.14 There is an existing grant scheme to encourage the development of recycling projects. In the light of the "Recycling for Ireland" strategy launched by the Government in 1994 this scheme should be reviewed to take account of the distinct approach of the Traveller community to recycling.

GR.15 Door to door collections of household waste could make an important contribution to the diversion of waste from landfill sites. This area has potential for further development and expansion. Travellers already play a role in this area. Recycling credits schemes as proposed in the "Recycling for Ireland" strategy should include an incentive for Traveller recycling in this area.

GR.16 The local authority should investigate and take advantage of opportunities for the involvement of Travellers and recycling organisations in the arrangement of junk collection schemes in order to maximise the amount of material recycled.

GR.17 The Department of the Environment should support Travellers and Traveller organisations in researching and introducing appropriate and safe technologies for the processing of copper wire waste.

GR.18 The "Recycling for Ireland" strategy states that *"waste management plans of local authorities and the business sector should aim at harnessing and engaging the contribution of community and residents' associations"*. It is important that Travellers and Traveller organisations be consulted in the development of these plans and that regard is taken of Traveller recycling activities.

GR.19 Where Traveller families keep horses, they should be required to secure adequate grazing areas for their animals. In the urban areas, there can be no requirement on local authorities to provide for this, due to lack of space. In other areas, local authorities have been able to assist in the provision of grazing facilities. This should continue and where possible, be expanded with the support of the relevant Department.

GR.20 Within the training and work schemes provided for Travellers, there should be support in developing their skills at breeding and caring for horses in order to create employment for young Travellers and to ensure the continuation of a tradition that is culturally important to them. This should be explored within FÁS and the VECs.

GR.21 The Departments of Education and of Enterprise and Employment, in conjunction with the relevant third level institutions, should develop special access measures for Traveller entry into third level education and into mainstream training. These measures should include preparation courses, adequate grants, and special tutorial assistance.

GR.22 The Department of Enterprise and Employment, in conjunction with FÁS and Traveller organisations involved in enterprise development, should develop a new funding strategy to support community enterprise, whose primary market is local supply, within communities such as the Traveller community which experience social exclusion. This funding strategy should be of a long term nature and should take account of special needs in relation to access to start-up capital and premises, and in relation to training requirements.

GR.23 The local partnership companies in the designated areas of disadvantage should be supported and encouraged to develop programmes of private sector purchasing from local community enterprise, including Traveller community enterprise.

GR.24 The public service should take a lead role in the recruitment of Travellers into the mainstream labour force. This role should be played in three ways:

- setting targets for Traveller inclusion in general recruitment strategies. These would include a rolling programme for recruitment to identified posts over the next five years and a target of 100 for the employment in non-identified posts during the same period;

- the nomination of existing posts as identified positions with specific Traveller sensitive selection criteria, particularly in education, health and local authority recruitment;

- the development of new posts as identified positions, particularly in education, training, health and local authorities;

- the Department of Finance should have overall responsibility for monitoring the implementation of these targets. It should review them after five years in consultation with the Equality Authority/Commission and relevant Traveller organisations. The Department of Finance should also prepare an annual report on the achievement of recruitment targets in respect of Travellers.

GR.25 The Department of Enterprise and Employment, in conjunction with FÁS and Traveller organisations with experience in this field, should develop a Traveller apprenticeship scheme within the broader apprenticeship model. The Traveller apprenticeship should be designed around the skills, knowledge and attitude required for particular identified positions.

GR.26 The Department of Education, in conjunction with relevant funding agencies and Traveller organisations, should develop the special additional funding supports required to promote and support the further employment of Travellers as youth workers.

GR.27 The proposed Equality Authority/Commission should have a role in reviewing, evaluating and making recommendations in relation to these and future affirmative action measures to promote greater access for Travellers to the mainstream labour force. This role should be played in conjunction with the relevant government departments and Traveller organisations.

GR.28 The FÁS Employment Incentive Scheme sets an important precedent in specifically facilitating Traveller access, by naming them as a special category and waiving entry requirements. The same flexibility in relation to Travellers in the structure of and regulations governing other schemes, in particular the Community Employment Programme, should be implemented to enhance access for Travellers and Traveller organisations.

GR.29 In view of the difficulty of access to mainstream training, education and employment, the life span of all schemes for Travellers should be extended to a three year programme to facilitate skills development, planning and progression into mainstream provision.

GR.30 To encourage greater participation the level of allowances should be increased to cover the full costs associated with participation and to ensure an appropriate increase in comparison with social welfare payments.

GR.31 The number of programmes and places available through the Women's Training Programme for Traveller women and Traveller groups, sponsored by FÁS through the External Training budget, should be increased.

GR.32 Traveller groups should have access to schemes on a multi-annual basis, with guaranteed funding for core staff and facilities.

GR.33 Partnerships between funding agencies and Traveller groups should be developed at national level so that Traveller groups have an input into policy and procedures relating to training and employment schemes.

GR.34 Pilot programmes for Travellers using YOUTHREACH and the Vocational Training Opportunities Scheme should be designed and implemented in partnership with Traveller organisations. This would facilitate greater Traveller participation on these programmes.

GR.35 In-service training, focusing on anti-discriminatory practices and Travellers' culture, should be made available for people providing training and employment scheme opportunities for Travellers.

GR.36 A number of strategies including links with the private sector should be developed to ensure progression for Travellers on schemes both into the mainstream labour force and within the Traveller economy.

GR.37 Within the Local Development Programme for non-designated areas, particular attention should be given to the inclusion of Travellers.

GR.38 In drawing up the Local Action Plan, Travellers and Traveller groups should be consulted.

GR.39 Local Development Partnership Companies should be supported and encouraged to develop strategies in support of the social economy in their area. This would include local purchasing strategies.

GR.40 County Enterprise Boards are focussed on job creation. Supports appropriate to a range of different forms of economic activity, including that of the Traveller Economy with its income focus rather than a job creation focus, should be developed.

GR.41 The Boards should provide resources for job creation in the social economy particularly in the area of local services. This should also include funding strategies of a long-term nature for service enterprises located within disadvantaged communities and serving primarily a local market.

Section H: Traveller Women

HR.1 In implementing each of the recommendations addressed in this report the gender dimension should be examined in order to ascertain how policies and practices in each area contribute to or block progress for Traveller women. Proposals for future initiatives in each area must be monitored in terms of their impact on equality for Traveller women. Each must outline its objectives, targets and likely outcomes for Traveller women.

HR.2 The Government should make resources available for the collection and collation of data on Traveller women through specific research projects. In these projects Traveller women and Traveller women's groups should be subjects rather than objects of the research. The research should build on local profiles and accounts already produced and on other research underway so that any study complements rather than repeats, and addresses gaps not heretofore the subject of detailed scrutiny.

HR.3 In line with the recommendations of the Second Commission on the Status of Women, Government policies on this matter and EU Directives, progress for Traveller women is recognised as a priority in the move towards equality for all women. It is also recognised as essential if progress is to be made for all Travellers. This necessitates a particular focus on Traveller women by any body set up as a consequence of the Task Force Report and in all Government Departments concerned with its implementation. It also requires a particular focus on Traveller women in procedures and legislation adopted towards the implementation of the Report of the Second Commission on the Status of Women.

HR.4 The special needs of different groups of Traveller women should be looked at separately acknowledging that not all Traveller women are the same e.g. the specific situation of young Traveller women.

HR.5   **(i)**   Particular issues which affect the human rights of Traveller women must be urgently addressed. Institutionalised violence towards Traveller women requires detailed examination and responses. Culturally appropriate ways to support Traveller women who experience violence within their community, and to respond to the issue of male violence, need to be worked on with Traveller women. Such work should take into account the responses already being made by voluntary groups, refuges and Women's Aid. The Department of Health should provide resources for pilot projects in this area.

       (ii)   There should be no discrimination or exclusion of Traveller women wishing to access these services.

       (iii)   Resources should be made available by the Department of Health to expand and improve existing facilities in these areas. This should ensure provision for family units of different sizes.

       (iv)   Those working in this area should have access to training in order to ensure their understanding of Travellers and their way of life.

       (v)   The child care needs of Traveller women should be researched and addressed.

HR.6   Traveller women's economic roles in their community should be acknowledged and resourced so that any economic progress for Travellers is supportive of, rather than at the expense of, Traveller women.

HR.7   **(i)**   Targeted responses to Traveller women's needs in a variety of areas such as health, education, training and personal development are required as a pre-requisite towards progress and equality. These should be designed and delivered in partnership with Traveller women's organisations. They should be flexible and capable of integrating local work already underway and building on the knowledge of existing groups.

       (ii)   Ongoing targeted initiatives for Traveller women, as outlined above, should be built into mainstream programmes of FÁS and other State agencies. Staff on such programmes should be selected and managed by Traveller women's organisations.

Section J: Travellers with a Disability

JR.1   The relevant Government Departments and State Agencies should make resources available:

– to ensure that the premises of Traveller groups in their area are accessible to people with a disability;

– to develop a programme for care service providers, Traveller groups or organisations of people with a disability, to train and employ personnel as Traveller advocates. These advocates would play a role in ensuring that the buildings and resources of Traveller groups are accessible, ensuring that the policies and practices of care service providers are sensitive and appropriate to cultural difference, and are supportive of Travellers with a disability, enabling them to express their double identity with confidence. It is envisaged that funding this work would be the responsibility of the Department of Health, and local health boards as appropriate;

– to further research the particular experience and needs of Travellers with a disability.

JR.2   Those responsible for the provision of care services to people with a disability should be required by the various health boards and the Department of Health, as appropriate, to develop appropriate responses to the particular needs of Travellers with a disability including initiatives to reduce their isolation, and programmes to assist those who wish to affirm their Traveller identity and to challenge any discrimination experienced.

JR.3 The various health boards and the Department of Health, as appropriate, should support and resource care service providers to develop in-service training on intercultural work practices in co-operation with Traveller groups.

JR.4 (a) The Commission on the Status of People with Disabilities should make specific reference in its work and reporting to the distinct needs of Travellers with a disability.

(b) In the implementation of the National Health Strategy, the Health Development Sectors should provide resources and opportunities for Travellers and Traveller groups and, within this, specific mention should be made of the needs of Travellers with a disability.

Section K: Co-ordination of services/implementation of Report

KR.1 In order to oversee the implementation and monitoring of this Report, the Task Force recommends that the following arrangements be put in place by the Minister for Equality and Law Reform or his successor:

(a) The Minister for Equality and Law Reform as part of his/her responsibility for co-ordinating Government policy in relation to Traveller issues should monitor and co-ordinate the implementation of the recommendations contained in this Report.

(b) A Traveller Unit with adequate resources should be established within the Department of Equality and Law Reform to assist the Minister in regard to (a).

(c) An annual progress report should be published on the implementation of the Task Force's Report and a formal mechanism should be established for discussion of that progress report with all relevant interests.

Section L: Sport and other recreations, Culture and the Arts

LR.1 In relation to all forms of recreational activity and access to the venues in which these activities take place, the Task Force recommends that discriminatory practices of a direct and indirect nature, should be prohibited against any group particularly vulnerable to discrimination, including Travellers. The Task Force notes, in particular, that legislative proposals in this regard are being drawn up by the Minister for Equality and Law Reform.

LR.2 The Task Force welcomes the provisions of the European Sports Charter adopted by Member States of the Council of Europe in 1993 and recommends that in line with that Charter, special emphasis should be placed on encouraging greater involvement by those who are disadvantaged, including members of the Traveller community, in sporting activities at all levels.

LR.3 The Department of Education should draw up a statement of practice in relation to access to and participation in sporting activities by all members of the Traveller community.

LR.4 There should be an increased commitment on the part of the Department of Education and Vocational Education Committees in relation to the provision of funding, including funds from the National Lottery, to enable Traveller groups to participate in sporting activities.

LR.5 Present arrangements operated by the Department of Education for the allocation of grant-in-aid approvals in respect of sports facilities should include a reference to Travellers' right of access to such facilities.

LR.6 National sports organisations should issue statements of practice to their members on the same lines as recommended at Recommendation LR.3 above.

LR.7 In making grant allocations, sporting organisations including VEC sports committees, should assist less well known sports pursued by Travellers, such as road bowling and trotting, to ensure greater standards of safety in appropriate locations.

LR.8   The Task Force recommends, in relation to Traveller involvement in and the development and administration of cultural policy, including participation in the arts and access to cultural facilities such as museums, theatres etc. that:

– The statements of the Arts Council and in the White Paper on Cultural Policy "Access and Opportunity" quoted in the main Report should act as fundamental principles to be implemented, developed and built upon as necessary in relation to the Arts;

– The Arts Council should publish a Code of Practice for access by Travellers to the Arts along the lines of that published in 1985 for people with a disability;

– Increased funding should be provided, at national and local levels, by the relevant statutory agencies, including the Arts Council, in order to assist and encourage Travellers to develop their artistic and cultural potential and to participate fully in the cultural and artistic life of the State particularly at community level;

– Museums, galleries and other institutions in which artistic work is displayed, should accommodate the work of the Traveller community.

GLOSSARY OF TERMS

TERM	EXPLANATION
Bay	the area within a site allocated for the use of a family, usually walled, with space for caravans and with a small service block.
Group housing	a purpose built scheme of bungalows or houses.
Halting site:	
– Permanent	site with individual bays, with full range of services provided in a small structure on each bay;
– Temporary	short term site, providing basic facilities, for families awaiting permanent accommodation;
– Transient	site providing the basic facilities, for short term use by families pursuing a nomadic way of life, or visiting relatives.
Housing/Local Authority	for the convenience of the reader, the term "local authority" has been used throughout this Report, even where the term "housing authority" would technically be the more appropriate term.
National Programme	will be drawn up by the Traveller Accommodation Agency in consultation with local authorities, and monitored by it.
National Strategy	the sum of the Task Force's recommendations on Accommodation.
Single house	either built or purchased by a local authority, to meet the needs of a specific family.
Standard housing	in standard local authority housing, in local authority housing schemes.
Traveller specific accommodation	group housing and halting sites built specifically for Travellers.
Units:	
– roadside	household on an unofficial site;
– serviced	household on an official site.

"The Task Force on the Travelling Community" is referred to briefly as "The Task Force".

"The Report of the Commission" and "the Commission" refer to the Commission on Itinerancy established by the Government in June 1960 and which published its report in August 1963.

"The Report of the Review Body" and "the Review Body" refer to the Travelling People Review Body established by the Ministers for the Environment and for Health and Social Welfare in January 1981 and which published its Report in February 1983.

Introduction

1.   The Traveller Community Today

1.1   The Traveller community in Ireland today is experiencing high levels of social exclusion and disadvantage. This requires an urgent and planned response.

1.2   The principal features of the serious difficulties being faced by Travellers include:

–   insufficient accommodation with 1,085 Traveller households residing on the roadside and another 257 households on temporary sites many of which are without the basic services such as toilets, electricity and proper washing facilities, services which are taken for granted by the vast majority of the 'Settled' population;

–   infant and adult mortality rates which are over twice those of the 'Settled' community and a general health status which is much lower than for members of the 'Settled' community;

–   extremely low education participation rates among Traveller children particularly at second-level. For example, it has been estimated that eighty per cent of Traveller children in the twelve to fifteen year old age group do not attend any school;

–   high levels of illiteracy which present a major barrier to full Traveller participation in society and to Traveller participation in adult education programmes;

–   the disappearance of the traditional economic activities of Travellers and difficulties faced in pursuing new economic initiatives;

–   a very low rate of participation in the mainstream labour force with high levels of unemployment and reliance on social welfare payments;

–   direct and indirect discrimination against Travellers, which is experienced at many levels.

2.   The Task Force on the Travelling Community

2.1   As provided for under the Programme for a Partnership Government (1993 - 1997), (Ref.1) the Task Force on the Travelling Community was established by the Minister for Equality and Law Reform, Mr. Mervyn Taylor, T.D. in July 1993 with a brief to examine, advise and make recommendations on the needs of Travellers and on Government policy generally in relation to the Traveller community. The terms of reference of the Task Force which were wide ranging are on page 10 of this Report.

2.2   The Task Force submitted an Interim Progress Report to the Minister for Equality and Law Reform in January 1994.

2.3   On 9th January, 1995, Senator Mary Kelly was appointed Chairperson of the Task Force following the resignation of Ms. Liz McManus, T.D. as Chairperson on her appointment as Minister for Housing and Urban Renewal.

2.4 Procedure:

2.4.1 Since its establishment in July, 1993, the Task Force met on thirty occasions in full plenary including its inaugural meeting on 9th July, 1993. It established five sub-committees which met on 94 occasions to deal with Accommodation (29), Education and Training (28), Health (10), Traveller Economy (11) and Discrimination (16) and which comprised Task Force members or their substitutes.

2.4.2 A number of research reports and papers were commissioned and a significant number of submissions from individuals, groups and organisations were also received following public advertisement.

2.4.3 During its deliberations, visits were undertaken by members of the Task Force or its sub-committees to a number of locations in Ireland and meetings were also held with various interests to discuss issues of relevance to the work of the Task Force. Full details are contained in the appendices to this Report.

2.5 This Report and, in particular, Section F (5) on primary education, draws on a number of the submissions to the Task Force because of their particular relevance and the expertise of the authors in relation to the subject matter referred to. The Task Force wishes to thank all those who made submissions during the course of its deliberations and, where these are drawn upon in its Report, hopes that this general acknowledgement will be a sufficient expression of gratitude for the assistance provided.

3. Recent Demographic Trends

3.1 The five-yearly Central Statistics Office (CSO) Censuses of Population are the main source of data concerning the size of the population. Unfortunately, for a number of reasons including the manner in which people are categorised, it is not possible to extract accurately data relating to Travellers from the returns in respect of either the 1986 or 1991 Censuses of Population. Accordingly, apart from the Annual Count of Traveller Families which is carried out by the local authorities, collated by the Department of the Environment and published in the Annual Housing Statistics Bulletin of that Department, there are no detailed statistics on the exact size of the Traveller population in Ireland today. However, it is clear from the various statistics that exist that there has been an increase in the Traveller population in the last decade. The last complete census of Travellers was undertaken in late 1986 as part of a Travellers' Health Status Study carried out by the Health Research Board and published in 1988 (Barry J. and Daly L. H.R.B. 1988) (Ref. 2) recording a population of about 16,000 Travellers, distributed among 2,800 households.

3.2 Recent statistics from the Annual Count, which enumerate families rather than individuals, are contained in Table 1 below. Statistics from the Annual Count report a total of 3073 families in 1986. In 1994, according to comparable Department of the Environment statistics (Ref. 3), there were 4083 Traveller families enumerated. The Annual Count of Traveller families between the years 1986 and 1994 indicates an approximate thirty per cent increase. It should be noted, however, that the Annual Count is aimed at estimating accommodation needs of Travellers and, accordingly, is not entirely reliable for predicting the actual size of the Traveller population or for projecting population increases. This requires a census which enumerates individual Travellers.

3.3   The areas of Ireland in which the largest population of Traveller families are located are Dublin, Galway, Cork, Limerick, Kerry and Wexford.

Table 1	
Total Number of Traveller Families	
1986	3073
1987	3069
1988	3125
1989	3513
1990	3705
1991	3850
1992	3906
1993	3998
1994	4083
Source: Annual Count of Traveller Families:	
Annual Housing Statistics Bulletin, Department of the Environment	

3.4   Research carried out for the Task Force has projected an annual Traveller population increase of 3.3 per cent up to 1999. Allowing for net immigration from the United Kingdom and some under counting in the Annual Count, a projection of a population increase of four per cent per annum is used in Section D of this Report for the purposes of predicting Traveller accommodation needs during the period 1995 - 2000.

4.   Task Force Report

4.1   In order to meet its terms of reference, this Report examines and makes recommendations in relation to three principal areas, as follows:

– key policy issues of relevance to Travellers namely accommodation, health, education and training, and economic development including the co-ordination of policy approaches by the relevant statutory agencies;

– relationships between Travellers and 'Settled' people;

– the experience of Travellers with a particular focus on culture and on discrimination.

4.2   Within each section, this Report recommends strategies to tackle the problems of social exclusion and social disadvantage which are faced by the Traveller community today. The main elements of these strategies include:

– the need to provide 3,100 units of additional accommodation by the year 2000, with supporting administrative and legislative changes to meet the needs of the existing and projected population of the Traveller community.

–   the introduction of measures to improve the health status of the Traveller community and to remove the obstacles to Traveller access to the health services;

–   the re-organisation and development of the education services in order to provide for increased participation levels by Travellers;

–   the encouragement and undertaking of new initiatives to support the development of the Traveller economy and increased levels of Traveller participation in the mainstream labour force;

–   the adoption of measures which address the problem of discrimination faced by the Traveller community;

–   the introduction and/or, where necessary, the improvement of mechanisms in order to ensure that statutory agencies which provide services that impact on Travellers do so in a co-ordinated manner;

–   the need to increase participation by Travellers and Traveller organisations in the decision making process in areas which affect Travellers' lifestyle and environment.

–   the need to recognise and take into account the distinct culture and identity of the Traveller community in policy making and service delivery.

4.3.1   This Report also examines mechanisms for facilitating improved relationships between the Traveller and 'Settled' communities particularly at local level and makes recommendations with a view to reducing conflict and strengthening mutual respect and understanding which it is hoped will merge into a Strategy for Reconciliation. The Traveller community has a fundamental contribution to make to a Strategy for Reconciliation, in particular, by appreciating the anxieties of the 'Settled' population arising from actions which include the illegal occupation of public open space land or using land in a manner that alienates local residents.

4.3.2   The 'Settled' community will also have to accept that their rejection of Travellers is counter-productive and that incidents of social exclusion and discrimination against the Traveller community, such as the refusal of service in hotels, public houses and other establishments and the segregation of Travellers in the provision of facilities, must end.

4.3.3   The Task Force believes that in addition to initiatives and actions taken by the statutory sector, the development and improvement of relationships between the Traveller and 'Settled' communities through the mechanisms recommended in this Report will have an impact in tackling the problem of social exclusion and disadvantage being experienced by Travellers.

4.4   Nomadism is a feature of the Traveller lifestyle and has a relevance for Traveller accessability to health, education and other services. The implications of Traveller mobility have, as far as is possible, been taken into account in drafting this Report.

It has not, however, been possible for the Task Force to quantify the exact frequency of Traveller mobility. Research carried out for the Task Force indicated that several factors were of particular significance in determining the extent and patterns of movement such as family networking, standard of living conditions and services and economic activity. That research also indicated, however, that the patterns of movement have changed.

In addition, it has not been possible for the Task Force to exactly project the impact of the provision of adequate accommodation on the level of nomadism among the Traveller community. However, in Section D on Accommodation, the recommendations relating to the provision of a network of transient sites attempt to meet the estimated needs of existing transient households, the projected increase in their numbers, and to cater for the nomadic way of life of Travellers.

5.   Need for an Integrated and Urgent Response

5.1   In preparing this Report, the Task Force has been increasingly conscious of the many interconnections between all the areas covered and of the urgent need for action in all those areas. The recommendations in any single section likewise cannot be viewed in isolation from other sections. The Report seeks to be an integrated response to the many different dimensions of the situation of Travellers and, as such, progress cannot be made in one area in isolation from progress in the other areas.

5.2   The Task Force is also aware that apart from meeting the requirement under its terms of reference to provide an estimate of cost in relation to the provision of accommodation for the Traveller community by the year 2000, the costs of implementing the recommendations contained in this Report have not been estimated. However, in putting forward various strategies and recommendations, the Task Force recognises that their implementation as well as requiring the re-direction of some existing expenditure, will require an appropriate increase in government funding in the policy areas in question which will in turn place an additional demand on the Exchequer. This is inevitable given the level of exclusion and disadvantage experienced by the Traveller community. However, in the long term, the implementation of many of the recommendations in this Report should also result in savings to the Exchequer as Travellers are, for example, provided with better social and living conditions with a resultant improvement in their health status leading to a reduction in demand for health and other related services.

5.3   The Task Force points to the sense of urgency involved in implementing its recommendations so as to enable the present level of social exclusion and disadvantage experienced by Travellers to be addressed and, at the same time, remove the current causes of friction between the Traveller and 'Settled' communities. In achieving these objectives, the Task Force believes that Travellers will be enabled to take their place and make their full contribution as citizens in Irish society.

References

1.   Programme for a Partnership Government (1993 - 1997). Dublin 1993.

2.   Barry Joseph and Daly Leslie: The Travellers Health Status Study: Census of Travelling People - November, 1986: The Health Research Board Dublin 1988.

3.   Annual Housing Statistics Bulletin: Department of the Environment . Stationery Office: Dublin (Annual).

Section A: Relationships between the Traveller and 'Settled' Communities

1. Introduction

1.1 The purpose of this section on relationships between Travellers and the 'Settled' community is to consider the nature and principal characteristics of the relationship between the Traveller and 'Settled' communities in Ireland today. It endeavours to show that this relationship is, to some extent, based on lack of contact and knowledge on the part of each community about the other. Ways in which mutual understanding and respect can be developed between Travellers and 'Settled' people are explored.

1.2.1 This section also examines mechanisms for facilitating improved relationships between Travellers and 'Settled' people at local level. These mechanisms need to build on experiences of positive contact and co-operation and must elicit mutual understanding between both communities.

1.2.2 Finally, the section contains recommendations, with a view to reducing conflict and strengthening mutual respect between the two communities. It is hoped that these recommendations will merge into a strategy for reconciliation.

1.3 The task of developing relationships between the two communities is a mutual responsibility. Both communities, Traveller and 'Settled' and their associated organisations, have a fundamental role to play in pursuing this objective.

1.4 Attitudes on the part of each community towards the other and relationships between the two communities are influenced by external factors. This section focuses in particular on two of these factors; namely, the role of the media and the influence of the education process in forming attitudes.

2. Nature of the Relationship Between Traveller and 'Settled' Communities

2.1 The relationship between the Traveller and 'Settled' communities in Ireland today is complex. It is influenced by a number of factors including:

– lack of contact and knowledge on the part of each community about the other;

– social exclusion of Travellers by the 'Settled' community;

– lack of provision of appropriate accommodation facilities for the Traveller community;

– illegal parking of caravans on public and private land;

– incidents of inappropriate behaviour.

2.2.1 The Report of the Travelling People Review Body, (Ref. 1) noted that *"the general population of the country has very little detailed knowledge of travellers and the problems they face. Only a small number of people have more than cursory contact* *with travellers and fewer still are on sufficiently friendly terms to engage freely in conversation with them"*. The Report of the Commission on Itinerancy (1963), (Ref. 2) stated that *"the majority of the settled population wish to avoid any contact with itinerants in any form and break off any contact that is established as soon as possible"*. The 1983 Report (op. cit, 1) makes a similar statement to the effect that *"due to lack of communication between Travellers and settled people, the vagabond image tends to predominate in the minds of the majority of settled people"*. It is evident to the Task Force that this position still pertains today.

2.2.2   Minimal contact between both communities contributes to barriers of prejudice based on fear and ignorance on both sides. In addition, it often contributes to the creation of phobias, intolerance, misconceptions, hostility and aggression.

2.3   Incidents of social exclusion and discrimination against Travellers include:

–   refusal of service in hotels, public houses and other establishments;

–   reluctance to share facilities with Travellers;

–   hostility and aggression against Travellers;

–   segregation of Travellers in the provision of facilities.

2.4   Actions by some Travellers which give rise to hostility in the local 'Settled' population include:

–   illegal occupation of public open space land for living purposes without due consideration for the use of that land by the local residents;

–   using land in a manner that alienates the local residents - (rubbish, scrap cars, grazing horses) - and damages the local environment;

–   incidents of harassment and intimidation of passers-by, causing fear in local people, particularly for their children;

–   unruly behaviour from time to time of large numbers of Travellers on special occasions which tend to create fears among the 'Settled' community that this type of activity will be a regular occurrence in every proposed halting site.

2.5   The Task Force believes that whereas all members of society, including Travellers, have the right and responsibility to take an active part in the affairs of the community in which they live and are entitled to enjoy full rights in that community, Travellers often find themselves in an impossible situation. On the one hand, they are subjected to criticism and abuse because of the unsightly and insanitary conditions in which they are forced to reside. On the other hand, when efforts are made to improve their social and living conditions, through the provision of improved accommodation, the same people within the 'Settled' community make strenuous efforts to frustrate and delay those very endeavours which will remove the unsightly and insanitary conditions.

2.6 A successful programme will call for changes in attitudes and behaviour among both communities. An acceptance by the 'Settled' community that refusal to accept a network of sites nationwide can only mean perpetuation of dreadful living conditions for Travellers and their children, and a similar acknowledgement and acceptance by the Traveller community that activities such as those outlined at paragraph 2.4 above are obstacles to the provision of proper living accommodation for Travellers.

3. A Strategy for Reconciliation: A Two Way Process

3.1 The Task Force believes it is imperative that both communities play a role in fostering understanding, consideration and respect for each other's culture. The State also has a key role to play in this process.

3.2 It is essential for the success of any strategy for reconciliation and for improving relationships, to ensure that the statutory authorities gear their efforts and provide sufficient resources to uphold the rights of Travellers as citizens. The foundation for improved relations between the Traveller and 'Settled' communities, is the provision by the relevant statutory authorities of good living conditions and a permanent base which gives Travellers the opportunity to avail of education, health and other statutory services. In time, these improved conditions should lead to better health standards, improved levels of school attendance and greater job opportunities, and effectively lead towards the closure of the gap in living standards between the 'Settled' and Traveller communities as well as removing many of the current causes of friction between the two. Many of these issues of social concern are addressed by the Task Force in other sections of this Report.

3.3 The Task Force wishes to emphasise its belief that Travellers have a fundamental contribution to make to a strategy of reconciliation and to the process of relationship building, and, in particular, must appreciate the anxieties of the 'Settled' population through the exercise o their responsibilities as citizens for the betterment of society as a whole.

3.4 Finally, in order for any process of bridge building to succeed, the 'Settled' community will have to accept that their fears and rejections of all Travellers are extremely negative and discriminatory. As part of a two way process of reconciliation, the 'Settled' community must take responsibility for addressing the social exclusion experienced by Travellers. They must recognise that objecting to and thus obstructing the provision of proper services for Travellers, is counter-productive. Such objections contribute to the creation of unsightly, insanitary and inappropriately placed Traveller camps which upset the 'Settled' community and which also seriously affect the health, living conditions and social and educational prospects of the Traveller community.

4. Traveller Organisations

4.1 The past decade has seen significant growth in the number of Traveller organisations. This growth has been accompanied by change in the nature and role of these organisations. This change can be seen in a number of areas including:

- A shift in focus has taken place, from a welfare approach inspired by charity to a more rights based approach inspired by a partnership process, in seeking to improve the living circumstances and general welfare of Travellers.

– There is an increase, that is both quantitative and qualitative, in Traveller participation in Traveller organisations. This increase is related to the more developmental approaches and work methods that have evolved within Traveller organisations.

– The recognition of the importance of concepts of culture, ethnicity, racism and discrimination has entered in the debate about the situation of Travellers. This has resulted in a redefinition of the Traveller situation in terms of cultural rights as opposed to simply being a poverty issue.

– The emergence of a range of more conflictual relationships with statutory bodies is evident. These relationships were preceded by earlier consensus around a welfare agenda. The present thrust is now towards a new partnership based on a common understanding of the cultural rights of Travellers and of the urgent need to respond to the situation of Travellers.

4.2 The Task Force acknowledges the important role played by Traveller organisations. They have made a significant contribution to creating the conditions needed for new initiatives to be developed in response to the situation of the Travellers and for these new initiatives to succeed. It is important that this acknowledgement is tempered by a realism as to what can be expected of Traveller organisations. Ultimately, only the statutory sector can resolve the major problems being experienced by the Traveller community. Traveller organisations can complement this effort through the different roles they play.

4.3 Traveller organisations working at local level have played a range of different roles. These include:

– Creating a forum where Travellers, with the support of 'Settled' people, can come together to formulate their interests and needs and to define a policy agenda that reflects these.

– Providing new opportunities for Travellers. This has involved providing a range of training opportunities in areas such as personal development, women's issues, enterprise development and employment related skills. It has also included promoting and supporting the creation of Traveller community enterprises and the development of youth and community work projects within the Traveller community.

– Developing new relationships between Travellers and 'Settled' people. This has involved training in intercultural skills and in anti-racism. It has included supporting Travellers to develop contacts with 'Settled' people in a range of settings such as schools, youth clubs, women's groups and community groups. This has involved Travellers in supporting 'Settled' people on their issues and vice-versa.

– Pursuing campaigns, lobby work and media work to highlight and communicate a Traveller policy agenda. This advocacy work has been an important contribution to democracy in ensuring that the Traveller voice is heard in public debate.

4.4   It is useful to identify a number of features common to these Traveller organisations:

–   They are non-governmental and independent of the statutory sector although many of their activities are funded by the state.

–   They are organised with a membership of Travellers and 'Settled' people seeking to work together as equal partners and can also be organised with a membership made up solely of Travellers. The effective participation of Travellers is the key feature of these organisations.

–   They have taken up unambiguous supportive positions in relation to Traveller issues and to the improvement of the living circumstances and general welfare of Travellers.

4.5.1   Traveller groups are organised at both local and national level. A range of co-ordination mechanisms have been put in place. These include national resourcing and group development services, as well as networking between groups and the development of national platforms on issues. Access to resources specifically for such a purpose has been an obstacle in the development of national networking.

4.5.2   In terms of national networking, the Irish Traveller Movement provides co-ordination and a national platform for Traveller organisations around the country. The National Traveller Women's Forum provides a similar facility for Traveller women and groups working on Traveller women's issues. The National Federation of Travelling People, which was another national network, was disbanded during the life of the Task Force. Some members of this network are now organising the Federation of Irish Travellers. Pavee Point has been developed as a national resource centre for Travellers and Traveller organisations and has been resourced to promote the growth and development of Traveller organisations at a local level.

4.6   The National Traveller organisations should develop procedures of co-operation so as to ensure their ability to organise their representation on the various relevant bodies now being recommended by the Task Force.

5.   Improving Relationships

Recommendation

AR.1   The improvement of relationships between the Traveller and the 'Settled' communities through the development of mutual understanding and respect requires an adjustment in attitudes towards one another and an acceptance of each other's culture. In order to achieve this key goal, the Task Force recommends that every opportunity must be taken to increase levels of contact between the Traveller and 'Settled' communities at national level and more particularly at local community level. It is the view of the Task Force that improved levels of contact will :

–   result in a better understanding on the part of the 'Settled' population of the general needs of Travellers, their culture and aspirations and also of the contribution which cultural diversity makes to society;

–   enable Travellers to understand more about the anxieties of the 'Settled' population;

–   contribute to the reduction in the present levels of conflict and tension which exist between both communities by helping to eradicate misconceptions, intolerance and hostility.

5.1   It is important that attention is also given to the process by which increased contact can be achieved. The identification of common ground in terms of common interests, issues and concerns provides the best basis for good quality contacts. The objective of quality contact will also require that increased contact is based on a mutual respect for cultural diversity and not on notions of assimilation of one community by the other. This in turn requires that groups prepare for contact by developing their knowledge of each other and by developing their skills in relating across cultural boundaries. The conditions should thus be created for both groups to enter into, and set the terms for, new relationships on a basis of equality. Without adequate attention to the manner in which these contacts are developed, there is a real danger that increased contact will merely serve to confirm negative perceptions already held by each group.

5.2   Increased levels of contact both formal and informal must be encouraged, in particular at local level. Traveller organisations and training centres can make an important contribution to this process by:

–   identifying common issues with local 'Settled' organisations and working alongside them on these issues;

–   reaching out to local 'Settled' organisations and supporting them, even when the issues concerned may not be of direct relevance to Travellers;

–   encouraging Travellers to respect 'Settled' people's needs and anxieties and creating the right conditions to work positively in co-operation with relevant statutory bodies on issues which affect their interests.

Recommendation

AR.2   In widening the focus of their activities to include the work outlined above, Traveller organisations should have access to additional resources.

5.3   Local voluntary and community organisations involving 'Settled' people, can contribute to the process of relationship building through actions such as:

–   setting out their opposition to acts of exclusion or violence against Travellers;

–   raising awareness within the local 'Settled' community through providing opportunities for people to explore issues of cultural difference, equality, discrimination and anti-racism;

–   identifying and pursuing common issues in partnership with Traveller groups and supporting them on their issues.

5.4   Travellers should be encouraged to join local community associations, sports clubs, youth groups, school boards of management, residents' associations and other similar organisations. It is hoped that these groups will welcome and encourage local Travellers to join and to participate in their activities for the overall betterment and development of relationships and improvement of living conditions in the local community.

Recommendation

AR.3 The statutory sector has a contribution to make in terms of providing institutional support and resources for the above initiatives and also, through its activities, in conveying a more positive attitude to the Traveller community and to issues affecting the well-being of Travellers. In particular, the Government should make these issues the focus of a sustained and committed media campaign.

5.5 The Task Force believes that church groups have a significant role to play in this area, particularly in the improvement of relations between 'Settled' and Traveller populations.

5.6 The role of the non-statutory social partners has become more important in recent years through the work of such fora as the NESF and NESC and also as part of the process of economic and social planning, for example, in the negotiation of national agreements such as the Programme for Competitiveness and Work. The voluntary and community sector is increasingly represented as a partner in these fora. As part of this process national Traveller organisations are making an important contribution and should continue to be facilitated to do so.

Recommendation

AR.4 The Task Force recommends that the social partners, in drawing up future National Agreements, should take account of the needs of disadvantaged groups such as Travellers and should involve Traveller organisations where the needs of Travellers are being discussed.

5.7 Conflict Resolution

Reconciliation strategies, combined with a changing policy context and improved living conditions for Travellers, will greatly improve the relationship between Travellers and 'Settled' people. However, conflict resolution strategies will continue to have a relevance at particular moments of tension or where incidents have taken place or seem likely to take place. Conflict resolution has much to offer reconciliation strategies by ensuring that moments of tension do not lead to violence or a hardening of attitudes or responses.

The Community Relations Service in the United States has developed a model of mediation which is based on three principles, namely:

– mediation is an informal process to resolve disputes and is not judgmental;

– the mediator acts as facilitator and problem solver;

– the parties are responsible for the ultimate resolution of the dispute.

This model is being explored by Pavee Point with the assistance of the Department of Social Welfare.

The advantages of mediation include the possibility of an early and quick settlement, limited expense and enhanced relationships through the direct involvement in negotiation of all parties. Conflict resolution will involve Travellers and 'Settled' people. It will involve Traveller groups and residents' and tenants' associations. The statutory sector also has an important contribution to make.

Recommendation

AR.5 The Task Force recommends that the Department of Equality and Law Reform, in conjunction with other relevant Departments and non-governmental organisations, taking account of previous work in this field, should play a role in exploring and devising a framework for mediation.

6. A Strategy for Reconciliation: Additional Elements in the Process

6.1 The final part of this section looks at two external influences on the process of bridge building between Traveller and 'Settled' people, namely, the role of the media and the role of education institutions.

6.2 The Role of the Media

The media is a prime source of information for people and therefore has an important role to play in addressing relationships within a culturally diverse society. The media can challenge or reinforce racist images, attitudes and behaviour. In a situation of minimal contact, 'Settled' people obtain most of their information about Travellers from the media. Travellers are often portrayed negatively and stereotypically in the media. Travellers can be presented as a problem or a threat. Media reports focus on events related to crime, violence and conflict and they also tend to be reactive to events with less concentration on a pro-active approach to issues and events involving members of the Traveller community.

6.3 The European Parliament has carried out a number of inquiries into racism and xenophobia which draw attention to the role and responsibility of the media. The most recent was the Ford Report in 1991, (Ref. 3) which stated:

> *"Whilst acknowledging that the media can play a positive role in forming knowledge about ethnic minority communities, it is undeniable that currently, media presentation overall, perpetuates a negative image of these communities"* and *"Members of ethnic minorities should be involved in the communication process at all levels, in the elucidation of what information is needed, through planning how information is to be collected, presented, packaged and distributed, through active participation in those decision making processes involved in the production and distribution of information (and cultural productions)".*

6.4 The National Union of Journalists' "Guidelines on Race Reporting", (Ref. 4) provide useful principles and practical suggestions which should inform all media. In relation to Travellers, the Guidelines state that the word Gypsy or Traveller should only be mentioned if strictly relevant or accurate and that reporting on Traveller issues should be balanced seeking Travellers' views as well as those of other members of the community. The Guidelines also recommend journalists to:

– *"Resist the temptation to sensationalise issues involving Travellers, especially in their relations with settled communities over issues such as housing, settlement programmes and schooling.*

– *Try to give wider coverage to Travellers' lives and the problems they face.*

– *Strive to promote the realisation that the Travellers' Community is comprised of full citizens of Great Britain and Ireland whose civil rights are seldom adequately vindicated, who often suffer much hurt and damage through misuse of media and who have a right to have their special contributions to Irish and British life, especially in music and craftwork and other cultural activities, properly acknowledged and reported".*

6.5 In relation to the approach adopted by the media the Task Force makes the following recommendations:

Recommendations

AR.6 The media should adopt a more pro-active approach on issues of concern to and relating to the Traveller community, in consultation, where necessary, with Traveller organisations. This could include the provision of more programming time on television and on radio (both at national and local levels) and more print features on such issues as Traveller culture, lifestyles and achievements.

AR.7 The National Union of Journalists' "Guidelines on Race Reporting" if followed more consistently, could make an important contribution to the development of better relations between Travellers and the 'Settled' population. It is recommended that these Guidelines be developed into a Code of Practice to be adopted by the various media institutions.

AR.8 The proposed White Paper on Broadcasting Policy offers another important opportunity to develop the media's contribution to better relationships between Travellers and the 'Settled' community. The White Paper should give a firm commitment to the following:

– Highlight the role and responsibility of public broadcasting in the development of interculturalism and anti-racism.

– Point to the need for programmes which promote respect for cultural diversity, and the rights of minorities including Travellers.

– Emphasise the importance of a code of practice and guidelines which encourage broadcasters to avoid sensationalism and negative stereotypical images of Travellers and other minority groups.

- Encourage education programmes which challenge intolerance, racism, xenophobia and discrimination and which provide a voice for communities experiencing exclusion such as Travellers.

- Broaden the concept of 'Equal Opportunities' to include Travellers.

- Encourage and support Traveller groups and other organisations representing communities experiencing exclusion, to have access to the production and delivery of public broadcasting.

6.6 The Role of Third Level and Adult Education Courses

While the question of education provision for the Traveller community and of access to education facilities is addressed elsewhere in this Report, it should be noted that courses provided by third level education institutions, have an important role to play in forming public opinion and in influencing public policy on Traveller issues. In particular, such courses have a contribution to make in:

- raising levels of awareness about the living circumstances and culture of Travellers;

- providing a sound information base, as part of the process of combating any role 'Settled' people might play in the social exclusion of Travellers;

- analysing the bases and mechanisms of social exclusion/marginalisation in Ireland;

- training and informing the policy makers of the future and in the public sector in particular, who will be charged with the task of the formulation and implementation of policy which will have an influence on the lives of Travellers as well as the rest of the community.

6.7   A wide range of courses are provided by third level education institutions at both under-graduate and post-graduate levels which address, in some way, issues of concern to the Traveller community. These courses are mainly in the social policy and practice areas. Particular examples include Community Work courses in St. Patrick's College, Maynooth, Social Work courses in UCC, TCD, UCD, UCG and in some of the Regional Technical Colleges and Women's Studies and Equality Studies courses in UCD. Many contain anti-racist modules which focus on Travellers' lives.

Recommendations

AR.9   Anti-racist modules have a particular relevance to the professional training of people who will have contact with Travellers in their work situation. They should be an obligatory component of all courses in professional training where this contact is likely. Traveller groups should be involved in the design and delivery of such modules.

AR.10   Modules dealing with Traveller issues should be extended, as far as is practicable, to courses other than Social Policy/Social Science, for example, to Political Science and Business Studies, which are pursued by many of the policy makers of the future.

AR.11 Guidelines should be developed in relation to the collection and use of academic research relating to Travellers by education institutions. These guidelines could be modelled on the code of ethics for Aboriginal health research in the Australian National Aboriginal Health Strategy, (Ref. 5).

6.8 Public Service Training

The Institute of Public Administration (IPA) has an important role to play in the professional formation and development of management and policy-making skills among public servants.

Recommendation

AR.12 The Task Force recommends that every opportunity be taken by the IPA to include specific modules on Traveller issues and anti-racism in its courses of professional training for public servants and that Travellers and Traveller organisations should be involved in the design and delivery of such modules.

References

1.   Report of the Travelling People Review Body, Stationery Office, Dublin 1983.

2.   Report of the Commission on Itinerancy, Stationery Office, Dublin 1963.

3.   European Parliament Committee of Inquiry on Racism and Xenophobia, (Ford Report): Office for Official Publications of the European Communities: Luxembourg 1991.

4.   Guidelines on Race Reporting: National Union of Journalists, London 1984 (re-printed)

5.   Centre for Health Promotion Studies UCG and P. McCarthy and Associates (Dublin): Health Service Provision for the Travelling Community in Ireland (Study commissioned for the Task Force on the Travelling Community) 1995.

Section B: Culture

1. Introduction

1.1 Everybody has a culture. It is the package of customs, traditions, symbols, values, phrases and other forms of communication by which we can belong to a community. The belonging is in understanding the meanings of these cultural forms and in sharing, values and identity. Culture is the way we learn to think, behave and do things.

1.2 Knoeber and Kluckhohn, in "Culture: A Critical Review of Concepts and Definitions" (1952), (Ref.1) state:

"Culture consists of patterns, explicit and implicit, of and for behaviour, acquired and transmitted by symbols, constituting the distinctive achievements of human groups, including their embodiment in artefacts; the essential core of culture consists of traditional (i.e. historically derived and selected) ideas and especially attached values".

This defines culture as a largely intangible aspect of human society located in the realm of ideas, symbols and values. Culture is defined in terms of the way people interpret, use and perceive artefacts and material objects to express and define themselves.

1.3 The Traveller culture lies in the values, meanings and identity that the Traveller community shares. It is clear that the Traveller community's culture is distinct and different. 'Settled' people generally recognise the difference but fail to understand it as cultural difference. This is a phenomenon, characteristic of many societies, where the majority culture sees itself as holding a universal validity or norm in relation to values, meanings and identity.

1.4 It is difficult, given its intangible nature, to define a particular culture. We can only describe Travellers' culture in terms of what we see as different from 'Settled' society. However, a culture exists in terms of values, customs, identity, belonging and the exclusion of non-members. It is at the level of communication that a culture is kept alive, and it changes to meet new social and economic circumstances. Culture is dynamic, complex, changing and not static. Thus, to define the Traveller culture it could only be defined at one particular time and only then if those defining it were within it and fully understood all the values and meanings in the intercommunication and identity.

1.5 The Travelling People Review Body which reported in 1983 (Ref. 2) captured the concept of cultural difference in its very useful definition of Travellers:

"They are an identifiable group of people, identified both by themselves and by other members of the community (referred to for convenience as the 'settled community') as people with their own distinctive life style, traditionally of a nomadic nature but not now habitual wanderers. They have needs, wants, and values which are different in some ways from those of the settled community".

1.6 More recent affirmation of the culture of the Traveller community comes from the report to Government of the Second Commission on the Status of Women in January 1993 (Ref. 3). They stated that:

71

"Travellers have their own culture and a strong sense of community, facts which are often unappreciated by the settled community"

1.7 The Irish Government reported to the Human Rights Committee of the United Nations in October 1992 under the terms of the International Covenant on Civil and Political Rights. In its presentation to the committee the Attorney General stated that *"While Traveller culture and traditions have many positive traits such as strong sense of family they also have patriarchal elements"* and *"it is also the case that there is a growing awareness among the Travellers of their own rights and cultural heritage. This, it is hoped, will facilitate their participation in public life"*. (Ref. 4).

1.8 At the level of the European Union clear affirmation of the distinct culture of the Traveller community is contained in the "EC Resolution of the Council and the Ministers of Education meeting within the Council of 22nd May 1989 on School Provision for Gypsy and Traveller Children" (Ref. 5) to which the Irish Government was a party. This document states that:

"Gypsies and Travellers currently form a population group of over one million persons in the community and that their culture and language have formed part of the community's cultural and linguistic heritage for over 500 years".

The resolution goes on to recommend *"consideration for the history, culture and language of Gypsies and Travellers"* in teaching methods and teaching materials.

2. Visible Manifestations

2.1 Traveller nomadism, the importance of the extended family, the Traveller language and the organisation of the Traveller economy all provide visible or tangible markers of the distinct Traveller culture.

2.2 The Council of Europe report "Gypsies and Travellers" (Ref. 6) which was prepared by J.P. Liegeois in association with experts from a range of member countries including Ireland highlights the importance of Traveller nomadism. The report states:

"nomadism is neither entirely the product nor the producer of culture, it is a basic component which confers on the whole a marked flavour".

Traveller nomadism, as with its counterparts across Europe, takes a range of forms. It includes those who are constantly on the move, those who move out from a fixed base for a part of any year, and those who are sedentary for many years and then move on. Traveller nomadism contributes to the social organisation of the community as it provides for contact and communication within a dispersed community. It plays an important economic role in providing Travellers with access to markets broad enough to make marginal economic activities viable. It also plays a psychological role which is described as follows in the Council of Europe report "Gypsies and Travellers":

"Nomadism is more a state of mind than an actual situation. Its existence and importance are frequently more psychological than geographical".

2.3   Nomadism is, as described, a feature of the Traveller economy. A number of other features also serve to highlight the distinct nature of the Traveller economy and to make this another area where cultural difference is visible. These features include:

* **Flexibility.** In moving from one economic activity to another as opportunities for profit emerge. This contrasts with the more specialised career oriented approach dominant within the 'Settled' community.

* **Self employment.** In the Council of Europe report "Gypsies and Travellers", this emphasis on self employment is described as "one of the most marked elements which make up the identity of Gypsies and Travellers".

* **Income basis.** The Traveller economy is based on immediate payment for goods or services provided. This contrasts with the focus on jobs and job creation within the 'Settled' community.

* **Home base.** The extended family is the basic economic unit within the Traveller economy. Home space and working space tend to be one and the same.

2.4   The Traveller language is called Gammon or Cant. In academic circles it is referred to as Shelta. Study of the language has revealed a vocabulary which is used in a somewhat simplified English grammatical structure. Some of the vocabulary consists of Irish words which have been transformed or disguised.

It is these latter words that formed the basis for the conclusion, in the studies of John Sampson of the University of Liverpool and the German folklorist Kuno Meyer in the early 1900s, that the Traveller language was very old. They found:

– archaic words preserved in disguised form in the language;

– words formed from pre-aspirated Irish;

– methods of disguising words identical to those employed in monastic manuscripts.

Research into the Traveller language (Ref. 7) has interpreted the manner in which the language has developed as a product of a nomadic group, the members of which were only in intermittent contact with each other. In this way the vocabulary is well developed while the grammar is borrowed from the majority 'Settled' community. The development of a grammar requires a fixed stable community.

2.5   The Irish Travellers in North America have been found to use the Gammon despite over a century of separation from Irish Travellers in Ireland. It is estimated that between 4,000 and 7,000 Irish Travellers are scattered across the southern states of Alabama, Georgia, Tennessee, South Carolina, Mississippi, Louisiana and Texas. The ancestors of the Irish Travellers were themselves Irish Travellers who were part of the mass emigration from Ireland in famine times. Despite the years of separation they have maintained an identity and culture that still has much in common with Irish Travellers in Ireland. Self-employment, mobility, burial customs and the extended family still serve as the visible markers for this culture. (Ref. 8)

3. Importance

3.1 The recognition of Travellers' culture and identity has an importance for Travellers and their status in Irish society. Identity and belonging is vital to everybody and is equal to physical wants and needs. Identity and sense of community cannot be ignored because identity is fiercely cherished by everyone and community is vital for everyone's sense of belonging.

3.2 Frederico Mayer, the director-general of UNESCO, emphasises the importance of culture in stating:

"All thinking and all action concerning Gypsies and Travellers must be based on an essential parameter: culture, its existence, its dynamics, its past and future. When this parameter is ignored, be it through oversight, lack of reflection, or deliberately, policies run aground and actions do not produce the desired effects".

This position was also reflected by President Robinson in a speech given in 1990:

"When we talk about the Travelling community it's not just a question of whether they want housing or whether they would prefer serviced halting sites. It's that they want their culture recognised, they want their dignity respected, they want to be full citizens of this country. I think that that's the most important thing - that there is real space for the Travelling community, for their own culture, for their own self development and self expression; that we have space for them and that we value them; and then other things like the appropriate kind of houses, services and facilities are provided to the best of our ability as a nation. But perhaps the most important thing is that we value them as a distinct community within our larger community". (Ref. 9).

3.3 It is impossible to wipe out one's culture, the values one has, the ways of evaluating, of communicating with and understanding others. While, in normal circumstances, cultures are dynamic, change cannot be imposed and must come from within. Communities, 'Settled' or Traveller cannot give up their values and customs and beliefs totally and adopt others. Earlier housing or settlement projects did not grasp this and results achieved were not compatible with the investments involved.

3.4 Cultural difference therefore is a key element to be taken on board in policy design and in the procedures by which resources are made available. The Council of Europe report "Gypsies and Travellers" which comments from a range of experiences across Europe, highlights the consequences of failure in this regard in concluding:

"The forced process of settling, frequently carried out under poor conditions, means less psychological, social and economic adaptability. When travel becomes just a dream, a long-delayed dream for the Traveller, despair and its effects set in (illness, break-up of the family, aggressiveness and delinquency). The result is a crisis in the society of Gypsies and Travellers". (op.cit.6)

3.5 The important contribution of cultural diversity to the well-being of a society should also be acknowledged. Cultural diversity provides a society with a broader range of

74

perspectives and frames of reference. Cultural diversity in a context of mutual respect means that communities with different cultures can provide different approaches and solutions to common problems.

Cultural diversity allows for communities with different cultures to contribute to each others' well-being. An example of this is in the field of Irish traditional musical heritage (Ref. 10). In the past, Travellers have contributed to musical expression within the settled community through:

- bringing tunes, songs, and dances from town to town;

- making and repairing instruments;

- their particular style of playing the uilleann pipes and the fiddle which influences many of today's practitioners.

4. Intercultural Contact and Conflict

4.1 While the relationship between Travellers and 'Settled' people is dealt with in more detail in Section A, it is important to reiterate some key elements of the debate as it relates to culture. Minimal contact contributes to the formation of barriers of prejudice based on fear and ignorance. Contact is largely confined to economic transactions, statutory service providers, and, increasingly, Traveller groups making links and networking with schools and community based groups.

4.2 Conflict and tension are other characteristics of the relationship between the two communities. Conflict can arise where communities with different cultures share limited resources. This can be accentuated where these resources are not designed in a manner that accommodates cultural difference.

4.3 Anti-discrimination legislation can play an important role in increasing the contact between the Traveller and 'Settled' communities by removing the discriminatory exclusion of Travellers from many areas of social life. This legislation can also improve the quality of the contact through affirming Travellers' status in Irish society in terms of their distinct culture and identity.

4.4 Planning can play an important role in reducing conflict and tension. Resources provided in a manner that recognises and incorporates the distinct Traveller needs can reduce the basis for hostility, rejection and fear that exist. By reducing the basis for hostility, fear and rejection, real integration can be realised, where the values, customs and beliefs of all are respected by all.

4.5 The public sector, in terms of its planning function, can therefore play a key role in reducing conflict and tension. The public sector can also foster Traveller participation and partnership in planning. This will give Travellers a sense of belonging, in the broader Irish society, as Travellers. It will strengthen integration, respect and sense of ownership and responsibility. The commitment to such participation was clearly made in the Attorney General's presentation to the UN Human Rights committee (op.cit,4) *"it is Government Policy that the Traveller community will participate in policy decisions which affect them".*

4.6 The provision of appropriate resources and the recognition of cultural difference carry with them obligations and responsibilities. Such responsibilities and obligations should be enforced on the Traveller community as on the 'Settled' community.

5. Conclusion

5.1 Everybody has a culture. Culture is the way we learn to think, behave and do things. The Traveller culture is that distinct complex mix of values, traditions, customs and patterns of behaviour that are shared by the Traveller community and practised in their daily lives. This involves a specific field of communication, meaning and belonging.

5.2 Traveller nomadism, the importance of the extended family, the Traveller language and the structure of the Traveller economy all provide visible or tangible markers of the distinct Traveller culture. The Traveller way of life is an adaptation of culture and circumstances. It is important that culture and circumstances are not confused.

5.3 Nobody's culture can be destroyed, wiped out or assimilated. A person's cultural reality is not capable of complete or immediate change. While, in normal circumstances, cultures are dynamic, change cannot be imposed and must come from within. Communities, 'Settled' or Traveller, cannot give up their values and customs and beliefs totally and adopt others.

5.4 There is minimal contact between the Traveller community and the 'Settled' community. The relationship between the two communities is characterised by conflict and tension. Legislation and planning based on an acknowledgement of cultural difference can reduce this conflict and tension. Such initiatives carry with them obligations and responsibilities which should be enforced on the Traveller community just as they are on the 'Settled' community.

6. Recommendation

BR.1 That the distinct culture and identity of the Traveller community be recognised and taken into account.

References

1. Knoeber and Kluckhohn, Culture: A Critical Review of Concepts and Definitions. Vintage Books, N.Y. 1952.

2. Report of the Travelling People Review Body. Stationery Office, 1983.

3. Report of the Second Commission on the Status of Women. Stationery Office 1993.

4. United Nations Human Rights Committee, Geneva, 12-13 July 1993. Response by Attorney General of Ireland, Harold A. Whelehan.

5. EC Resolution of the Council and the Ministers of Education meeting within the Council of 22nd May 1989, on School Provision for Gypsy and Traveller Children. (89/C153/02)

6. Jean Pierre Liégeois, Gypsies and Travellers Dossiers for the Intercultural Training of Teachers: Council of Europe, Strasbourg 1987.

7. Binchy, Alice, in Irish Travellers: Culture and Ethnicity, edited by McCann, O'Síochain, Ruane, Institute of Irish Studies, 1994.

8. Lockwood, William G. and Salo, Sheila, Gypsies and Travellers in North America. An Annotated Bibliography, Gypsy Lore Publication No.6., U.S.A. 1994.

9. Speech to the Joint Irish Association/DTEDG Seminar, President Mary Robinson. Pavee Point, Dublin, December 1990.

10. The exhibition "Pavee Pipers and Players" Travellers Cultural Heritage Centre, Pavee Point, 46 North Great Charles Street, Dublin 1, 1994.

Section C: Discrimination

1.   Introduction

1.1   The Travelling People Review Body, (Ref. 1) highlighted a range of discrimination experienced by the Traveller community. At the level of the individual or interpersonal, it stated:

"A local continuing hostility on the part of the settled population in many areas is identified by the Review Body as the greatest factor hindering the provision of accommodation".

At the level of the institutions of Irish society the report made reference to:

"punitive action against Travellers without recourse to the due process of law"

and

"In recent years a more subtle form of harassment has been practised by certain local authorities. This takes the form of fencing off parking areas, even traditional camping sites, or digging trenches around them"

and

"continuing infringement of the scheme of letting priorities resulting in the denial to Travellers and especially the married children of housed Travellers, the same rights as other applicants for local authority housing".

The Travelling People Review Body decided not to seek the enactment of legislation "to outlaw discrimination against Travellers as a minority group". This was because it was considered that *"the implementation of such legislation would be fraught with many difficulties, especially in the absence of a precise legal definition of 'Traveller."* However, since then, Travellers have been specifically named within two pieces of legislation - the 1988 Housing Act and the 1991 Prohibition of Incitement to Hatred Act - without such difficulties becoming apparent.

1.2   Over the past decade discrimination against Travellers has not diminished. Such a scenario requires new initiatives and new approaches. Public debate has increasingly focused attention on the need for legislative initiatives.

This debate has been encouraged by developments within the European Union. In 1991 the European Parliament Committee of Inquiry on Racism and Xenophobia (Ref. 2) reported that, in Ireland:

"The single most discriminated against ethnic group is the 'Travelling People'".

The Committee, referring to Ireland, recommended:

"That the only Member State which has not already signed the UN Convention on the Elimination of All Forms of Racial Discrimination, do so as soon as possible".

In this context the Task Force acknowledges the commitment in the Programme for a Partnership Government, (1993 - 1997), (Ref. 3) to *"pass Equal Status Legislation which will prohibit discrimination,"* and to *"ratify the U.N. Convention on ending all forms of discrimination"*. More recently this commitment was reaffirmed in the Programme for Competitiveness and Work, (1994), (Ref. 4) which states that *"Equal Status Legislation will be introduced in 1994 with a view to combating discrimination beyond the employment field."*

1.3 The approach in the Programme for a Partnership Government coincides with developments in Northern Ireland. In March 1992 the Standing Advisory Commission On Human Rights (Ref. 5) recommended:

"That the Travelling People, together with the other ethnic minority groups in Northern Ireland, should be brought within the scope of race relations legislation applicable to Northern Ireland and that the Travelling People should be specifically identified in the legislation as an ethnic group".

In December 1992 the Central Community Relations Unit published a discussion document on "Race Relations in Northern Ireland" (Ref. 6) as a precursor to legislative change there. Pressure for this change was further reinforced in September 1993 by the Report of the Committee on the Elimination of Racial Discrimination of the United Nations (Ref. 7) which expressed *"concern about the absence of legislation prohibiting discrimination on racial grounds in Northern Ireland and the ensuing lack of adequate protection available to ethnic minorities including, in particular, Travellers and persons of Chinese origin"* .

1.4 Academic debate and various international fora focus attention on the link between racism and cultural difference particularly in scenarios of unequal power relationships. The forms of prejudice and discrimination experienced by the Traveller community equate with racism in the international context.

The European Union has taken a growing interest in promoting and co-ordinating anti-racist measures. Racism is a growing phenomenon across Europe. The European Union Green Paper on European Social Policy, (Ref. 8) states that:

"The fight against racism and xenophobia is echoed in the protection of fundamental rights confirmed in the Single European Act".

Travellers, in their view, should be clearly located within this European Union commitment.

1.5 Travellers experience discrimination at the individual or interpersonal level and at the institutional level.

Discrimination at the individual level is most common when a Traveller seeks access to any of a range of goods, services and facilities, to which access is denied purely on the basis of their identity as Travellers. Examples abound of public houses refusing to serve Travellers, hotels refusing to book Traveller weddings, bingo halls barring Traveller women, leisure facilities barring access to Travellers, and insurance companies refusing to provide motor insurance cover. This experience can also include physical and verbal attacks and intimidation.

At the institutional level three mechanisms are identifiable whereby discrimination against Travellers may occur:

— Procedures and practices can reflect a lack of acceptance of Travellers' culture and identity and can involve controls placed on Travellers in excess of those placed on members of the 'Settled' community in similar circumstances.

— Travellers can be segregated in the provision of various services. Segregation is an imposed setting apart of a group. Segregation is therefore different from provision which is designed to advance positive resourcing and affirmative action policies, where participation is by choice.

— Legislation, policy making and provision can be developed without account being taken of their potential impact on a minority cultural group such as the Travellers. In this way policy and practice can develop in a manner that only reflects the 'Settled' community's culture and identity and can therefore be inappropriate for the Traveller community. The nomadic way of life, through not being named, is marginalised, as resources and services which are provided, are inappropriate to this aspect of the Traveller culture and identity.

1.6 This discrimination experienced by Travellers can be direct and indirect. At the level of the individual it is more often conscious and direct. At the level of the institution it can more often be indirect and without intent.

Direct discrimination consists of treating Travellers, on the grounds that they are Travellers, less favourably than others are or would be treated in the same or similar circumstances. This would include segregation of Travellers in the provision of goods, services and facilities.

Indirect discrimination consists of :

— applying a requirement or condition which, although applied equally to all persons, is such that a considerably smaller proportion of Travellers can comply with it and which cannot be shown to be necessary on other grounds,

or

— pursuing policies or practices which, although applied equally to all persons, are such that they produce outcomes that adversely affect a significantly higher proportion of Travellers.

Indirect discrimination is complex. It involves treatment that seems on the surface to be fair, but where the effect or result is unequal. A good rule of thumb is that where the effect or result shows a twenty per cent or greater disparity between the Traveller community and the majority 'Settled' population, then indirect discrimination could be a factor and should be investigated (Ref. 9).

Possible examples of indirect discrimination against Travellers are:

– unwarranted reliance upon qualifications and requirements which are not essential to a job being offered or a service being provided;

or

– an understanding or requirement that a service or facility is to be accessed only by persons of fixed residence;

or

– policies or procedures of relevance to Travellers that do not acknowledge and respond appropriately to the distinct Traveller culture, identity, and way of life.

1.7   Discrimination also occurs where a person is victimised for making a complaint in relation to discrimination, for supporting anyone making such a complaint, for giving evidence or information in relation to such a complaint, or for intending to do any of these things.

1.8   Positive action targeted on Travellers to eliminate discrimination, to promote equality, and to relieve hardship and the impact of past discrimination is necessary. Positive action programmes should be developed and implemented in partnership with Travellers and Traveller organisations. Access to such programmes should be on the basis of voluntary participation.

1.9.1   Discrimination generates a crisis for the Traveller community. The crisis can end up perpetuating many of the negative stereotypes of Travellers held by the majority 'Settled' population. Inadequate and inappropriate provision for Travellers contributes to conflict at a local level between Travellers and 'Settled' people over the use and abuse of resources. Discrimination at an institutional level creates conditions for discrimination at an individual level.

1.9.2   Stereotyping and conflict cannot be dealt with through attitudinal change alone. A new environment needs to be created through change in legislation, policy and procedures in provision of services for the Traveller community. This changing context will present an opportunity and a challenge to the Traveller and the 'Settled' community in developing new relationships of mutual respect, trust and responsibility.

2.   Equal Status Legislation

2.1   While legislation alone will not put an end to the discrimination faced by the Traveller community, it will make an essential contribution to this task. It will provide a catalyst for changing the context within which conflicts and stereotypes are generated. It will give Travellers a legal means of redress against discrimination. It will be a statement of significant weight from Government of the Travellers' status in Irish society and of the unacceptability of discrimination. In this it will provide a basis for changing attitudes within the 'Settled' community and the Traveller community, and for new relationships between the two communities.

2.2   Recognition of the distinct culture and identity of the Traveller community will make a significant contribution to this community enjoying equal status in Irish society. The Travelling People Review Body Report in 1983 (op.cit,1) defined Travellers in a manner that acknowledges their distinct culture, identity and way of life:

"They are an identifiable group of people, identified by themselves and by other members of the community ... as people with their own distinctive lifestyle, traditionally of a nomadic nature but not now habitual wanderers. They have needs, wants and values which are different in some ways to those of the settled community".

Recommendation

CR.1   That the Equal Status legislation would define Travellers in a manner that acknowledges their distinct culture and identity.

2.3   The indirect nature of much of the discrimination faced by the Traveller community can be difficult to address legislatively. Experience in Britain and Northern Ireland has shown that defining indirect discrimination as *"the imposition of terms or conditions that a substantially higher proportion of a particular group cannot comply with"* (op.cit,6) is not adequate or broad enough.

Recommendations

CR.2.1   That the Equal Status legislation would define indirect discrimination in a manner that incorporates not only terms and conditions set for the provision of goods, services and facilities but also policies or practices governing or relevant to these.

CR.2.2   That the Equal Status legislation would identify a twenty per cent differential between communities in their access to goods, services and facilities as the point beyond which indirect discrimination requires to be investigated. The experience of British Race Relations legislation indicates that this figure would be appropriate.

2.4   The content of Equal Status legislation must be adequate to address the nature of the discrimination experienced by the Traveller community which is described in sub-section 1. above. In this it is important to draw on the experience of the Commission for Racial Equality in Britain, the Fair Employment Commission in Northern Ireland, and the Employment Equality Agency in Ireland. The Task Force has drawn from these sources in developing the recommendations set out below.

Recommendations

CR.3.1   That the Equal Status legislation would prohibit:

– policies and procedures that discriminate against Travellers' culture and identity;

– the exclusion of Travellers, just because they are Travellers, from the normal benefit of goods, services and facilities;

– the segregation of Travellers in the general provision of goods, services and facilities unless this is for reasons of positive action.

CR.3.2 That the Equal Status legislation would specifically name the statutory sector as being bound by its provisions, as this sector is the predominant provider of goods, services and facilities to the Traveller community and experience in Britain has demonstrated that it is necessary to specifically name this sector. Any exemption in this area should be strictly necessary and subject to regular review by the Equality Authority/Commission.

CR.3.3 That the Equal Status legislation would ensure equality of treatment for all citizens in the areas of law enforcement and the judicial process.

CR.3.4 That the Equal Status legislation would ensure protection from victimisation for those making a complaint of discrimination under the legislation, supporting such a complaint, giving evidence in relation to a complaint, or intending to do any of these things.

CR.3.5 That the Equal Status legislation would ensure that Travellers can continue to benefit from affirmative action to prevent discrimination, promote equality, and redress past discrimination.

CR3.6 That the Equal Status legislation would ensure protection from victimisation for those who support, work with or resource the Traveller community.

CR.3.7 That the Equal Status legislation would provide a legislative basis for the Equality Authority/Commission's Codes of Practice and for Equal Status policy programmes so that these can be taken into account in the deliberations around any complaint.

2.5.1 The Task Force has also drawn from research commissioned from the Human Rights Centre in the University of Essex (Ref. 10). One section of this research focused on the application of British Race Relations legislation to Travellers. This research found that:

"anti-discrimination law upon British lines is capable of providing protection to the Travelling community especially if it is made explicit that ethnic groups are intended to benefit from protection afforded by the legislation.".

2.5.2 The British Courts initially faced problems in deciding what constitutes an ethnic group. The issue was settled by the Courts in the speech of Lord Fraser in "Mandla v. Dowell Lee" (1983), (Ref. 11) where he stated :

"For a group to constitute an ethnic group in the sense of the Act of 1976, it must, in my opinion, regard itself and be regarded by others, as a distinct community by virtue of certain characteristics. Some of these are not essential but one or more of them will commonly be found and will help to distinguish the group from the surrounding community. The conditions which appear to me to be essential are these:

(1) A long shared history, of which the group is conscious as distinguishing it from other groups, and the memory of which it keeps alive;

(2) a cultural tradition of its own, including family and social customs and manners, often, but not necessarily associated with religious observance.

In addition to those two essential characteristics the following characteristics are, in my opinion, relevant:

(3) either a common geographical origin or descent from a small number of common ancestors;

(4) a common language, not necessarily peculiar to the group;

(5) a common literature peculiar to the group;

(6) a common religion different from that of neighbouring groups or from the general community surrounding it;

(7) being a minority or being an oppressed or dominant group, for example a conquered people (say the inhabitants of England shortly after the Norman conquest) and their conquests might both be ethnic groups."

2.5.3   This judgement of Lord Fraser cited with strongest approval a fragment from Richardson J.'s judgement in the New Zealand Court of Appeal in "King-Ansell v. Police", (Ref. 12) which stated:

"a group is identifiable in terms of its ethnic origins if it is a segment of the population distinguished from others by a sufficient combination of shared customs, beliefs, traditions and characteristics derived from a common or presumed common past, even if not drawn from what in biological terms is a common racial stock. It is that combination which gives them a historically determined social identity in their own eyes and in the eyes of those outside the group".

2.5.4   For the purposes of British law it is clear from these judgements that the Traveller community could be identified as an ethnic group. In the Irish context, it is important that Equal Status legislation in specifying its protection of ethnic groups would also specifically name the Traveller community as being protected. The relevance of the provisions in British Race Relations legislation is clear and the research commissioned by the Task Force provides the basis for two further recommendations in relation to Equal Status legislation. These relate to the protection of cultural identity and to economic justifications for discrimination.

2.5.5   In relation to cultural identity the research highlights arguments regarding indirect discrimination and what *"can comply with"* means where indirect discrimination is defined as *"applying a requirement or condition which, although applied equally to all persons, is such that a considerably smaller proportion of a protected group CAN COMPLY with it"* (op.cit,10). Lord Fraser, again in the Mandla v. Dowell Lee (op.cit, 11) case is quoted as settling this discussion in stating that *"can comply"* should be read as *"can comply consistently with the maintenance of his cultural traditions"*. The intention of the Act is therefore understood as being to protect cultural identity by rendering unlawful discrimination based upon cultural norms.

Recommendations

CR.4.1   That Equal Status legislation would specifically identify its intention to protect cultural identity.

CR.4.2   That Equal Status legislation would ensure that Travellers are protected from indirect discrimination where they are unable to comply with requirements, conditions, policies or practices consistent with the maintenance of their cultural norms.

2.5.6   The research also highlights contradictory judgements in relation to whether indirect discrimination can be justified upon economic grounds. Direct discrimination cannot be justified in this way but there is a lack of clarity in relation to indirect discrimination.

Recommendation

CR.5.1   That Equal Status legislation would clearly identify that neither direct nor indirect discrimination against Travellers could be justified on the grounds of potential financial disadvantage to the provider.

3.   **Equality Authority/Commission and Equality Court**

3.1   The effectiveness and impact of Equal Status legislation depends on the quality of the institutions created to promote and implement such legislation. Existing equality legislation focuses on sexual harassment and on equality of opportunity and elimination of discrimination in employment as between men and women in the workplace. The institutions relevant to this legislation are the Employment Equality Agency and the Labour Court.

Equality legislation in the employment area will now be extended to cover other groups including the Traveller community. Equal Status legislation will protect Travellers and other groups from discrimination in non-employment areas.

These new challenges cannot be met merely by expanding the remit and powers of existing institutions. A re-structuring of these existing institutions is a minimum requirement to ensure new expertise is developed and that new areas and experiences of discrimination are addressed with equal rigour.

3.2   In making recommendations in relation to the institutions required for effective Equal Status leislation, the Task Force has analysed the experience of the existing Employment Equality Agency and of the Labour Court. These recommendations are presented in the knowledge that a range of new groups are to come under the protection of equality legislation. The Task Force stresses the importance of involving Traveller organisations that can represent Traveller interests in such institutions. The Task Force has framed these recommendations conscious of the reality of financial constraints. Financial resources available can therefore determine the exact implementation of these recommendations. However, to be effective, the implementation of the new legislation will require appropriate and significant investment.

3.3   Re-structured institutions should reflect the broad range of groups to be encompassed within equality legislation. They require a specific body of expertise in relation to discrimination in non-employment areas to match that existing in relation to employment areas. They also require a specific body of expertise in relation to the particular experience of discrimination faced by the Traveller community.

Recommendations

CR.6.1   That an Equality Authority/Commission be established based on a re-structured Employment Equality Agency. The Equality Authority/Commission is to be comprised of an Employment Board and a Non-Employment Board.

CR.6.2   That the Employment Board of the Equality Authority/Commission would include representation from Traveller organisations.

CR.6.3   That the Non-Employment Board would include Travellers and Traveller organisations along with representation from the appropriate Government Department with responsibility for co-ordinating services to the Traveller community.

CR.6.4   That an executive committee would be drawn from both the Employment and Non-Employment Boards to co-ordinate policy and to control resources and administration.

CR.7   That the Equality Authority/Commission would have legal powers and necessary resources to:

CR.7.1   Initiate and pursue investigations into instances and patterns of discrimination.

CR.7.2   Receive complaints and provide advice and support to those taking a case under the legislation.

CR.7.3   Take cases on its own initiative.

CR.7.4   Develop codes of practice to set standards in relation to Equal Status policy programmes to be implemented in private, voluntary and public sector institutions and organisations. (This point is developed in sub-section 4 below).

CR.7.5   Monitor and evaluate the quality and impact of Equal Status policy programmes put in place by institutions or organisations, to ensure consistency and minimum standards for these Equal Status policy programmes, and to provide support and advice to institutions or organisations designing, implementing or reviewing such programmes.

CR.7.6   Require an institution or organisation to develop and implement an Equal Status policy programme. (This point is developed in sub-section 4 below).

CR.7.7   Secure affirmative action where discrimination has been identified, to correct this discrimination and to redress its past impact.

CR.7.8   Proof legislation, existing and new, to ensure that it takes account of its impact on Travellers.

CR.7.9   Develop an information service on relevant international instruments, and taking into account needs of Travellers and Traveller organisations.

CR.7.10   Form consultative groups to assist it in its work.

CR.7.11   Develop educational projects on equality issues and rights under equality legislation.

CR.7.12   Review on a regular basis all equality legislation and any exemptions therein.

CR.8.1   That the Non-Employment Board of the Equality Authority/Commission would establish a distinct Traveller unit which would ensure cohesive action on Traveller issues, which would encompass officers in the following areas; legal, enforcement, information, legislation, positive action and research, and which would have adequate clerical and financial support. The research officer would initiate in-house research, co-ordinate with research commissioned in other sections of the Equality Authority/Commission and make an input into such research.

CR.8.2   That the staff training programme for all officers of the Equality Authority/Commission would include intercultural methods, anti-discriminatory practices, and an appreciation of the importance of identity and cultural difference.

CR.8.3   That the Non-Employment Board would operate through sub-committees dealing with legislation, positive action, enforcement, information and research to facilitate decision making between Board meetings and to ensure a consistent and co-ordinated approach. The officers assigned to these functions in the Traveller unit would participate in the relevant sub-committees.

CR.8.4   That the Equality Authority/Commission would be able to recruit outside the Civil Service.

CR.8.5   That the Non-Employment Board would put in place a programme to create the conditions for the recruitment of staff from the Traveller community. This programme would include a form of Apprenticeship Scheme as a step towards this goal.

CR.8.6   That the nomadic element of the Traveller way of life would be accommodated in the delivery of information and case support through initiatives such as a 'free phone' service and regular outreach clinics, and that all relevant materials developed by the Equality Authority/Commission would be in a format and medium appropriate to the Traveller community.

3.4   The District Court system is not the appropriate institution for hearing cases in the non-employment area of discrimination. The process in the District Court is too slow, intimidating, and too closely linked to criminal prosecutions. The District Court does not have the officers or specific expertise to deal with this new area of casework. This has been the experience in Britain where the Commission for Racial Equality (op.cit,9) has recommended that *"the County Court jurisdiction for non-employment cases should go"*.

3.5 The nature and magnitude of awards open to the Fair Employment Tribunal in Northern Ireland is widely acknowledged as providing new standards. Practice there should be used as a guideline in framing the awards open to a new Equality Court.

Recommendations

CR.9.1 That an Equality court would be established, similar to, but separate from, the Labour Court, to deal with cases of discrimination in the non-employment area.

CR.9.2 That the right to redress throughout the court system would not be precluded by the establishment of an Equality Court.

CR.9.3 That the Free Legal Aid Scheme would be expanded to cover those taking action on the grounds of discrimination in both employment and non-employment areas.

CR.9.4 That respondents to a case before the Equality Court would be required to show that their action was necessary on grounds other than those prohibited by Equal Status legislation once differential treatment is established.

4. Code of Practice and Equal Status Policy

4.1 The development of Codes of Practice will be the responsibility of the Equality Authority/Commission. The Codes should set out the central objectives of an Equal Status Policy and the key commitments required in an Equal Status Policy.

While a Code of Practice has a general relevance, an Equal Status Policy is specific to a particular institution or organisation. An Equal Status Policy in relation to Travellers aims to ensure that an institution or organisation and its employees:

– do not engage in direct or indirect discrimination or victimisation;

– establish procedures to enable complaints of such discrimination to be thoroughly investigated, appropriate remedial measures to be taken where discrimination is found to have occurred, and disciplinary measures to be imposed against defaulters as necessary;

– acknowledge and respect the distinct culture and identity of Travellers;

– promote positive action in support of equality and equal status for Travellers;

– work to clear targets and timescales in developing and implementating actions appropriate to each of the above headings.

While it is recommended that public, private and voluntary sector institutions and organisations prepare an Equal Status Policy, it is acknowledged that such a policy has a particular relevance for public sector institutions, given:

– the scale of operations in this sector;

– the role of the public sector as sole provider of certain services;

- the essential nature of many of the goods, services and facilities provided by the public sector;

- the function of the public sector in social planning;

- the potential for the public sector to play a lead in promoting equality in Irish society.

4.2 The concept of an Equal Status Policy builds on the work of the Employment Equality Agency in promoting Employment Equality Programmes in various public and private sector institutions and organisations, and extends this work into the non-employment area of discrimination.

Recommendations

CR.10.1 That each government department, semi-state body, State agency, local authority, private sector and voluntary sector organisation would adopt, implement and monitor an Equal Status policy appropriate to the nature of its function and, that public and voluntary sector organisations and institutions would be adequately resourced to meet their obligations in this regard.

CR.10.2 That, while an Equal Status policy is the responsibility of management, it would be designed in co-operation with employees and their trade unions, and that the Equal Status Policy would be clearly communicated to all staff within the institution or organisation and to the general public served by the institution or organisation.

CR.10.3 That individual employees would be encouraged to draw the attention of management and their trade union to areas and incidents of suspected discrimination - a staff suggestion scheme with incentives could be developed similar to the present Input Scheme operating in the Civil Service.

CR.10.4 That an Equal Status policy would include the following commitments as appropriate to the size and nature of the institution or organisation:

- a member of senior management to be given responsibility for implementation and monitoring of the Equal Status policy. (In the public sector this could be an extension of the present functions of Equality Officers. However, it is preferable that this role be established outside of the personnel department.);

- goods, services and facilities to be provided in a manner that respects and is appropriate to the distinct culture and identity of the Traveller community;

- materials to be developed that are appropriate to the Traveller culture and identity, within services and facilities availed of by this community;

- communications with the general public to be couched in a language and imagery that reflect the commitments in the Equal Status policy and that is accessible to the Traveller community;

- training to be provided for all staff to ensure an understanding of the Equal Status policy;

- training to be provided for staff with responsibility for Traveller issues and services to ensure an understanding of the Traveller culture and identity and a knowledge of intercultural and anti-discrimination work methods;

- Travellers and appropriate Traveller organisations to participate at the relevant level within the institution in decision-making processes that impact on the Traveller community and on the implementation of the Equal Status policy;

- where the institution or organisation is involved in the creation of policy fora or task forces, any Traveller dimension be recognised and Traveller and Traveller organisation representation ensured;

- positive action programmes to be developed for Travellers, including programmes for the recruitment of Travellers into the institution or organisation, and creating the conditions for this to happen;

- existing policies and procedures, including the Equal Status Policy, to be reviewed on a regular basis and changed wherever the potential for discrimination is discovered or where scope for further or alternative positive action is identified;

- annual reports, or other appropriate reporting mechanisms engaged in by the institution or organisation, to include details of equality issues arising during the year, including implementation of work done, complaints of discrimination dealt with and positive action taken.

Recommendation

CR.11.1 That the Department of Equality and Law Reform, or its successor, in its work of co-ordination in relation to services to Travellers, would promote and support the introduction of an Equal Status policy, based on the above recommendations, within the various public sector institutions that provide services of an essential nature to the Traveller community, as a matter of priority.

5.   **International Standards**

5.1   International standards on human rights at the universal and regional levels have an importance for the Traveller community. These standards, many of which are a matter of binding treaty commitment for the Irish State, are directed at both the elimination of discrimination and the recognition and positive valuing of minority cultural identities.

Given the importance of these international standards the Task Force commissioned research from the Human Rights Centre in the University of Essex (op.cit,10) to identify the instruments of key relevance to Travellers and to assist in formulating recommendations in relation to these.

5.2   United Nations Standards

(a) International Covenant on Civil and Political Rights, 1966

Article 2 of this Covenant obliges the Irish Government to legislate for the prevention of discrimination and provides a framework from which to judge the adequacy of this legislation. It requires anti-discrimination law to ensure an effective remedy against discrimination, to encompass discrimination by public authorities and by private individuals or organisations, and to allow vindication before a competent authority preferably a judicial authority.

Article 27 of this Covenant reads :

"In those States in which ethnic, religious or linguistic minorities exist, persons belonging to such minorities shall not be denied the right, in community with the other members of their group, to enjoy their own culture, to profess and practise their own religion or to use their own language".

In October 1992 the Irish Government presented its first report to the Human Rights Committee in relation to this Covenant. The Committee's published comments on this report stated:

"The Committee suggests that the State party undertake affirmative action aimed at improving the situation of the 'Travelling community' and in particular facilitating and enhancing the participation of 'Travellers' in public affairs, including the electoral process." (Ref. 13).

Recommendation

CR.12.1   That the Irish Government in responding to this report of the Human Rights Committee as it relates to cultural minorities, would take particular cognisance of Article 27 of the Covenant and that future reports from the Irish Government to the Human Rights Committee on this Covenant would make specific references to the application of Article 27 to the Traveller community.

(b) International Covenant on the Elimination of all Forms of Racial Discrimination 1965[1]

The Programme for a Partnership Government 1993-1997 (op. cit, 3) states that the Government will ratify this Convention Article 5 of which states:

"State Parties undertake to prohibit and eliminate racial discrimination in all its forms and to guarantee the right of everyone, without distinction as to race, colour, or racial or ethnic origin, to equality before the law notably in the enjoyment of the following rights..."

which rights include economic, social and cultural rights.

---

[1] Adopted in 1965, entered into force in 1969.

The work of the Committee on the Elimination of Racial Discrimination (established under Article 8 of the Covenant) in its consideration of the United Kingdom 1993 report (op.cit, 7) expressed concern at the experience of Travellers in Northern Ireland particularly in relation to the *"lack of adequate protection available to ethnic minorities including, in particular, Travellers and persons of Chinese origin"*. This demonstrates that Travellers are considered an ethnic group for the purpose of this Covenant.

Recommendation

CR.13.1   That the Irish Government would ratify the Covenant on the Elimination of all Forms of Racial Discrimination.

CR.13.2   In ratifying this Covenant the Irish Government should accept the right of individual petition under Article 14.

(c) The International Covenant on Economic, Social and Cultural Rights 1966[2]

This Covenant safeguards many of the vital economic, social and cultural rights of citizens and includes an anti-discrimination provision in Article 2(2). Rights safeguarded include respect for family life, adequate standard of living, health, education and cultural life.

The Irish Government will shortly be required to report on the application of this Covenant.

Recommendation

CR.14.1   That the Irish Government, in preparing its report on this Covenant, and those reports required by other international instruments, would pay due regard to the involvement of Traveller organisations.

(d) Declaration on the Rights of Persons Belonging to National or Ethnic, Religious and Linguistic Minorities, 1992

This declaration was adopted by the United Nations General Assembly in December 1992. Article 1 of the Declaration states that:

"States shall protect the existence and the natural or ethnic, cultural, religious, and linguistic identity of minorities within their respective territories, and shall encourage conditions for the promotion of that identity."

This Declaration adds an important content to the duty of the Irish State to not only protect but to *"encourage conditions for the promotion"* of the Traveller community's identity including by appropriate laws.

---

[2] Adopted in 1966, entered into force in 1976.

Recommendations

CR.15.1 In contributing to reports being made under these International Instruments by the Irish Government and in making direct petitions and submissions to the relevant United Nations Committees, Travellers' organisations should be assisted appropriately by the Government.

CR.15.2 The Government should, through the appropriate statutory bodies, in partnership with Traveller organisations, develop appropriate actions in response to the requirements of this declaration to *"encourage conditions for the promotion"* of the Traveller identity.

(e) Convention of the Rights of the Child 1989[3]

This Convention contains a number of rights of relevance to Traveller children. It also contains a powerful non-discrimination clause.

5.3   European Regional Standards

(a) European Convention on Human Rights, 1993

The Vienna summit meeting of the States of the Council of Europe (October, 1993) agreed that a new Protocol on Minority Cultural Rights would be drafted for the European Convention of Human Rights.

Recommendation

CR.16.1 That the Irish Government would press for the specific inclusion of the cultural rights of nomadic groups including Irish Travellers within this Protocol and that this would be done in consultation with Traveller organisations.

(b) Conference on Security and Co-operation in Europe, 1990

The document of the Copenhagen meeting of the Conference on the Human Dimension of the CSCE (1990) represents the high point in standard setting on minority issues. The position of nomadic groups such as the Roma has been recognised and discussed at CSCE meetings.

Recommendation

CR.17.1 That the Irish Government would continue to participate in CSCE Human Dimension conferences and similar conferences and would involve Traveller organisations.

6.   Access to Voting

6.1 The Electoral Act of 1992 makes residence within a Constituency a prerequisite for registration and as such nomadism can disenfranchise Travellers as the legislation stands.

---

[3] Adopted in 1989, entered into force 1990

Recommendation

CR.18   The Department of the Environment should introduce procedures and any necessary amendments to legislation to ensure that this situation does not continue. They should also satisfy the requirements of the Human Rights Committee of the United Nations as referred to in para. 5.2(a) previously.

References

1.   Report of the Travelling People Review Body. Stationery Office, Dublin 1983.

2.   European Parliament Committee of Inquiry on Racism and Xenophobia. Report on the Findings of the Inquiry. Rapporteur: Mr. Glyn Ford. Office for Official Publications of the European Communities, Luxembourg 1991.

3.   Programme for a Partnership Government, 1993 - 1997. Stationery Office, Dublin 1993.

4.   Programme for Competitiveness and Work. Stationery Office, Dublin 1994.

5.   Standing Advisory Committee on Human Rights. Religious and Political Discrimination and Equality of Opportunity in Northern Ireland. HMSO 1990.

6.   Central Community Relations Unit. Race Relations in Northern Ireland. HMSO 1992.

7.   Report of the Committee on the Elimination of Racial Discrimination of the United Nations. Supplement No. 18 (A/48/18). United Nations 1993.

8.   European Social Policy Options for the Union. Office for Official Publications of the European Communities. Luxembourg 1993.

9.   Second Review of the Race Relations Act, 1976 Commission for Racial Equality. London 1992.

10.   Boyle, Prof. K. and Watt, B. (University of Essex), International and United Kingdom Law relevant to the Protection of the Rights and Cultural Identity of the Travelling Community in Ireland. Paper commissioned by the Task Force. Task Force Report 1995.

11.   Lord Fraser: Mandla v. Dowell Lee [1983] 2 AC 548, [1983] 1 A11 ER 1062.

12.   Richardson J. New Zealand Court of Appeal. King-Ansell v. Police [1979] 2NZLR 531.

13.   Report of the Human Rights Committee of the United Nations CCPR/C/79 Add, 21 United Nations 1992.

Section D: Accommodation

1. Introduction

1.1 Review of 1963 and 1983 Reports

1.1.1 Background

1.1.1.1 In formulating its proposals regarding the provision of accommodation for the Traveller community, the Task Force was informed by the experience of its predecessors, who produced the Report of the Commission on Itinerancy (Ref. 1) and the Report of the Travelling People Review Body, (Ref. 2). The Task Force and its two predecessors in turn have sought to address the issue of Traveller accommodation needs. While their approaches have differed, each has been conscious of the fundamental importance of accommodation to the current and future well-being of Travellers. The different approaches of the three bodies reflect an evolving understanding of the needs and rights of the Traveller and 'Settled' communities, at local and national level.

1.1.2 Quantifying Accommodation Needs

1.1.2.1 The 1983 Report reflected on the 1963 Report. In 1960 there were c. 1,150 Traveller families living on the roadside. Over the next twenty years that number had been housed or allocated serviced sites. However, in the meantime, the population had doubled, and again, c.1,150 Traveller families were living on the roadside. The 1983 Report recommended:

"Local authorities must avoid the concept of the problem being finite....traveller settlement will be ongoing, even when the backlog from previous decades is cleared"; and "It is not enough for housing authorities to meet the present backlog of accommodation needs among travellers. In planning, they must also project demand for housing and sites due to new family formation."

1.1.2.2 The experience of the succeeding ten years has confirmed this forecast. In recognition of this, the Task Force has prepared its accommodation strategy on the basis of research into population projections and demographic trends within the Traveller community.

1.1.3 Accommodation Needs

1.1.3.1 Types of Accommodation

1.1.3.1.1 The 1983 Report favoured standard housing as the best accommodation for Travellers, and believed that this was the preferred option of the great majority of Travellers.

1.1.3.1.2 Group housing schemes were still seen as experimental and this Report made recommendations regarding their design.

1.1.3.1.3 It was strongly against caravans as a long-term option, regarding them as dangerous, damp, and generally unhealthy. It was its view that halting sites should be kept to a minimum, and that provision should be on the basis of:

–   a particular family wanting to remain mobile;
–   a learning experience for a family who ultimately wanted to settle in a house;
–   to facilitate a group who wished to settle together.

1.1.3.1.4 In reviewing the provision of chalets/tigeens, this report stated that: *"Although experience has shown that this type of facility is now inadequate, in its time it was forward thinking"*, and does not include it among the approaches which it puts forward.

1.1.3.1.5 Where the next generation of Travellers was concerned, the emphasis of this report was on treating as *"housed"* the adult children of housed Travellers, even if they had left home and were now living in a caravan. They should therefore be placed on the waiting list for houses as if 'settled'.

1.1.3.2   Location of Accommodation

1.1.3.2.1 The 1983 Report shows that the Review Body was aware of the force of local opposition to providing facilities for Travellers. While similar opposition to provision for other groups, such as the Simon Community and women's refuges, could be allayed or circumvented in time, opposition to the provision of accommodation for Travellers in a locality would be more difficult to overcome. The 1983 Report concluded that: *"(Local authorities) must reconcile the need for consultation with the need to take effective action to meet the accommodation needs of families in their areas"*. It recommended that Traveller families be housed in new estates where there would not be organised resistance.

1.1.3.3   Approaches to the Issue

1.1.3.3.1 The 1963 Report had assumed that housing all Travellers would lead to integration and absorption. Instead, the 1983 Report indicated that absorption would be a matter of choice for each Traveller family and that individual choice must be respected. This view informed its recommendations concerning the types and location of accommodation to be provided.

1.1.3.3.2 It is the Task Force's view that the accommodation which is provided to Traveller families must be appropriate to their needs, and must be met through the provision of a range of accommodation types.

1.1.4   Ensuring Implementation

1.1.4.1   Both the 1963 and 1983 Reports recommended the establishment of a Corporate Body to *"accelerate and smooth"* the provision of services needed by Travellers. Neither recommendation was accepted by the then Governments. In both instances, a substitute *"advisory"* function was created, neither of which proved effective. However, neither Report recommended that the proposed Corporate Bodies have any specific powers in relation to accommodation.

1.1.4.2   The 1963 Report took the view that responsibility for accommodation should continue to be left solely with the local authorities. When it reviewed the situation, the 1983 Report indicated that this approach had been ineffective:

"A policy based on advice and financial inducements was insufficient to overcome local political and community indifference. No penalties were laid down in the event of low performance by a local authority, and no system of surveillance was introduced...".

Nevertheless, its view was that primary responsibility must remain with the local authorities but that the Minister for the Environment should have responsibility to investigate instances where they were inactive. The Minister would check that all Local Authority Housing Programmes included adequate provision for Travellers and should monitor their implementation. The Minister was expected to avail of the existing range of sanctions to deal with instances of non-provision.

1.1.4.3   It is clear to the Task Force that these previous approaches have not been adequate to meet accommodation needs. In addition, the Government has set itself a target of providing permanent, serviced caravan site accommodation for all Traveller families who require such homes by the year 2,000. In order to address the situation, the Task Force sets out in this section proposals for a Traveller Accommodation Agency, which will supplement the existing structures at local and national level. The Task Force recognises that at local level responsibility must continue to rest with the local authorities to provide accommodation for Travellers. Their role in this regard should be carried out within the framework of a national programme, under the auspices of the national body.

1.1.5   'Indigenous' Travellers

1.1.5.1   The 1983 Report noted that local authorities, where they took responsibility for Travellers, focused on those families who spent the greater part of the year in their area. These were *"their"* families, regarded as indigenous to the area. The Report had little to say about other families.

1.1.5.2   The Task Force has taken into account the needs of these *"other"* families. Its recommendations later in this section are intended to meet their accommodation needs, for example, through the provision of a national network of transient sites.

1.2   Role of the Department of the Environment

1.2.1   Relevant Legislation

(1)   The statutory framework in relation to the accommodation of Travellers is set out in the Housing Acts particularly Section 13 of the Housing Act, 1988, which empowers local authorities to provide halting sites for Travellers. The provision of sites under Section 13 is excluded from the procedure of public notice and comment under Part 10 of the Local Government (Planning and Development) Regulations, 1994.

(2)   Other Legislative measures

These are mainly of a regulatory nature related to controls over the parking of temporary dwellings (including Travellers' caravans). The legislation for which the Minister is responsible is as follows:-

– Local Government (Sanitary Services) Act, 1948

Part (iv) of this Act imposes controls over camping, the parking of temporary dwellings and empowers local authorities to prohibit the parking of temporary dwellings in particular areas (prohibition orders). Where objections to the making of prohibition orders are received the Minister has the function of confirming or otherwise the prohibition orders.

– Housing (Miscellaneous Provisions) Act, 1992

Section 10 of the Housing (Miscellaneous Provisions) Act, 1992, gives the housing authorities power to take direct action in relation to temporary dwellings parked, without lawful authority, in a public place within five miles of a site provided under Section 13 of the Housing Act, 1988, which could in the opinion of the authority be appropriately accommodated on the site. In the first instance a local authority may serve notice on the owner requiring him/her within twenty four hours, to move the dwelling on to the site. Failure to comply with the notice, or to relocate the dwelling to a place where the authority would not be entitled to serve another such notice in respect of it, constitutes an offence and allows the authority to move the dwelling on to the site or, if prevented from so doing, to a place of storage.

– Roads Act, 1993

(a) Section 69 of the Roads Act, 1993, prohibits the placing of temporary dwellings on national roads, motorways, busways, protected roads and other roads or classes of roads prescribed in regulations by the Minister. Local authorities and the Gardaí have powers to enforce these new provisions and to take immediate action to deal with offenders.

(b) Section 71 of the Act gives powers to local authorities and the Gardaí to deal with unlawful trading on public roads. It prohibits, and provides for the immediate removal of, unauthorised caravans and vehicles used for the sale of goods or provision of services on any public roads.

1.2.2 Overview of the Role of the Housing Division

(i) Delivery of Housing Services

The Housing Acts, 1966 to 1992, place responsibility on the individual local authorities for the delivery of housing services including the provision of serviced caravan parks (halting sites) for Travellers. Local authorities, as elected bodies, are accountable to their local electorates for the delivery of their services.

(ii) Department's Role and Responsibilities

The Department's role is to provide the legislative framework for the service, provide funding as necessary, and to guide and co-ordinate the housing programme, including the provision of halting sites for Travellers, at national level. Thus, the Department's main functions in relation to housing are:

* to monitor the national housing situation and develop appropriate policy responses;

* to provide the legislation (both primary and secondary);

* to provide the resources for certain functions, (such as house/halting site construction which is funded one hundred per cent from the Public Capital Programme);

* to lay down the terms and conditions within which the schemes are operated by local authorities;

* to provide general guidance and assistance to authorities in relation to certain of their functions;

* to monitor the performance of local authorities in the implementation of housing policies;

* to gather and publish information on national trends in housing needs and the housing activities of local authorities and other housing sectors.

In exercising its functions, the Department must strike a balance between, on the one hand, local democratic autonomy, including the devolution to the greatest extent possible of responsibility to local authorities, and, on the other, consistency of approach nationally. Generally the Department ensures that the same set of options are available to each local authority.

However, the emphasis that an individual local authority might place on the implementation of one particular option as opposed to another, is a matter for local discretion. Judgements on the quality of delivery of housing services by an authority must relate to the results achieved over the full range of options available to them rather than to individual programmes.

(iii)   **Monitoring by Department**

In monitoring the performance of the local authorities, the Department's primary concern is to evaluate the success of the various options available and investigate possible causes of uneven levels of implementation. Apart from the collection of statistical data there is feedback to the Department on the quality of service provided by the authorities, through members of the Oireachtas, other public representatives, the media, representative groups and individuals.

(iv)   The Department recoups local authorities and voluntary bodies ninety per cent of the cost of employing social workers to work with Travellers, also miscellaneous costs, such as fifty per cent of the cost of providing caravans in exceptional cases and the payment of the first time special house purchase grant. Expenditure of £1.21 million was incurred in 1994. The 1995 provision is £1.3 million.

1.3   The Role of the Local Authority

1.3.1   There are two elements to the statutory role of the local authority in catering for the Traveller community:

(i) To identify the number of Traveller families in its administrative area and to determine the accommodation needs of these families;

(ii) To develop programmes for the provision of accommodation for those families.

To meet the first requirement the local authority carries out an annual count of Traveller families in November each year, which is collated at national level by the Department of the Environment and currently published in the Housing Statistics Bulletin. The procedures for the provision of accommodation for Travellers follow a well established pattern and can be summarised as follows:

(1) Acquisition of land by agreement or by Compulsory Purchase Order;
(2) Design of lay-out of an appropriate housing scheme or halting site when land becomes available;
(3) Presentation of proposal to the elected members of the local authority prior to submission to the Department of the Environment;
(4) Following approval, tenders are invited in the public press for construction of the scheme.

These procedures are followed by the local authority against the background of an identified need for Traveller specific accommodation for the Traveller community. This need is currently expressed in three ways:

(i) Group housing schemes where a number of Traveller families are identified as being interested in being accommodated in a purpose - built scheme of houses/bungalows;
(ii) Halting sites with individual bays with full services provided in a small structure on each bay;
(iii) Single houses/sites.

Some Travellers apply for standard housing in the same manner as the 'Settled' community.

1.3.2 Generally, local authorities employ one or more social workers who are involved in a variety of activities with the Traveller community as part of the local authority service. This is further elaborated in the sub-section entitled "The Support Structure in the Local Authority for Travellers": Part 5 of this Section.

2. Traveller Accommodation

2.1 Achieving the Government's Target

2.1.1 The terms of reference of the Task Force include a requirement to *"report on implementation of measures to meet the Government target of providing permanent serviced caravan site accommodation for all Traveller families who require it by the year 2000. Pending the realisation of that target, to report on arrangements whereby temporary serviced caravan sites should be provided by local authorities for Traveller families who require them; and to examine and report on the costings of such sites and to advise and report on the most efficient use of resources in the provision of such sites"*.

2.1.2 In its approach to this section of its terms of reference the Task Force, as in its Interim Progress Report published in January, 1994, took the view that all types of accommodation, including permanent halting sites, should be available to Travellers and accordingly, identified a two pronged approach to Traveller accommodation in the period 1995 to 2000.

2.1.3 The first is the provision of Traveller specific accommodation. This is accommodation designed around the distinct needs of Travellers. Within this approach three categories are required:

(i)   group housing;
(ii) permanent halting sites;
(iii) transient sites.

2.1.4 The second is the inclusion of Travellers in mainstream housing programmes. This principally relates to Traveller accommodation in local authority estates.

2.1.5 It is clear that Traveller mobility as it is structured at present has meant that many Travellers experience a range of different types of accommodation over their lifetime. It is important to recognise this in the provision of Traveller accommodation. Equally, it is important to recognise that the provision of Traveller specific accommodation is the desired option of many Travellers; for them it cannot therefore be viewed as an interim solution prior to settlement.

2.1.6 The Task Force has considered the structures for the provision of accommodation for Travellers and the obstacles, legal and other, encountered in the process. The Task Force acknowledges the contribution made by some local authorities over the years in providing accommodation for the Traveller community. In particular, the Task Force acknowledges the contribution of individual councillors and officials for their commitment in this regard. However, performance has been uneven and accommodation remains a major issue for Travellers.

2.1.7 Research (Ref. 3) carried out by the Task Force highlights significant deficiencies in the following areas:

–   Insufficient accommodation for 1,085 Traveller households on the roadside and the 257 households on temporary sites;

–   Lack of provision for transient families;

–   Facilities inappropriate to the distinct needs of Travellers;

–   Lack of planning for the projected Traveller population increase;

–   Absence of a comprehensive plan to achieve the Government's target and timescale for implementation.

2.1.8 Combining the existing need, the projected growth rate in Traveller families and the need for transient sites, 3,100 units of various types of additional accommodation will be needed by the year 2000. It is clear from the research (op. cit, 3) that the current initiatives of the local authorities will not adequately address this need. This is particularly true where the efforts of some local authorities have been dismal. The

Task Force therefore considers that a National Strategy is required. It is also clear that any such national strategy cannot come from current structures and approaches.

2.1.9 To achieve the Government's target for the provision of Traveller accommodation, the Task Force proposes a National Strategy on Accommodation for the Traveller Community which would include the following elements:

–   the provision of 3,100 units of additional accommodation which will be needed by the year 2000, with a commensurate increase in Government funding, by the provision of a range of types of accommodation, including Traveller-specific accommodation, of an appropriate standard, and the provision of a network of transient sites throughout the state;

–   the establishment of a new statutory body which will draw up, in consultation with local authorities, and monitor, a National Programme of Accommodation;

–   the responsibility for the provision of accommodation to remain with the local authorities;

–   the amendment of the Planning Acts and other legislation to facilitate the provision of accommodation;

–   increased executive power for local authority management;

–   amendments to legislation and procedures to improve local authorities' powers in relation to anti-social behaviour among tenants, and illegal camping;

–   increased participation from Traveller tenants and Traveller organisations at local level and balanced representation at national level on the Board of the proposed statutory body, all of which are developed further in this section.

2.1.10 This National Strategy on Accommodation for the Travelling Community is based on a recognition that all individuals of the Traveller and 'Settled' communities have rights and responsibilities which, when observed, enable both communities to co-exist in harmony. It is the failure to acknowledge rights and to observe responsibilities which leads to conflict and discrimination. In this regard, it is envisaged that all the recommendations in the Task Force's Report including the "Strategy for Reconciliation", as outlined in Section A, and those in Section G the Traveller Economy, will complement and contribute to he process by which the National Strategy will lead to the achievement of the Government's target for the provision of Traveller accommodation.

2.2   Population and Accommodation Projections to end of Year 2000[1]

2.2.1   Projected population increase

As indicated previously, an annual count of the number of Traveller households is the source of information on the Traveller population in this country. The accuracy

---

[1] The Statistics of population etc. do not include "Traders", who are enumerated separately in the Annual Count.

of the count is limited by difficulties in carrying it out in each county, having regard to general Traveller movement.

A research project carried out for the Task Force (Ref. 4) projected an annual Traveller population increase of 3.3 per cent up to 1999. Allowing for net immigration from the United Kingdom and some under counting in the annual count, a projection of a population increase of four per cent per annum is used here, which gives an overall increase of twenty-six per cent over six years 1995 - 2000. This is the same as the percentage increase over the previous six year period. There is some evidence that the size of Traveller households is beginning to decrease but this new trend will not impact on accommodation requirements up to the year 2000.

As partly illustrated in Table D.1., the overall population increase projection to the year 2000 is as follows:

1988	3066 households
1994	3878 households (+812)
2000	4905 households (+1027)

Table D1 - Current Accommodation Units (1994) and Projected Requirements by Type of Accommodation (Source: D.O.E. and Research)			
Location	1994 Annual Count	2000 projection*	Projected increase (rounded)
Housing (group Housing and standard housing)	1,814	2,295	480
Serviced Units			
— permanent	722	915	195
— temporary	257	325	70
Roadside Units			
— idigenous	890	1,125	235
— transient	195	245	50
Total	3,878	4,905	1,030

* Presuming no change in rate of provision

2.2.2 Estimated Accommodation Requirements

In planning for the provision of accommodation for Traveller households to the year 2000, it is necessary to provide, in the first instance, for households which are residing on the roadside, those on temporary halting sites and the general increase in these two categories. In addition, the general increase in households in housing and on permanent halting sites must also be accommodated. Provision of transient sites is also required to cater for those households which prefer to live on transient sites and to provide for the nomadic aspects of Travellers' way of life. On the basis of Table D1, the number of accommodation units required in the period 1995 to 2000 is set out in Table D2 as follows:

Table D2 - Estimate of Accommodation Units required 1995 to 2000 (Source: Research)	
Households on roadside excluding transients	1,125
Households on temporary sites	325
General increase (housed/permanent sites)(rounded)	650
Transient units – roadside at present 245 – nomadic demand 755*	1,000
*Ratio of 1 per 2.56 permanent sites in 2000	
Total	3,100

Apart from the 1,000 transient units, 2,100 units of accommodation, either permanent units or housing (single, group and standard housing) will be required (see Table D2). It is presumed that the policy of existing temporary sites will be phased out as early as possible and be replaced with permanent sites and housing as appropriate.

Table D3 - Location of Households Units in 1994 (Source: Research and 1994 Annual Count)			
	Dublin area % of column total	Rest of Country % of column total	No of households/units in category
Housing (group housing and standard housing)	219 (25%)	1,595 (54%)	1,814 (47%)
Serviced Units			
– permanent	218 (24%)	504 (17%)	722 (19%)
– temporary	184 (21%)	73 (2%)	257 (6%)
Roadside Units			
– indigenous	252 (28%)	638 (21%)	890 (23%)
– transient	16 (2%)	179 (6%)	195 (5%)
Total	889	2,989	3,878

Table D3 provides a breakdown of the present accommodation situation of the estimated 3,878 families enumerated in the 1994 Annual Count.

The 1994 Count showed 889 households (twenty-three per cent) residing in the Dublin area (Table D3 above) and this number is expected to increase to 1,125 by the end of the year 2000 on the basis of the projected population increase outlined at Para 2.2.1 above. Similarly, the number of households (2,989) living in the rest of the country in 1994 is projected to increase to 3,770 by the end of the same period. On the assumption that the ratio of houses to serviced bays required is 25:75 in the Dublin region (at present twenty-five per cent in housing) and 50:50 in the rest of the country (at present fifty-four per cent in housing), the number of houses and serviced units required is set out in Table D4 as follows:

Table D4 - Estimate of Accommodation Units Required 1995 - 2000 (Source: Table D2)	
Type	**Total**
Houses (Standard and Group Housing)	900
Serviced Units	1,200
Transient Units	1,000
Total	3,100

2.2.3   Cost of Accommodation[2]

2.2.3.1 Houses (Standard and Group Housing)

In the five year period 1989 to 1993, local authorities provided accommodation for an annual average of over 200 Traveller households divided nearly evenly between housing and serviced caravan sites. If the Local Authority Housing Programme is maintained at its existing level, the number of Traveller households housed annually should increase above the annual average (1989-1993) of 115. The decision to exclude group housing from the general Local Authority Housing Programme from 1995 should assist in this matter. This change in policy should not be operated by local authorities so as to reduce the number of standard local authority house lettings to Traveller households. The number of houses required over the period 1995 to 2000 is 900 and the cost of these will vary considerably depending on whether group housing, individual special houses or houses in local authority housing schemes are involved. In addition, the generally large size of Traveller families requiring housing and the larger than average size of house required will increase the cost of such housing. While the average cost of providing a three bedroomed local authority house in 1994 was approximately £40,000, having regard to the larger size of house required and other considerations, (parking for caravans), an average figure of £60,000 (1994 prices) per house is assumed. The

---

[2] Based on estimates of costs provided by the D.O.E.

cost of providing the 900 houses would be approximately £54 million (1994 prices). In 1994 the estimated cost of an annual average of 152 houses let to Traveller households was about £6 million.

2.2.3.2 Permanent Sites

The cost of providing a serviced caravan site for Travellers depends on a range of factors including the cost of the land, topography of site, the cost of bringing services on to site, the number of bays and the ancillary buildings and facilities being provided. Consequently, the cost per bay can vary appreciably from one site to another.

The number of permanent serviced units required is estimated at 1,200. It is estimated that the present average cost of providing a caravan unit is £50,000. It is considered, having regard to the increasing difficulty of obtaining sites, movement to urban areas, the concentration of Traveller households in the Dublin area and improved/larger serviced blocks being provided, that for future projection purposes the average cost per unit should be reckoned at £60,000 (1994 prices). This figure could increase with additional facilities (sub-section 2.3 refers). Therefore the cost of 1,200 units over the six year period (1995 - 2000) is estimated at £72 million (1994 prices). The Task Force shares the general concern at the high cost of providing serviced units (Table D5 refers) and it considers that the Traveller Accommodation Agency (see sub-section entitled "Traveller Accommodation Agency) should review the reasons for such high costs. Of course, it is also important to point out that, while the cost per unit on a halting site is high, the cost per bed space is actually the more relevant figure. Given the level of occupancy on a unit, the cost per bed space is not abnormally high.

Table D5 - Average Cost of a Unit on a Serviced Caravan Site							
Land £000	Piped Services £000	Pavings £000	Buildings £000	Walls & Fencing £000	Fees £000	Other* £000	Total Cost £000
5	6	7	14	6	3	9	50

* Including preliminary expenses, site clearance, landscaping, external electrical work, telephone, insurance, bond and other miscellaneous expenses.

2.2.3.3 Transient Sites

A research project for the Task Force (op. cit, 4) stated that a network of transient sites would have to provide a total number of units greater than the number of transient households and suggested a factor of 1.25 to 1.5 units per household might need to be adopted. The 1,000 transient units proposed are intended for the 195 transient households in the 1994 census, and projected increase of fifty families to the year 2000; and the balance of 755 units is intended to cater for the nomadic way of life of Travellers and is based on a ratio of 1:2.56 of permanent units in the year 2000. On the basis of an average cost of £20,000 per unit the cost of these sites would be £20 million (1994 prices). Transient and permanent sites must be provided very rapidly and simultaneously.

106

2.2.3.4 Cost of Provision

The cost of providing the accommodation as outlined previously is estimated at £146 million (1994 prices) or an average of £24 million per year as against about £10 million expenditure in 1994 (£6 million on standard houses and £4 million on halting sites).

2.2.3.5 Cost of Maintenance/Management

The annual cost of maintenance and management of serviced caravan sites is generally much higher than comparable expenditure on public housing. As well as extra maintenance, caretakers are required (full time or part time) for sites. It is estimated that annual maintenance and management costs will increase from a level of about £5 million in 1994 (considered inadequate) to about £10 million per annum (1994 prices) if the new serviced units (1,200) are provided. It will also be necessary to carry out remedial works on some of the existing permanent sites during the six year period. It is difficult to estimate the cost of such works. If an average of ten per cent of existing 700 permanent units need refurbishment, the annual cost would be approximately £2 million. This would give an annual maintenance (including refurbishment) and management cost of about £6 million in 1994 rising to £12 million in the year 2000. (1994 prices). It is estimated that the cost of maintenance and management (including refurnishment) for the period 1995 - 2000 inclusive would be £72 million.

2.2.4 Summary

The estimated cost of meeting the accommodation needs of the Traveller community in the period 1995-2000 is £218 million, (1994 prices) as set out in Table D6 below. The figure of £218 million over six years includes £90 million (for standard housing and the provision and maintenance of halting sites) based on an estimate of what is currently provided. In other words, the net extra expenditure over the period is £128 million (1994 prices). The Task Force also wishes to emphasise that the size of this figure must be considered in the context of the following factors:

(i)   The considerable backlog of needs. Once this backlog is addressed, it is expected that average annual costs will thereafter be signficantly reduced.

(ii)   It is expected that the Task Force recommendations in relation to "Traveller Tenant Participation" and "Local Authorities - Extension of Powers" will reduce the incidence and cost where such facilities are abused.

Table D6 - Projected Cost of Accommodation (1994 prices)			
	1994 estimated expenditure £m	1995/2000 estimated cost £m	Average Annual Cost 1995/2000 £m
Housing (Group housing and standard housing*)	6	54	9
Serviced Units	3	72	12
Transient Units	–	20	3
Refurbishment of Units	1	12	2
Maintenance/Management of Units	5	60	10
Total	15	218	36

* standard housing comes out of the normal Local Authority Housing Budget

Recommendation

DR.1   The Task Force recommends the provision of 3,100 units of additional Traveller accommodation. The investment in Traveller accommodation should therefore be substantially increased to meet the Government target of accommodating all Traveller families in need of accommodation.

2.3   Approaches to Accommodation for Travellers

2.3.1   Types of Accommodation

2.3.1.1   The 1983 Report of the Traveller People Review Body (op. cit, 2) identified a three pronged approach to Traveller accommodation. It stated that:

"It is recommended that in future plans for accommodation, three main approaches would be recognised and followed:

(i)   standard housing;
(ii)   group housing;
(iii)   serviced sites for caravans".

2.3.1.2   The Council of Europe report "Gypsies and Travellers" (Ref. 5) also identified the need for a range of approaches to the accommodation of Travellers. It found that:

"While in housing, as in other fields, there are certainly trends, there is also an infinite variety of situations and wishes: from those determined to live entirely as nomads - in accordance with their social and economic organisations - to those who would like to live in small adjoining houses or have a mobile home near such a house, from those who like a properly equipped site to those who want 'simply a piece of land, as untouched as possible, where they may stop' "

108

2.3.1.3 The approach adapted by the Task Force as outlined in sub-section 2.1 above is that all types of accommodation, including permanent halting sites, should be available to Travellers.

2.3.2 Design of Traveller Specific Accommodation

2.3.2.1 There is a close link between accommodation and identity. The design of Traveller specific accommodation should reflect the distinct culture and identity of Travellers. These issues were a focus for The President Robinson Awards for the Design of Travellers' Accommodation. The Awards were presented on February 2nd 1993 and winning entries were published in the same year. In her preface to the publication, President Robinson wrote:

"When you apply a sense of excellence to a housing problem, when you try to design a home for someone else, I think you are forced to imagine their lives. Through that act of imagination, the inheritance of the Travellers - and their particular housing needs - cease to be objects of suspicion and become objects of great interest and sources of instruction" (Ref. 6)

The Council of Europe Report "Gypsies and Travellers" (op. cit, 5) noted the importance of linking the design of Gypsy and Traveller accommodation to the way in which Gypsies and Travellers use their living space:

"At present, there is too great a gap between the spontaneous occupation of space by Gypsies and Travellers and institutionalised dwellings on organised sites. Many of these are avoided by those able to do so. Sites felt to be acceptable, where the gap between spontaneous and institutionalised dwelling has been reduced, quickly become known and favoured, particularly since in a hostile environment the possibility of finding a place in which to rest and be free gives a sense of security".

2.3.2.2 The 1983 Report of the Travelling People Review Body (op. cit, 2) acknowledged the need for a Traveller perspective on the design of accommodation. It stated that:

"It is of the utmost importance in designing programmes for the accommodation of traveller families that plans should be based on a thorough knowledge of the needs and wishes of the families in each locality........"

2.3.3 Design and Provision

2.3.3.1 Recommendations

DR.2 The location of Traveller specific accommodation will depend on a number of variables. These will include land availability and technical and planning considerations. Consideration should also be given to the preferences and needs of the prospective Traveller tenants. Equally, it should include good access to services, schools and shops.

DR.3 The design of particular accommodation schemes will vary from locality to locality. However, a number of principles can be identified as usefully informing the final design of all schemes. The accommodation provided should:

(i) acknowledge the distinct needs and identity of Travellers;

(ii) cater for the work patterns of Travellers in accordance with the recommendations of Section G: The Traveller Economy and take account of technical and planning considerations;

(iii) take cognizance of the needs and compatibility of extended family groupings, and of the different population structure of the Traveller community with over fifty per cent under the age of fifteen;

(iv) contribute to improving relations between Travellers and 'Settled' people;

(v) include proper landscaping to ensure the site is not only functional but also pleasant to live on and aesthetically pleasing to look at. This should include not only the site itself but also the outer boundary;

(vi) have adequate public lighting for security and safety purposes;

(vii) ensure an appropriate balance between personal privacy and communal needs compatible with the requirements of the Fire Officer;

(viii) allow for the integration of the family caravan with the accommodation facilities provided for each family as well as adequate parking space for vehicles used by the family;

(ix) include facilities for play space, caretaker's office, communal meeting rooms, and public telephone;

(x) where possible cater for changing family structures;

(xi) be accessible and appropriate for Traveller tenants with a disability.

DR.4 Traveller tenants and Traveller organisations should be involved at an early stage in the design of Traveller accommodation.

DR.5 The Traveller Accommodation Agency should stimulate dialogue on the design concepts of Traveller accommodation as exemplified in "The President Robinson Awards for the Design of Travellers' Accommodation" (op.cit.6). This dialogue should include the Department of the Environment and local authorities, Travellers and Traveller organisations, private sector architects and architectural students.

DR.6 Permanent Halting Sites

Recommendations

DR.6.1 A network of permanent sites is required across the country. The final parameters of this network should be defined by the Traveller Accommodation Agency based on local authority programmes approved by the Agency.

DR.6.2 The bay should allow for safe fuel storage with electricity, sewerage services and water supply provided.

DR.6.3 Accommodation provided should include kitchen, toilets, bathroom, washing and drying facilities, and family room.

DR.6.4 While the size may vary with the requirements of particular areas, it is recommended that the focus should be on moderately sized sites, having regard to the compatibility of families and size of extended family.

DR.7 Transient Halting Sites

Recommendations

DR.7.1 **(a)** A network of these sites is required across the country. These sites should be provided simultaneously with the other types of accommodation facilities as an integral part of a National Programme.

The final parameters of this network should be defined by the Traveller Accommodation Agency based on the following:

(i) A network of transient sites should be provided in each local authority administrative area.

(ii) The specific locations of these sites should include:

(a) cities, towns, villages and other centres of population;

(b) other areas where there is a tradition of Traveller transient camping.

The Agency should be informed by the advice/information from the local authority and should take account of appropriate linkages between the provision of transient and permanent accommodation. These linkages should ensure that visiting families can be accommodated on a transient site within a reasonable distance.

(b) Bays on transient sites should provide access to electricity, running water, sewage disposal and refuse collection. A suitable hard surface should be provided. While the size may vary with the requirements of particular areas, it is recommended that the focus should be on small sites.

(c) Guidelines should be developed for transient sites covering design features, management issues and appropriate size by the Traveller Accommodation Agency.

DR.8 Caravan Design

Recommendation

DR.8.1 It is recognised that caravans are not designed for long term living. The Traveller Accommodation Agency should develop a research project to develop a caravan design that continues to allow mobility while improving its capacity for long term occupation as well as increasing its fire safety features.

2.3.3.2 Funding Issues

Recommendations

DR.9 A specific capital allocation, separate from the general housing construction allocation should continue to be provided annually for the construction of Traveller specific accommodation. This allocation should therefore cover group housing, single housing, permanent sites and transient sites.

DR.10 Given the importance of this investment, local authorities should be provided with seventy-five per cent funding from central government to cover the cost of managing and maintaining existing and new Traveller specific accommodation, including costs of a caretaker service where this is provided.

DR.11 In addition to direct provision of accommodation by local authorities, the Traveller Accommodation Agency should investigate the possibility of direct provision of accommodation by Travellers themselves or by Traveller organisations. Such schemes could include low interest rate house purchase loans, the provision of houses and/or serviced caravan parks by approved bodies under Section 6 of the Housing (Miscellaneous Provisions) Act, 1992, use of Capital Assistance and Rental Subsidy Schemes.

2.3.3.3 Other Issues

Recommendations

DR.12 In the context of the National Strategy, where each local authority is playing its part, local authority approaches should be flexible and should avoid determining specific numbers of Travellers to be accommodated within particular areas. This does not in any way preclude the need for all areas to be included in the local authority's plan for Traveller specific accommodation.

DR.13 It is recognised that local authorities must be allowed to exercise control over unauthorised Traveller encampments and this is provided for in sub-section 7. However, in the absence of adequate provision local authorities should be required to deal sensitively with such cases and use the option of eviction only as a last resort.

DR.14 Traveller families who are provided with accommodation in the functional area of one local authority cannot expect duplicate provision to be made by other local authorities, save where they avail of transient halting sites, for stays of short duration.

DR.15 Where private firms are used in a caretaker role, they should operate to clear guidelines and should not be employed in contradictory roles, including evictions.

DR.16 Existing temporary sites should be replaced with permanent sites and housing as appropriate or should be adapted as permanent or transient sites.

2.4 Travellers in the Dublin Area

2.4.1 Introduction

2.4.1.1 The particular experience and needs in the greater Dublin area are focussed upon here. Given the concentration of population of Traveller and 'Settled' communities within this relatively small area and the experience of recent decades in Dublin in relation to accommodation, the Task Force considers it necessary to examine the Dublin situation and makes recommendations on a strategy for the future.

2.4.2 Historical Background

2.4.2.1 The move from a rural to an urban setting is a phenomenon shared by both Travellers and 'Settled' people, for similar reasons, including:

– economic opportunities;

– perceived benefits of life in the urban setting;

– increased mobility and improved communications.

2.4.2.2 There are other reasons for the move from a rural to an urban setting which have specific relevance to Travellers, including:

– relative availability of facilities in the 1960s and 1970s in the Dublin area, compared to the rest of the country;

– the greater availability of publicly owned land (including road developments).

2.4.3 The Current Dublin Situation

2.4.3.1 The Dublin situation is characterised by the presence of large numbers of families either in unofficial locations or on temporary sites, in addition to families on permanent sites, and families in group housing schemes and standard housing.

2.4.3.2 The annual count by Dublin's Local Authorities for 1994, (Ref. 7) indicated that the number of families in the range of accommodation categories is as set out in Table D7 below:

	Dublin Corporation	Fingal	Dublin South	Dun Laoghaire/ Rathdown	Total
Table D7 - No. of Families in Range of Accommodation Categories (1994) **(Source: Dublin Local Authorities Census 1994 (unpublished))**					
(A) Families in housing etc.					
Standard Housing	35	13	42	16	106
Group Housing	72	3	14	24	113
Chalet Sites	9	–	–	2	11
Sub-Total (A)	**116**	**16**	**56**	**42**	**230**
(B) Families on Permanent Halting Sites					
Permanent Halting Sites	118	35	55	22	230
Sub-Total (B)	**118**	**35**	**55**	**22**	**230**
TOTAL (A) & (B)	**234**	**51**	**111**	**64**	**460**
(C) Families in need of accommodation					
Temporary Halting Sites	–	64	97	–	161
Roadside	37	79	62	26	204
Overcrowding* in Group Housing Schemes	60	–	–	–	60
Sub-Total (C)	**97**	**143**	**159**	**26**	**425**
OVERALL TOTAL (A) & (B) & (C)	**331**	**194**	**270**	**90**	**885**

* Families living in caravans in places such as driveways

2.4.3.3   Excluding those living in standard and group houses and recently developed permanent sites, most of these families live in conditions where they lack one or more of the basic services. A number of reports have been published in recent years (op. cit, 1, 2, 3) which have highlighted these conditions, and their impact on Travellers' lives.

2.4.3.4   Over the past twenty-five years, the Dublin local authorities have made positive efforts to provide accommodation and refurbish existing facilities for the Traveller community. Despite this progress, the Dublin region continues to be the area with the greatest need of accommodation arising from the movement from the rural to the urban setting described above and the natural increase in the Traveller population during that period. As shown in paragraph 2.4.3.2, 425 families are in need of permanent accommodation today in the Dublin region and this figure increases to 545 (+120) if the need is to be addressed by the year 2000 as envisaged in the Programme for a Partnership Government, (1993 - 1997), (Ref. 8).

2.4.3.5   The number of Traveller families to be accommodated however, is only one aspect of the problem in the Dublin region. The physical capacity of the area to cater satisfactorily for such large numbers is a constraint on the ability of the local authorities to meet the needs of the Traveller community; a constraint that needs to be taken into account in seeking solutions for the Dublin area. The high cost of infill sites is another problem.

2.4.3.6   There are 97 families on the roadside or on overcrowded sites in the Dublin Corporation area, despite the fact that the Corporation has provided accommodation for 234 families since the programme started in the sixties. Most of the sites provided are on the perimeter of the city where, in terms of space, the best opportunity exists to develop more sites. However, this cannot be done through the creation of ever bigger sites. Some opportunities do exist for infill type sites, like the one developed off Basin Street Upper.

2.4.3.7   South Dublin County Council has an accommodation need for 159 families today. In the programme adopted for 1995, four sites are proposed which, when completed, will result in the total provision of twelve sites accommodating ninety-four families. Allowing for these developments and applying a projected population increase of four per cent per annum over the next five years, the accommodation need to be addressed over that period by South Dublin County Council is approximately 190 families. There are major difficulties associated with implementing a programme of this dimension in a county of twenty-two square kilometres (55,170 acres) of which approximately forty per cent is a rural hilly landscape including the foothills of the Dublin/Wicklow Mountains.

2.4.3.8   The number of Traveller families requiring accommodation in the administrative area of Fingal County Council is 143. Applying the four per cent projected increase factor this places a requirement of 180 (+37) units to be provided over the next five years. While the area of Fingal County Council is larger than South Dublin (111,179 acres) a very large part of it is rural agricultural land in which it is difficult to develop sites, many of which are considerably removed from services at present. It is generally accepted that sites for the accommodation of Travellers should not be provided in isolated areas.

2.4.3.9 In contrast to the other three authorities, Dun Laoghaire-Rathdown County Council does not have a major problem in meeting the needs of the Traveller community in their area. A number of proposals are currently planned to meet this need.

2.4.4   A Workable Strategy

2.4.4.1 In seeking to meet current and future accommodation needs of Travellers in the Greater Dublin area, the Task Force considers that for any strategy to be successful, it should take account of:

–   families who see their future in Dublin;
–   families who would prefer to live in other parts of Ireland if sites were available;
–   transient families:
      –   those coming to visit relatives;
      –   those coming for short-term visits or for other reasons;
–   future population growth;
–   returning families who emigrated to England over the years.

2.4.4.2 In determining a strategy for the Dublin region, a key factor will be the development of a network of permanent halting sites countrywide which would give the families in the Dublin area the option of moving back out of Dublin as well as minimising the drift to Dublin. Plans developed by the Dublin local authorities will need to take account of those choosing to relocate over the period to the year 2000.

2.4.5   Recommendations

DR.17   In view of the absence of open land in the city area, Dublin Corporation, should pursue a policy of identifying and developing a range of infill sites for Traveller specific accommodation.

DR.18   Co-ordinated strategies for the accommodation of Travellers over the Greater Dublin area are required between the four local authorities. A Strategic Planning Unit should be established drawing together relevant officials from the four councils chaired by a representative from the Traveller Accommodation Agency to ensure co-ordination and best use of resources. This Unit should also meet on a regular basis with relevant Traveller organisations.

DR.19   The Traveller Accommodation Agency should ensure even progress in the development of Traveller accommodation facilities across the country. This should be done in a manner to ensure that any drift towards Dublin due to lack of facilities in other areas would be eliminated.

DR.20   The Traveller Accommodation Agency should ensure that provision in other local authority areas should include any Traveller families that might now choose to relocate from Dublin. This should be done on the basis of a survey carried out independently by the Agency.

DR.21   Existing official temporary sites should be upgraded where appropriate, to the standard of permanent halting sites or transient sites, on the basis of consultation.

These sites should be phased out as permanent accommodation is provided, with a view to temporary sites not being required after the year 2000.

3. Traveller Accommodation Agency

3.1 Introduction

3.1.1 In the Programme for a Partnership Government (op. cit. 8), the Government committed itself to the target of providing permanent, serviced caravan site accommodation for all Traveller families who require such homes by the year 2000. The Task Force notes the continued commitment of the present Government to this policy as confirmed by the Minister of State with responsibility for Housing and Urban Renewal, Ms. Liz McManus, T.D., in an address to the Irish Traveller Movement's Annual General Meeting on 11th February, 1995 (Ref. 9).

3.1.2 In making this recommendation, the Task Force considers that responsibility for the provision of accommodation for Travellers must remain with local authorities. However, having surveyed the level and pace of provision of accommodation to date, it is the Task Force's view, as indicated previously, that the existing structures at local and central level should be supplemented by the establishment of a Traveller Accommodation Agency. The Agency is necessary to achieve a National Programme which cannot be achieved by the local authorities on their own. In making this recommendation, the Task Force is also conscious of the increasing involvement of the courts in local disputes regarding the provision of accommodation to Travellers.

3.1.3 The proposed Traveller Accommodation Agency should be established on a statutory basis. The establishment of the proposed Agency would, in the Task Force's opinion, be the most efficient and effective way to ensure that the Government's target is met. Its specific brief will be to support, co-ordinate and advance the implementation of the Government target. It will draw up, agree and monitor the annual National Programme of Accommodation. It is envisaged that the Agency would have an adequate complement of staff.

3.2 Establishment of Traveller Accommodation Agency[3]

3.2.1 Recommendation

DR.22 An independent statutory body, to be known as the Traveller Accommodation Agency, should be established to draw up, in consultation with local authorities, a National Programme for the provision of Traveller specific accommodation in order to achieve the Government's objective of provision of such accommodation by the year 2000.

---

[3] **Reservation by Mr. P. Greene**

I disagree with this recommendation. It would, in my view, delay the provision of urgently needed accommodation for traveller people by creating uncertainty in the responsibility and role of local authorities and by providing a further focus for opposition to halting site locations. The establishment of a further statutory body in the Local Government sector is not compatible with a programme of devolution and a widening of the role of Local Government. Other recommendations in this section, when implemented, will remove obstacles to the provision of halting sites except local community opposition which can only be addressed at local level - see Section A.

(a) Structure

The Agency, to be established by the Minister for the Environment should consist of a Chairperson to be appointed by the Minister for the Environment and nine directors to be drawn from the following three categories with balanced representation:

(i)   direct appointments of the Minister for the Environment, including elected local representatives;

(ii)   direct appointments of the Minister for Equality & Law Reform or his/her successor, with a specific expertise on equality issues; and

(iii)   nominations made by relevant National Traveller Organisations.

The right of Travellers to a presence on the Board should be recognised. The Ministers concerned should ensure appropriate balances on the Board in terms of gender and of Travellers/'Settled' people.

The right of Travellers to a presence on the Board should be recognised. The Ministers concerned should ensure appropriate balances on the Board in terms of gender and of Travellers/'Settled' people.

The Agency's Chairperson and directors should be part-time and appointed for a five year period. The Agency should have a Chief Executive Officer, appointed following public advertisement and sufficient staff as required by the Board of the Agency. The Agency should be designated a prescribed body for the purpose of Section 21 of the Local Government (Planning and Development) Act, 1963 and Article 5 of the Local Government (Planning and Development) Regulations, 1994.

(b) Functions

The functions of the Agency should be as follows:

–   draw up a National Programme for the provision of Traveller specific accommodation on the basis of programmes submitted by the local authorities;

–   monitor, assess, advise on and secure the implementation of the annual building and refurbishment programmes of local authorities for Traveller specific accommodation;

–   monitor and review local development plans under the Planning Acts to ensure they provide for the provision of Traveller specific accommodation;

–   develop guidelines for planning authorities for the appropriate inclusion of Traveller specific accommodation in development plans;

–   advise the Minister for the Environment on the information sought and the manner in which it is sought for the Assessment of Housing Needs under Section 9 of the Housing Act, 1988;

- carry out research as necessary into and advise on matters relating to the provision and refurbishment of accommodation of Travellers including the participation of Travellers in the management of same;

- organise and promote, where necessary, appropriate training in intercultural skills and similar issues relevant to work in this area for staff involved in the provision, refurbishment and management of Traveller specific accommodation;

- advise the Minister for the Environment on all legislation relevant to Traveller accommodation;

- advise regional authorities on the individual local authorities' proposals for Traveller accommodation to ensure a co-ordinated and integrated approach in each region;

- liaise as necessary with the other bodies which the Task Force proposes should be established, namely the Traveller Education Service, Traveller Health Advisory Committee and the Equality Authority/Commission;

- analyse patterns of movement of Travellers within the State;

(c) Powers

The Agency should have the following powers:

- where a local authority fails to draw up an annual programme for the provision and refurbishment of Traveller specific accommodation, or where the Agency finds the local authority's annual programme is inadequate the Agency should issue a directive to the local authority to rectify the identified problem;

- where the Agency is of the opinion that a local authority fails to meet the annual targets agreed with the Agency without reasonable cause, it should direct the authority to carry out the necessary works within a time specified by the Agency;

- where the Agency is of the opinion that a planning authority fails to include appropriate provision for Traveller specific accommodation in its development plan or a revision of the plan, the Agency shall direct the authority to make such provision within a time specified by the Agency;

- in the event of a local authority or planning authority failing to carry out a directive by the Agency without reasonable cause, it shall apply to the High Court for an appropriate Court order to compel compliance;

- other powers appropriate to statutory bodies such as employing staff, and having a seal.

4.   Traveller Tenant Participation

4.1   Statement of Policy

4.1.1 Local Authorities are required under Section 9 of the Housing (Miscellaneous Provisions) Act, 1992, to draw up and adopt a written statement of policy for the effective performance of their function of management of their rented housing stock. In March, 1993, the Department of the Environment circulated local authorities with a memorandum on the preparation of a statement of policy in housing management (Ref. 10).

4.1.2   One of the items covered by the Memorandum is 'Tenant Involvement'. It stated:

"Tenant consultation and participation in the running of their estates is now regarded as crucial to securing the best return from the scarce resources available, to safeguarding the investment in the provision and improvement of the housing, and to contributing to the quality of life in the estates".

4.1.3   On this basis, it is appropriate to include Traveller tenants of local authorities in halting sites and group housing schemes in any consideration of tenant involvement in housing management.

4.2   **Traveller Accommodation Committee**

4.2.1   Local authorities should have a Traveller Accommodation Committee, set up under the powers of the Local Government Act, 1991, representing a partnership, based on fair representation and the principle of equality, of local authority councillors, Travellers and Traveller organisations based in the local authority area. While each local authority Traveller Accommodation Committee will identify its own priorities, the key role of the Committee will be assisting in the development and implementation of the accommodation programme and of Traveller tenant participation strategies.

4.3   **Recommendations**

DR.23   In relation to Statements of Policy on Housing Management, local authorities should ensure:

(a)   the involvement of Traveller tenants in the development of a participation programme;

(b)   the statements contain an anti-discrimination commitment to ensure that tenant participation strategies cannot contribute to the exclusion of Travellers, purely because they are Travellers.

DR.24   Each local authority should establish a Traveller Tenant Accommodation Committee, as described at paragraph 4.2.1 above.

DR.25   The provisions of the Department of the Environment Memorandum relating to tenant involvement should be applied to Travellers in Traveller specific accommodation. The Task Force supports the piloting and promotion of tenant participation strategies.

DR.26   Letting agreements with Traveller tenants should show flexibility to ensure they are appropriate to the use of Traveller specific accommodation.

5. Support Structure in the Local Authority for Travellers (The Social Worker)

5.1 The Social Worker's Role at Present

The range of work involving the local authority social worker varies with the specific needs and aims of his/her client Travellers, the availability of facilities and services for them, their accommodation status, and the policy of the local authority.

The local authority social worker for Travellers generally performs roles across the following spectrum:

1. Advisor;
2. Negotiator;
3. Co-ordinator;
4. Supporter and Enabler.

1. Advisor

The social worker assesses their different accommodation needs and has an initial role in outlining the overall accommodation programme for Travellers. An accommodation programme is prepared by discussing their needs and preferences with individual families and family groups and by assessing the ongoing number of Travellers who are transient.

2. Negotiator

The social worker has emerged as a negotiator for individual Traveller families.

The difficulty for Travellers in accessing relevant local authority officials directly in some local authorities and the advantage of having a social worker to present their case has led Travellers to communicate with State agencies through the social worker. This has been accentuated by illiteracy among Travellers which leads to a very high number of all Traveller families seeking out the services of the social worker.

It can often happen that a local authority, a residents' group and Travellers are in conflict. The social worker can assist in negotiating in situations where there is conflict. The negotiator role is an opportunity to reduce direct conflict.

3. Co-ordinator

As co-ordinator the social worker has a role in facilitating the delivery of health, welfare, accommodation and education services to Travellers, especially those who are transient. Apart from the day to day work with medical card applications, requests for financial assistance, communication with Public Health Nurses and G.P.'s there is the longer term planning process of setting up structures, classes and facilities for education and health projects.

4. Supporter and Enabler

A fundamental aspect to social work is in empowering and enabling the client. For Travellers this requires acceptance of their culture. In the past, Travellers' culture was seen as just a sub-culture of poverty; they were seen as a people in need of rehabilitation. Social workers were expected to monitor child care and foster better standards in Travellers. Despite failure to provide basic services for so many Travellers, this rehabilitative role was expected.

The emergence of the debate on Traveller culture has helped social workers, in that the old rehabilitative model is generally discredited and social work can help Travellers to develop within their own culture.

5.2   Recommendation

DR.27   It is recommended that the social workers' formal duties be revised at national level by a Committee representing the social workers, local authorities, health boards, Department of the Environment, Department of Health, Travellers and relevant Traveller organisations. The Committee should take account of the need to shift the social workers' role from a rehabilitative focus to one of intercultural respect, and consider and make recommendations in relation to, inter alia, the following issues:

- job description and selection criteria;
- career structure;
- in-service training;
- management/reporting structure;
- liaison with other relevant agencies;
- harassment;
- case load size.

6.   Legislative and Procedural Changes

6.1   Background

6.1.1   The Task Force commissioned a paper on the legislation that governs the provision of accommodation for the Traveller community. This paper (Ref. 11) examined the case law in relation to Traveller accommodation and identified a range of issues in relation to the relevant legislation.

6.1.2   The Task Force met with a number of local authorities and representatives of the County and City Managers' Association. These meetings assisted in further clarifying the legislative changes that would be required to allow for an improvement in local authority responses to Traveller accommodation needs.

6.1.3.1   In relation to the Housing Code, the Task Force considers as a general principle that local authorities and the Department of the Environment, when making decisions under the Housing Code that concern Travellers, or that relate to Travellers, should give particular consideration to the welfare and accommodation needs of the Traveller community. In relation to the existing legislation, the Task Force would focus attention on Sections 8, 9 and 13 of the 1988 Housing Act. Sections 8 and 9 of the 1988 Housing Act require housing needs and requirements to be estimated.

These Sections are held to include Traveller accommodation. However, Traveller specific accommodation is not explicitly named in them. It is noted that these Sections do not include any specific provision for publishing the assessment or for giving relevant Traveller organisations the same consultative status as other voluntary bodies.

6.1.3.2 While the power to make provision for sites for Travellers under Section 13 of the 1988 Housing Act is an enabling one, it has been interpreted in the courts as a duty. The same applies to Section 111 of the 1966 Housing Act. This allows the Minister to intervene where local authorities are failing to perform any of their functions.

6.1.3.3 Travellers and Traveller organisations have concerns with the powers of eviction and removal under Section 10, Housing (Miscellaneous Provisions) Act, 1992 and Section 69, Roads Act, 1993. This is of particular concern in the absence of a network of transient sites.

6.1.4 A major element in the implementation of the National Strategy will be the speedy acquisition of suitable land by local authorities. A significant contribution to this process could be made by Departments and other State and semi-state bodies if the local authority had access to lands in the ownership of these bodies which are not required for their statutory purposes.

6.1.5 Article 44.2.6 Bunreacht na hÉireann (Ref. 12) states:

"The property of any religious denomination or any educational institution shall not be diverted save for necessary works of public utility and on payment of compensation."

It is necessary to explicate the fact that Traveller accommodation needs are part of the *"necessary works of public utility"*.

6.1.6.1 Development control is a statutory process under the Planning Code which encourages development to take place in an orderly and efficient manner to the benefit of the community at large. To assist in this process a system of land use zoning in the Development Plan is operated by planning authorities to indicate the planning control objectives for all lands in their administrative area.

6.1.6.2 This system of land use zoning as currently operated by the local authority as planning authority can cause difficulty for the authority when acting as housing authority. The zoning of land for particular usage in development plans has on occasion presented obstacles to the location of Traveller accommodation. There are also planning implications in the design of Traveller accommodation in a manner that incorporates living and working space in the one area, as recommended in Section G on the Traveller Economy. The Third Schedule of the Local Government (Planning and Development) Act, 1963 sets out certain categories of objectives to be catered for in the development plan. None of these categories relate specifically to the distinct needs of the Traveller community.

6.1.6.3 A number of court actions based on the zoning categories used in the planning code have been taken in efforts to stop the development of Traveller accommodation.

These include:

–   O'Leary and others -v- Dublin Co. Council (1988)
    High Court O'Hanlon J. unreported.

–   Mary Wilkinson -v- Dublin Co. Council (1991)
    ILRM 605

–   John Ferris and others -v- Dublin Co. Council (1990)
    Supreme Court 7th November, 1990 unreported.

–   Tom Chawke Caravans Limited and Patrick Hoare -v-Limerick Co. Council (1991)
    112/JR High Court, Flood J. unreported.

6.1.7   As far as possible, local authorities should acquire land for the provision of accommodation for the Traveller community by agreement. However, where it is not possible to acquire land by agreement, procedures for the speedy acquisition of land compulsorily should be available to local authorities.

6.1.8   There is a need to provide adequate controls and sanctions where owners allow their horses to wander, especially in built-up areas. The Government's undertaking in this regard, that: "We will introduce legislation to control wandering horses in urban areas", (Ref. 13) is noted.

6.2   **Housing Code**

6.2.1   **Recommendations**

DR.28   To amend Sub-Section (9) of Section (2) of the City and County Management (Amendment) Act 1955, which reads:

"Nothing in the foregoing provisions of this Section shall prevent the manager from dealing forthwith with any situation which he considers is an emergency situation calling for immediate action without regard to those provisions."

by the insertion of the following words at the end of the Sub-Section:

"or in the case of the provision of Traveller specific accommodation, where the members fail to agree with the Manager's proposals or with amended proposals within six months of being first presented by the Manager".

DR.29   To amend Section (27) of the Housing Act 1988, which reads:

"The City and County Management (Amendment) Act, 1955, is hereby amended by the insertion in Section 2 of the following Sub-Section after Sub-Section (9):

   "(10) An emergency situation for the purpose of Sub-Section (9) of this Section shall be deemed to exist where, in the opinion of the Manager, the works concerned are urgent and necessary (having regard to personal health, public health and safety considerations) in order to provide a reasonable standard of accommodation for any person".

by the insertion of the following words at the end of the Section:

"including Travellers who are parked in unserviced and unofficial locations without access to basic facilities which exist on a serviced site".

DR.30 That Section 8 of the 1988 Housing Act be amended:

– to have group housing and halting sites, permanent and transient requirements named as being included within the general estimate of requirements carried out by the local authority, including Traveller families likely to move into the functional area of the local authority within the time period of the estimate;

– to require the local authority to have regard to consultation with and submissions from Travellers and local Traveller organisations in making this estimate.

DR.31 That Section 9 of the Housing Act, 1988 be amended to require a local authority to give one month's notice of its intention to carry out a housing assessment to local Traveller organisations and to make this assessment available to these organisations upon completion.

DR.32 To facilitate the implementation of Section 10, Housing (Miscellaneous Provisions) Act, 1992 and Section 69, Roads Act, 1993, priority needs to be given to the implementation of the Task Force's recommendations concerning the network of transient sites. Each of these Sections should be amended to provide that Travellers whose temporary dwelling is removed to storage cannot be deemed to be deliberately homeless.

6.2.2 State Lands

Recommendation

DR.33 It is recommended that a statutory requirement be placed on public bodies including Government Departments that lands in their possession which are not clearly identified as being required for their statutory purposes within five years and which are deemed to be suitable by the local authority for the provision of accommodation for Traveller people be made available to the local authority for that purpose.

6.2.3 Land owned by a Religious Denomination or an Education Institution

Recommendation

DR.34 It is recommended that the necessary legislative changes be put in place to confirm that the term "necessary works of public utility" as used in Article 44.2.6 of Bunreacht na hÉireann, includes the provision of Traveller specific accommodation.

6.2.4 Planning Code

DR.35 It is recommended that the Third Schedule of the Local Government (Planning and Development) Act, 1963 be amended to include a reference to the provision of Traveller specific accommodation as an objective.

DR.36 Planning authorities should review and where necessary, amend their Development Plans immediately in order to allow the provision of Traveller specific accommodation in all land zones[4].

DR.37 It is recommended that Section 39 of the Local Government (Planning and Development) Act, 1963, be amended to provide that the provision of Traveller specific accommodation would not be regarded as a material contravention of the Development Plan. (This is a temporary measure pending revision of existing plans following enactment of amendment of the Third Schedule as recommended at DR.35 above).

DR.38 Where a system of land use zoning is not specified in a Development Plan to cover all land in the administrative area, the written statement of the Plan should clearly indicate that the provision of Traveller Specific Accommodation is permissible in all land whether zoned or unzoned[5].

DR.39 The Minister should issue a general directive under Section 7 of the Local Government (Planning and Development) Act, 1982 in relation to the inclusion in Development Plans for the provision of Traveller accommodation on the basis of Task Force Recommendations DR.35 and DR.36 above.

6.2.5 Compulsory Acquisition of Land for the Provision of Accommodation for the Traveller Community.

DR.40 Legislation should be amended to provide for the acquisition of land for the provision of accommodation for the Traveller community on the same model as set out in the Roads Act, 1993 (Section 47). The legislative procedures set out in the Roads Act, 1993 (Section 47) for the making of a Motorway, Busway and Protected Road Scheme represents the most expeditious procedures for compulsory acquisition of land for public purposes. It is recommended that this model should be applied to the acquisition of land for the provision of Traveller specific accommodation by appropriate amending legislation. The procedure envisaged would require each local authority to adopt a Traveller Specific Accommodation Scheme at specific times which would set out its programme of accommodation for Travellers for the following appropriate period.

6.2.6 Miscellaneous Legislation

Recommendation

DR.41 The provisions of the proposed Freedom of Information Act should apply to requests from Travellers and relevant Traveller organisations to local authorities, seeking relevant information in relation to the provision of Traveller accommodation.

DR.42 Legislation should be introduced to control wandering horses as promised in "A Government of Renewal" (op. cit, 13).

---

[4] Councillor Joan Maher does not agree that amenities/B & G zoning should permit Traveller specific accommodation.

[5] Councillor Joan Maher does not agree that amenities/B & G zoning should permit Traveller specific accommodation.

7. Local Authorities - Extension of Powers

7.1 General

The need for additional powers for local authorities in order to deal with anti-social behaviour, illegal camping on or adjacent to Traveller halting sites and group housing schemes is dealt with here. Anti-social behaviour also arises within the 'Settled' community and strategies should be formulated to address the issue in both communities.

7.2 Issues of Concern

Firstly, there exists a small number of families whose behaviour is anti-social and who, if living on a site with other families, can destabilise the site. Often the response of the other families on a site is to move away. This may lead to the phenomenon of empty bays, which roadside families refuse to occupy. Local authorities need to be able to prevent this situation arising in the first place, and to deal with it if it does arise.

Secondly, families which have not been allocated a bay, may arrive and stay on the site or on land adjacent to it. When there is a large number of these additional families or when additional families remain in position over a period of time, the services available at the site are inadequate and local residents may object to the presence of those additional families. Frequently, the result is a deterioration in the living conditions of the families who are official tenants of the site.

The Task Force accepts that the failure to provide adequate accommodation facilities on a country-wide basis for Traveller families has resulted in large numbers of such families moving to the limited number of sites/schemes which are available, in order to obtain access to the facilities provided at these locations.

Other factors that have a fundamental influence on the functioning of halting sites and group housing schemes are:

(i) the extended family system;
(ii) economic activities, including keeping of animals;
(iii) compatibility between families and family groups.

Within this context, local authorities have the responsibility to ensure that:

– there are adequate and secure tenancies for appointed tenants;

– there is proper management of the facilities, in order to prevent vandalism and intimidation; and

– that commitments to tenants and residents are upheld.

7.3 Present Legal Position

At present, the legal position is that a local authority must apply to the courts to have tenants whose behaviour is anti-social or who are illegally camped, evicted from halting sites and group housing schemes. The general experience is that this is a very slow and expensive process, often taking a number of months and in the interim considerable damage can be done to the facilities in question.

In some cases, families who make illegal entry onto sites and land adjacent to sites are unknown and names cannot be procured to take the required action, especially when large groups are involved in such activities. In addition, the lack of accommodation facilities elsewhere means that these families have no alternative locations in which to reside which can mean that the courts may not grant eviction orders.

In addition, while specific tenants whose behaviour is anti-social are usually well known to the local authority, there is difficulty in getting other residents and tenants to give evidence in court, in relation to any damage and intimidation which occurs, as most other families are afraid of reprisals.

7.4   Reasons Why Additional Powers are Required

In the case of Travellers, the need to consider additional powers to enable local authorities deal with families whose behaviour is anti-social or who are illegally camped on or adjacent to Traveller halting sites and group housing schemes arises for the following reasons:

–   The maintenance costs of these facilities are high. Vandalism and the misuse of facilities contributes to these costs;

–   Interference by such families with other tenants and residents can result in anguish, distress, depression, inconvenience and in some instances, intimidation;

–   Such actions have a negative impact on the response to proposals for future sites and schemes for Travellers;

There is the additional issue to be dealt with, of the specific harassment to which Traveller tenants in standard housing may be subjected by 'Settled' people.

7.5   Additional Powers Required

In view of the problems outlined above and the serious consequences to which they give rise for tenants, residents, maintenance and proposed new facilities, it is recommended that the following additional powers for local authorities should be considered:

Recommendations

DR.43   Legislation should be enacted to prevent parking of caravans and other temporary dwellings within one mile of Traveller specific accommodation. The local authority should be given powers to keep these areas clear of such parking. This legislation should not apply to existing families on long term unofficial sites, without prejudice to the provisions of Section 10, Housing (Miscellaneous Provisions) Act, 1992.

DR.44 Local authorities should be provided with powers of immediate access to the High Court to remove those who break into Traveller specific accommodation, or who park adjacent to such facilities, or who come in to use these facilities continually, without the permission of the local authority. One method to achieve this would be specific legislative procedures for short service of an interlocutory application to the High Court in these cases. The provision of a network of transient sites, which is dealt with elsewhere, is an essential element in dealing with this issue. These powers are not intended to be availed of by local authorities to cause Travellers, who are in their functional area, to move to an adjoining area, thus evading their obligations.

DR.45 In the case of existing tenants identified by the local authority as responsible for vandalising a facility or interfering with other tenants or residents of that facility, a speedy and effective response is required. A process incorporating the following elements is proposed:

(a) warning notice;
(b) interview;
(c) rehabilitation programme, where appropriate;
(d) if (a), (b) and (c) do not produce the desired result, then the ultimate sanction of eviction would be pursued.

Persistent anti-social behaviour should constitute a breach of the tenancy agreement and, following the procedure outlined above, the ultimate sanction should be eviction. Priority should be given to seeking court orders for this purpose. Given the difficulty of obtaining primary evidence in these cases, secondary evidence should be admissible.

The forging of links with the Traveller community and Traveller groups is important. Community support for a harassed family is invaluable in counteracting the effect of anti-social behaviour.

DR.46 Local authorities should develop responses to the specific experience of intimidation against Travellers moving into standard housing. This protection should be reflected in the general tenancy agreement.

8. Statistics

8.1 The Task Force makes the following recommendations in relation to certain statistics collected by or on behalf of the Department of the Environment and the Central Statistics Office:

The Annual Count

Recommendations

DR.47 The Traveller Accommodation Agency should review the necessity for an Annual Count and if found to be necessary, should take responsibility for its compilation and publication. Pending this review, the Annual Count should continue to take place.

DR.48 The 1995 Annual Count should be carried out on the basis of a partnership between the local authorities and local Traveller groups.

The Census of Population of Ireland

Recommendation

DR.49 The Task Force recommends that the Central Statistics Office include the Traveller community as a separate heading in its classification of households in all future Censuses of Population.

References

1. Report of the Commission on Itinerancy, Stationery Office, Dublin 1963

2. Report of the Travelling People Review Body, Stationery Office, Dublin 1983

3. Keane Liam: Surveys of Local Authorities. Report prepared on behalf of the Task Force, Task Force Report, 1995.

4. Butler, Paul. Accommodation Needs of Travellers in Galway 1994 to 2000. Report commissioned by the Task Force, Task Force Report, 1995.

5. Liégeois, Jean Pierre: "Gypsies and Travellers", Dossiers for the Intercultural Training of Teachers, Council of Europe, Strasbourg 1987.

6. The President Robinson Awards for the Design of Travellers' Accommodation. Pavee Point Publications, Dublin 1993

7. Annual Count of Travellers, 1994. Annual Housing Statistics Bulletin 1994. Stationery Office, Dublin 1995.

8. Programme for a Partnership Government, (1993 - 1997). Stationery Office, Dublin 1993.

9. Speech by Minister of State, Ms. Liz McManus, T.D. to Irish Travellers Movement AGM, February 11th, 1995.

10. "Management of Local Authority Housing: Statement of Policy" Circular HRT 4/93, Department of Environment, 1993.

11. Elder Shaun & Co., Solicitors: "Perspectives and Recommendations on Legislation relating to Accommodation, as relevant to the Travelling Community" and "How the System of 'zoning' under the Planning Acts may be standardised; Whether amendment to legislation is Required". Papers commissioned by the Task Force, Task Force Report, 1995.

12. Bunreacht na hÉireann, Stationery Office, Dublin 1990.

13. A Government of Renewal, A Policy Agreement between Fine Gael, The Labour Party, Democratic Left. Stationery Office, 1990.

Section E: Health

## 1.	Introduction

1.1.1	The provision of health services and, in particular, questions associated with access to and utilisation of those services, are of major concern to the Traveller community.

1.1.2	The needs of the Traveller community in relation to general health service provision have in the past been examined in two previous reports published on the Traveller community, namely, the Report of the Commission on Itinerancy, (Ref. 1) and in the Report of the Travelling People Review Body, (Ref. 2) and recommendations were included in both reports in relation to the improvement and development of health service provision for Travellers. The issue of Traveller health was also addressed in the National Health Strategy "Shaping a Healthier Future", (Ref. 3).

1.1.3	This section examines the current situation concerning the health of the Traveller community in Ireland. It contains a summary of the findings and recommendations in the health area of the 1963 Commission Report, the 1983 Review Body Report and the 1994 National Health Strategy (op.cit, 1, 2, 3). It examines and comments on the present position concerning the health status of Travellers and summarises the main elements and conclusions of a joint study on how public health services relate to the needs of Travellers (Ref. 4), a study undertaken jointly for the Task Force and the Department of Health.

1.1.4	It should be noted that the joint study was not intended as an examination of Travellers' health but rather placed particular emphasis on identifying barriers to gaining access to health services and on gaps in service provision that are of particular relevance to Travellers. The Task Force identifies access and utilisation as the central issues to be addressed and this section concentrates mainly on these areas.

1.1.5	Finally, the Task Force makes a number of recommendations in relation to the improvement of health service provision for the Traveller community.

1.1.6	An examination of, and a set of recommendations in relation to, two other issues are also included in this section; namely, Traveller children involved in begging and the role of the health board social work service in relation to Travellers.

## 1.2	The Commission on Itinerancy Report, (1963)

1.2.1	In Chapter VII of its Report published in 1963, (op. cit, 1) the Commission on Itinerancy examined various aspects of the health of Travellers such as: medical requirements, adult, infant and child health, family size, conditions at birth, hygiene, food supply, clothing, age structure and life expectancy.

1.2.2	While the Commission referred to the fact that the available evidence supported the view, in relation to adult health, *"that the health of itinerants is seriously affected by the rigours of the way of life"*, it was the opinion of the Commission that Travellers were generally healthier than one would expect of people who experienced a lot of hardship in their lives. A survey of the incidence of a number of illnesses among

Travellers was carried out, although the results were inconclusive and bronchitis and pneumonia were commonly reported. The Commission was satisfied that the incidence of tuberculosis was not higher than among the 'Settled' population and that of mental illness was probably lower.

1.2.3　The Commission commented that the nomadic way of life of Travellers made it difficult for them to avail of some health service provision such as ante-natal and maternity care, child health services and protective immunisation. While the conditions at the birth of the majority of children were not found to be unsatisfactory, because many Traveller children were born either in hospital or with the assistance of a doctor or midwife, the Commission indicated that Traveller mothers, at the time, left hospital far too soon after the births of their children.

1.2.4　Two health issues were the subject of particular comment by the Commission namely the low rate of life expectancy and the high infant mortality rates among the Traveller community. In the case of infant health, in particular, the Commission indicated that mortality rates of infants in the first year of life were much higher than the national average with the majority of deaths due to respiratory diseases arising from the harshness and rigours of Traveller living conditions.

1.2.5　Recommendations made by the Commission in the area of Traveller health care included the carrying out of frequent visits to Traveller encampments by health personnel to make Travellers aware of the health services available and to encourage immunisation, pre-natal and post-natal care.

1.3.　Report of the Travelling People Review Body, (1983)

1.3.1　The Report of the Travelling People Review Body, (op. cit, 2) also considered the issue of Traveller health and made a number of recommendations in this area.

1.3.2　The 1983 Report concluded that the level of fertility among members of the Traveller community was extremely high. It suggested that almost all Travellers marry at a young age and had a large number of children; the size of Traveller families was large compared with those of the 'Settled' population; the age profile of Travellers was exceptionally young. Life expectancy for Travellers appeared to be considerably shorter than for the population as a whole. There seemed to be a high level of avoidable deaths among infants and children.

1.3.3　The 1983 Review Body also drew attention to a survey of health boards which indicated the following:

– Much ill-health among Travellers was due to over-crowded accommodation, poor ventilation and insanitary conditions in which Travellers lived. These conditions resulted in medical problems such as respiratory conditions, gastric disorders and alcohol-related conditions.

– While most Travellers were aware of the health services to which they were entitled, there were problems of ensuring continuity of treatment due to the mobility of families. A low level of literacy also militated against the use of services.

133

- It was noted that most Travellers had medical cards and that the Public Health Nurse had an essential role to play in ante-natal and post-natal care and in health education. It was also indicated that, as school attendance among Traveller children in some areas was low, school health examinations were not being undertaken.

- Finally, while Travellers made good use of the health services in the case of acute illnesses or confinement, there were problems in the case of conditions requiring repeated visits and appointments, when families tended not to take full advantage of the services available.

1.3.4   It should be noted that the Survey referred to in paragraph 1.3.3 above was based on the responses of service providers rather than on the experience of Traveller recipients of the health services.

1.3.5   Recommendations made by the 1983 Review Body included: the strengthening of the Public Health Nurse service with particular emphasis on follow-up visits; the provision of a family planning service which is sensitive to Travellers' way of life; the regular collection of information on the health status of Travellers and the need for improved co-ordination between the relevant statutory bodies so as to ensure that the environment in which Traveller families lived was improved.

1.4   **The National Health Strategy, (1994)**

1.4.1   In April, 1994, the Minister for Health published a National Health Strategy entitled "Shaping a Healthier Future", (op. cit. 3) which indicated that a special programme would be implemented to address the particular health needs of the Traveller community. The Health Strategy recognised that there was scope for achieving considerable improvements in the health status of Travellers through concerted health promotion and health care initiatives.

1.4.2   The Strategy includes a commitment to undertake a number of initiatives in the area of Traveller health following the completion of the joint study on Travellers' health (details in sub-section 3 of this section). These include:

- The development, in consultation with Traveller groups, of a health education programme aimed specifically at Travellers.

- The development of models of Traveller participation in health promotion and prevention.

- Ensuring that health boards make special arrangements to encourage and permit Travellers to avail of primary care services.

- Simplifying services under the General Medical Services including eligibility, immunisation and general health records to ensure better continuity of care from one health board to another.

- Liaising closely with other relevant statutory and voluntary agencies providing services to Travellers to ensure better targeting of services.

1.4.3   Following publication of this Report, the Minister for Health has undertaken to publish a policy on Travellers' health which will take account of the recommendations contained therein.

2.   The Health Status of Travellers

2.1   Arising from the recommendations of the Report of the Travelling People Review Body in 1983, the Department of Health commissioned the Health Research Board to undertake a study of the health of the Traveller community. The Traveller Health Status Study had three principal objectives:

– to determine the mortality rate and life expectancy of Travellers of all ages;

– to measure the health of Traveller infants;

– to measure the uptake of ante-natal, post-natal and infant health services by Travellers.

The findings of the study were to be presented in three publications, two of which are already published. This Study is the most up to date statistical analysis of Travellers' health status.

2.2   The first report is entitled Census of Travelling People, (Ref. 5) and was prepared by Joseph Barry and Leslie Daly. This census *"was carried out to provide denominator data to enable rates to be calculated for vital events which would occur in 1987."* It enumerated 15,888 Travellers and found:

– a marked difference between the age structure of the Traveller population and the country as a whole, with the median age of Travellers being fourteen years compared to the national figure of twenty-seven;

– over fifty per cent of all Travellers were in one of four counties: Cork, Dublin, Galway and Limerick.

2.3   The second report is entitled Vital Statistics of Travelling People, (Ref. 6) and was prepared by Joseph Barry, Bernadette Herity and Joseph Solan. This report focused on Traveller fertility and mortality *"to provide an assessment of the current situation and a baseline from which to monitor progress"*. It found:

– *"For Travellers in 1987 the general fertility rate was 164.2 per 1,000 compared to 70.1 per 1,000 for the settled community."*

– *"The infant mortality rate for Travellers in 1987 was 18.1 per 1,000 live births compared to the national figure of 7.4."*

– *"Male Travellers have over twice the risk of dying in a given year than settled males, whereas for female Travellers the risk is increased more than threefold."*

– *"Travellers are only now reaching the life expectancy that settled Irish people achieved in the 1940s."*

2.4   The detailed work of the Health Research Board raises a number of issues that are useful to identify:

–   There continues to be a lack of information on the causes of the poor health status of Travellers. In particular, the relationship between social context and Traveller health remains to be explored. The 1982 Black report (Ref. 7) commissioned by the U.K. Government identified the clear link between social inequality and ill health, finding that:

"From birth to old age those at the bottom of the social scale have much poorer health and quality of life than those at the top. Gender, area of residence and ethnic origin also have a deep impact."

The context of Travellers' lives includes the stress generated by living in a hostile society where discrimination is a constant reality, and this is compounded by frequently enforced change in their way of life. This context impacts adversely on Travellers' health.

–   The Health Research Board was not set the objective of identifying causes. However, the data is presented in terms of "housed" and "unhoused" Travellers, which inadvertently suggests a link between the Traveller way of life and poor health status. This might usefully have been corrected were it possible to separate out those on serviced sites and those on roadside camps within the unhoused category. It would also be important to identify the accommodation history of respondents before using data in this manner.

–   Little work has been done in the area of Traveller perceptions of health. Traveller morbidity was not a focus for the Health Research Board. Accurate morbidity studies would require an understanding of health beliefs and perceptions of a given community. This work would have much to contribute to improving the health status of Travellers. The most significant work in this area has been carried out by the Eastern Health and Social Services Board in Northern Ireland (Ref. 8). (see paragraph 2.7 below).

–   The issue of consanguinity is mentioned in the second Health Research Board Report (1987) in terms of metabolic disorders. However, while the study found a raised Standardised Mortality Ratio for metabolic disorders in males aged zero to fourteen of 1250, the numbers involved were so small that the ninety-five per cent confidence interval for this figure is thirty-two to 6965 making it statistically insignificant. The same situation applies to females aged zero to fourteen. In effect, only one death in each category was found in the period surveyed, from which it is not adequate to draw any conclusions. Further work is required in this area.

2.5   The work of the Health Research Board is still to be completed with the publication of a third report. Interim findings presented to the Task Force (Ref. 8a) provide evidence of:

–   a low uptake of maternal health services, with less than a third of mothers attending hospital by the end of the first half of pregnancy;

136

–   a low uptake of infant health services, in particular immunisation uptake and attendance at development screening examination, both of which are considerably less than fifty per cent;

–   high mobility of the Traveller community with only fifty to sixty per cent of infants located by the Public Health Nursing service at the child's first birthday.

2.6   The Health Research Board has identified a situation which the Task Force considers to be of crisis proportions in the health status of Travellers and it has provided a baseline against which to measure progress. The first priority must now be to develop adequate responses within the health service. These, of course, must be combined with initiatives in a broad range of other areas to improve the living conditions and life experience of Travellers.

2.7.1   The Eastern Health and Social Services Board in Northern Ireland has also carried out in-depth research on Travellers' health. This was conducted by Pauline Ginnety and published under the title "A Report on the Health of Travellers" (op.cit, 8). The aims of this research were to:

–   provide a baseline of information about Travellers' health, knowledge of which is unavailable elsewhere;

–   inform policy making at all levels in the EHSSB;

–   ensure the development of appropriate health services for Travellers;

–   be used as a basis for any training initiatives which are developed for key staff working with Travellers;

–   inform the Traveller community of the findings regarding their collective health and illness experience.

2.7.2   The research method pursued was based on *"elicit(ing) the naturally occurring health knowledge which is used informally by Travellers themselves"*. As such, the report provides important insights into Traveller health perceptions. These can make a central contribution to developing appropriate responses to Traveller health status. Among the insights provided were:

–   *"surprisingly, given the statistics, the majority of adults consider themselves to be fairly healthy, many saying they feel healthy and have never experienced illness"*.

–   *"their (mothers of young children) acknowledgement that women neglect themselves and wait for others to notice they are ill, highlights a need for support for this group"*.

–   *"overriding this are the current living conditions of Travellers (i.e. restrictions on movement, enforced large group encampments, lack of basic facilities, unemployment) which are perceived as the major health hazard"*.

137

- *"Travellers perceive that the many pressures they face affect their mental health. The main stressors are characterised as a change of lifestyle, the current living environment, worry and bereavement".*

2.7.3   The Report makes a series of recommendations in relation to health care strategy. It sets these in a challenging context when it quotes the WHO in 1985:

"It is salutary to remind ourselves that barely any of the World Health Organisation's (European Region) prerequisites for health are met for Travellers in Belfast - peace and freedom from threat or violence; social justice and equal opportunities for all; adequate food; safe water and sanitation; decent housing; basic education and employment, in order to ensure that everyone has a valued and rewarding role in society".

2.7.4   Recommendations made in the EHSSB Report include the following:

(a)   *"The Board, Unit and Trusts should:*

- *take a lead role in bringing together the relevant agencies in the voluntary and statutory sector to address issues of importance;*

- *include a statement on the care of Travellers in strategic and business plans;*

- *ensure that contracts include targets to be met for Travellers, but must also ensure that Travellers are not stigmatised by the arrangements;*

- *liaise with local councils to update information about sites in the area;*

- *identify a named person (other than direct face to face workers) to co-ordinate information relevant to Travellers;*

- *consult and collaborate with Travellers before embarking on initiatives;*

- *review policies in order to identify discriminatory practices".*

(b)   "Units/Trusts should:

- *Actively lobby for fully serviced site provision using intersectoral networks. This provision should cater for all families living or moving through the area. They should also work with other agencies to alleviate conditions on existing sites"*

- *"Adopt a community development approach to working with Travellers"*

- *"Enable Traveller families to gain access to the whole range of mainstream health and social services in a way that is in keeping with their right and freedom to travel"*

- *"challenge prejudice and discrimination against Travellers in the service".*

(c) Hospitals in the area should:

- *"Review appointment systems, records etc. for their relevance and accessibility to Travellers"*

- *"Consider innovative ways of communicating with Travellers regarding the preceding point"*

- *"Fully use the Travellers' client-held records in order to ensure continuity of treatment and care"*.

(d) *"It is only by developing a strategic perspective that the health needs of Travellers will be met in a fair and comprehensive way. Any strategy must be concerned with empowering them to make their own choices and with ensuring that the services available bring such choices within their reach"*.

3. Access To and Uptake of Health Services by Members of the Traveller Community

3.1 Background

3.1.1 In order to assist the Task Force in making recommendations in relation to the use of and access to health services by the Traveller community, consultants were commissioned by both the Task Force and the Department of Health to carry out an assessment of how public health services relate to the needs of Travellers. In the study, emphasis was placed on identifying barriers to gaining access to health services and gaps in service provision that are of particular relevance to Travellers. The study, although providing some information on the subject, was not intended as an examination of Travellers' health status.

3.1.2 The survey, which was undertaken by the Department of Health Promotion, University College Galway, and by Patricia McCarthy and Associates, Dublin (op. cit 4) involved in depth interviews with 200 Travellers in Galway and Dublin during October and November, 1994. In addition, surveys of health service providers were also carried out in the period of September to December, 1994, which involved interviews with nominated community care personnel from each health board, a postal survey of Programme Managers of the special and general hospital services, and a telephone survey of General Practitioners in the GMS Scheme. A survey of health education personnel in each of the health boards was also conducted.

3.1.3 The research work also involved a review of the general literature in relation to health service provision for nomadc peoples with particular reference to the situation in Australia and Canada.

3.1.4 Due to the absence of comprehensive statistics on health service utilisation, very little quantitative data on Travellers' utilisation of the health services is available. However, in summary, the picture that emerges from the consultants' report is one that involves a high utilisation of general practitioners and accident and emergency services and a low utilisation of other hospital services including after care and preventive services.

3.1.5 The study also identified a range of specific obstacles to Travellers' access to health services:

- illiteracy, which leads to difficulties completing forms for the renewal of medical cards;

- lack of provision for tracing and transferring the health records of Travellers who are mobile, which makes referrals and continuity of care more difficult;

- prejudice on the part of the general public and service providers, resulting in Travellers being refused access.

A number of gaps in health service provision, or unmet needs, were also identified.

3.1.6 The remainder of this section on access and uptake contains a summary of the main findings of the consultants' research work. The full text of their report is included in a volume of research papers published separately with this Report.

3.2 Review of International Literature

The review of international literature in relation to health service provision for nomadic peoples, with particular reference to the situation in Australia and Canada, established that initiatives aimed at improving the health-status of nomadic aboriginal groups in Australia and Canada are based on a number of key principles as follows:

- the active participation of nomadic people in determining health policy priorities for their communities and in decision making regarding the allocation of resources;

- the development of broadly based strategies in relation to nomadic health, based on detailed consultation with nomadic communities;

- specialist community-controlled primary health care services that are complementary to and promote greater utilisation of appropriate mainstream services;

- the promotion of the training and employment of nomadic people in health service delivery;

- nomadic health research that is based on the active involvement of nomadic people and sound ethical practices;

- flexibility in health service infrastructure and facilities tailored to meet the needs of nomadic people;

- positive discrimination/action in relation to health benefits;

—   a clear emphasis on environmental health, in recognition of the environment-related nature of much nomadic mortality and morbidity.

3.3   Survey of Travellers

3.3.1   The vast majority of Traveller respondents who took part in the survey were women. Thirty-four per cent of these women resided in standard housing. The survey found that:

- 20 per cent of the respondents had no toilet facilities;
- 27 per cent had only a shared cold water supply;
- 32 per cent had no electricity;
- 40 per cent had no bath or showers;
- 18 per cent had no refuse collection;
- 47 per cent had no access to a telephone.

3.3.2   The Traveller lifestyle data revealed that fifty per cent of the respondents reported on-going health problems and forty per cent said their families had on-going health problems.

3.3.3   The main information to emerge in relation to the use by Traveller respondents of the General Medical Services, was that:

- 83 per cent held a medical card for a doctor in their locality;
- 21 per cent stated that Travellers had difficulties filling out forms needed to apply for a medical card;
- 17 per cent had experienced difficulties in getting doctors to accept them on their lists;
- 36 per cent had experienced difficulties in getting doctors to come out on call;
- 20 per cent had more than 10 consultations in the last year;
- 41 per cent had more than 10 prescriptions in the last year.

3.3.4   In relation to Public Health Nursing and Child Health Services, it was found that:

- there was a low rate of Public Health Nurse intervention, with most visits taking place at home as opposed to at clinics;
- there was a low rate of immunisation for example fifty-two per cent MMR, forty-six per cent HIB (Haemophillus Influenza);
- Seventy-five per cent of respondents had paediatric developmental checks, but there was a low take-up of school based medical services;
- no assistance was received from the home help service by Travellers;
- the number of children referred to specialist services is low at twelve per cent.

3.3.5   In the case of access to hospital services by Travellers, it was found that:

- Thirty-six per cent had used out-patient services and thirty-three per cent had used in-patient services in the past year.

3.3.6   Responses to survey questions in relation to women's health, revealed a low take up of post-natal services, a very low rate of breast feeding and a low rate of family planning advice. With reference to the birth of their last child, four per cent of respondents had attended ante-natal classes, twenty-seven per cent had attended post natal check ups and seventy-eight per cent had afterwards been visited by a Public Health Nurse.

3.3.7 Finally, the survey of Travellers also revealed that twenty-one per cent of respondents attended a health education programme. The survey pointed out that because a number of women had taken part in women's training courses, the uptake of cervical cancer screening was high in comparison with the take up of other services. This finding points to the benefits of the voluntary sector's role in health service provision. Thirty-five per cent of respondents felt discriminated against by the health services.

3.4 Community Care Services

3.4.1 All eight health boards reported that they experienced particular difficulties with the provision of community care services to the Traveller community.

3.4.2 In the case of medical records, none of the health boards was able to extract statistics on Travellers' utilisation of community care services from their general records, as there is no system in place for the identification of Travellers on medical records. In addition, none of the health boards has special provision for the transfer of Travellers' medical records from one health board to another.

3.4.3 With regard to the delivery of services to Travellers, the following problems were identified by health boards, although all the difficulties may not be common to each health board:

–   GMS: Problems in renewing medical cards, due for example, to nomadism or illiteracy; the reluctance of GP's to take Travellers onto their lists; the lack of established relationships with GP's; a reluctance by GP's to go out on call to Travellers.

–   Public Health Nursing and Child Health Service: Difficulties included low take up of child preventive services such as immunisation, developmental paediatric services and specialist child health services (all eight health boards); poor continuity of care; difficulties contacting Traveller families to ensure delivery of services; non-attendance for school medicals; fear for personal safety on the part of Public Health Nurses. The reluctance of some Travellers to seek support from the health services for children with mental disabilities was also mentioned.

–   Women's Health: All health boards reported a poor take-up of ante-natal and post-natal services and four referred to the low take-up of cervical screening.

3.5 Hospital Services

3.5.1 With reference to Hospital Services, it was reported by all health boards that the general hospital services that are most used by the Traveller community are accident and emergency facilities, obstetrics and paediatric services. However, none of the health boards was able to extract data on Travellers' utilisation of hospital services from their records, due to lack of identification of Travellers on records and due to lack of accurate record keeping.

3.5.2   All health boards had experienced difficulties in the utilisation and delivery of accident and emergency services including, "inappropriate" use of these facilities, failure to keep recall appointments, threatening behaviour and difficulties arising because Traveller patients are sometimes accompanied by large groups.

3.5.3   With regard to obstetrics, problems identified included low rates of take up of ante-natal classes, ante-natal check ups and post-natal services. Difficulties also arose because of poor continuity of care and due to early self discharge of Traveller patients.

3.5.4   Most health boards reported that Travellers tend to have a low uptake of out-patient services. In relation to in-patient services, all the health boards reported that the Traveller community had a high uptake of paediatric services. Particular difficulties identified in relation to the use of paediatric services included overcrowding in waiting areas, due to large groups of relatives visiting patients and discharges against medical advice.

3.5.5   The survey of health boards suggested that Travellers had a low rate of utilisation of special hospital services, including psychiatric services. Very little information was available in relation to Travellers' utilisation of mental handicap services.

3.6.   Special Initiatives for the Traveller Community

3.6.1   Special initiatives have been introduced by individual health boards to attempt to redress some of the difficulties with the delivery of health services to the Traveller community.

3.6.2   Examples of special primary health care initiatives for Travellers are set out in Table E1, as follows:

Table E1: Special Primary Health Care Initiatives	
Type of Special Initiative	**Example/Health Board**
Specialist out-reach clinics	Mobile Clinic (EHB) On-Site Clinic (MHB)
Specialist out-reach services	On-Site Immunisation (NEHB, SEHB)
Specialist Staff	Specialist Public Health Nurses (SEHB, WHB, EHB, MHB) Home Makers' Service (NWHB)
Peer Led Services (i.e. employing Travellers)	Primary Health Care for Travellers Project (EHB) Shared Rearing Service (EHB) Foster Care Initiative (MWHB) Home Help Service (WHB)
Parenting Support	Community Mothers' Scheme (EHB) Mother and Baby Group (MHB)
Funding Voluntary Traveller Organisations	Dublin Committee for Travelling People (EHB) Traveller Families' Care (EHB) Local Traveller Support Groups (SEHB) Traveller Visibility Group (SHB)

3.7   Other Services

Additional information to emerge from the consultants' report includes the following:

(i)   **Health Education:** Public Health Nurses are involved in informal health education for Travellers, addressing issues such as nutrition, parenting skills, women's health and child health. However, while three health boards are also involved in formal health education that is targeted at Travellers, no formal health education is provided specifically for Travellers in many parts of the country.

(ii)   **Community Work:** Two health boards employ Community Workers whose briefs include specific activities with Travellers.

(iii)   **Inter-Sectoral Collaboration:** All health boards reported that informal inter-sectoral collaboration takes place in relation to Travellers and that this primarily involves collaboration with local authorities and the education sector. However, only three health boards have formal structures in place for collaboration with other sectors in relation to service provision for the Traveller community and only three health boards address the importance of direct participation by members of the Traveller community in inter-sectoral committees.

3.8 Survey of General Practitioners

3.8.1 A telephone survey of eleven nominated General Practitioners who have Traveller patients, confirmed the fact that a high proportion of Travellers a current medical card, that Travellers had a very high consultation rate and that there tends to be a very high rate of prescribing medicines for Travellers.

3.8.2 The GP's who were interviewed agreed that General Practitioners tend to be reluctant to accept Travellers as registered patients because of fear that to treat them will result in loss of other patients and because of their high consultation rate. GP's are also reluctant to carry out domicilary consultations on halting sites for various reasons including practical, personal security and financial reasons and, because of the general movement away from the provision of such consultations to all patients.

3.9 Conclusion

The Task Force bases the recommendations which follow on the main findings of the research report.

4.1 Health Service Organisation

4.1.1 Tackling Inequity

Recommendation

ER.1 Equity has been defined as a fundamental principle of Irish health policy. Increased funding, commensurate with the scale of the issue, should be allocated to tackling the unacceptable health status of the Traveller community and the widespread obstacles to Traveller access to health services.

4.1.2 Environmental Health

Recommendation

ER.2 The immediate improvement of the accommodation situation of Travellers is a pre-requisite to the general improvement of the health status of Travellers. Health boards should periodically inspect all halting sites so as to report on health and safety matters. The resulting reports should be publicly available.

4.1.3 Structures

Recommendations

ER.3 The Task Force notes the Minister for Health's commitment, as stated in the National Health Strategy (1994), (op. cit. 3) to addressing the particular health needs of the Traveller community. It recommends that a Traveller Health Advisory Committee should be appointed by the Minister for Health. Its brief should include:

   –   drawing up a national policy for a health strategy to improve the health status of the Traveller community;

- ensuring that Traveller health is a priority area within the Department of Health and setting targets against which performance can be measured;

- ensuring co-ordination and liaison in the implementation of national strategies of relevance to the health status of Travellers;

- ensuring the co-ordination, collection and collation of data on Travellers' health;

- supporting health boards in developing strategies to improve Traveller access to health services;

- providing a forum for the discussion of health initiatives for Travellers and for ongoing consultation with Travellers and Traveller organisations on health service delivery to Travellers.

The Traveller Health Advisory Committee should be drawn from the various divisions in the Department of Health, representatives of the Traveller community, from Health Boards and national Traveller organisations. It should have a small staff attached to it and be provided with an adequate budget. It should have a direct reporting relationship to the Minister.

ER.4 Each health board should establish a Traveller Health Unit. The brief of such a Unit would include:

- monitoring the delivery of health services to Travellers and setting regional targets against which performance can be measured;

- ensuring that Traveller health is given prominence on the agenda of the health board;

- ensuring co-ordination and liaison within the health board, and between the health board and other statutory and voluntary bodies, in relation to the health situation of Travellers;

- collection of data on Traveller health and utilisation of health services;

- ensuring appropriate training of health service providers in terms of their understanding of and relationship with Travellers.

- supporting the development of Traveller specific services, either directly by the health board or, indirectly through funding appropriate voluntary organisations.

The health board Traveller Health Unit should have a committee drawn from the various sectors in the health board and from local Travellers and Traveller organisations. It should have a small staff attached to it. It should have a reporting relationship to each of the Programme Managers and to the new Directors of Public Health. These Units should incorporate existing inter-sectoral structures focusing on Traveller health issues at health board level.

4.1.4 Medical Records
Recommendations

ER.5 An improved health record keeping system should be introduced by the Department of Health and the health boards to collect more detailed socio-economic data and make provision for the identification of Travellers. Provision should be made for the identification of Travellers on notification of births, deaths, hospital morbidity and maternal and perinatal statistical collections. A strict code of practice should be designed to govern this. This code should be based on the code of ethics for Aboriginal health research in the Australian National Aboriginal Health Strategy (Ref. 9). It should ensure that identification is voluntary and should guarantee confidentiality and sensitivity. The code of practice should be approved by the Data Protection Commissioner.

ER.6 A system of patient held records should be introduced nationwide. These records should provide information on a patient's medical history, in addition to all hospital and general practice consultations, and details of prescribed medicines. This should operate on a voluntary basis. It is envisaged that it would make a particular contribution to improving continuity of care for Travellers who are nomadic.

ER.7 An improved system of transferring records, both within and between health board regions, should be introduced. The application of information technology systems, such as those used in the field of banking, should be explored to establish data bases of Traveller health records that would ensure this transfer of records between community care, hospital services and pharmacies within and between health board regions. The process should be approved by the Data Protection Commissioner.

4.1.5 Personal Communication System
Recommendation

ER.8 Given the various difficulties, identified in the research, of communication between Traveller patients and the health service, a system, whereby correspondence from health services is provided through personal communications, should be offered to Traveller patients. Where requested, an appropriate channel should be identified in consultation with the patient. The patient should make the nominated person aware of any change of address.

4.2 Health Service Delivery

4.2.1 Traveller Specific Services
Recommendations

ER.9 Traveller specific services should be designed to complement mainstream services and to improve Traveller access to these. Travellers should have the right to opt out of any Traveller specific service and to choose to use mainstream services. In the implementation and provision of these services, there should be no segregation of Travellers.

ER.10 Traveller participation in health service delivery at all levels should be supported. This is especially important in the area of primary health care. In particular:

– Peer led services (such as Traveller paramedics) such as that piloted in the Eastern Health Board, should be expanded. This expansion should be based on an independent evaluation of the initiative with the participation of Travellers and Traveller organisations.

– Support should be provided to encourage and resource Travellers to gain qualifications as health professionals and to take up careers in the health field.

ER.11 Primary health care services for the Traveller community should be delivered on an outreach basis. It is important to stress that these outreach initiatives should complement, improve, and encourage access to mainstream provision and not replace such provision. On-site clinics in Traveller specific accommodation facilities should be established and serviced by various members of the Community Care teams, including Public Health Nurses, Dental Nurses, Speech Therapists and Social Workers. Priority should be given to child health, the care of the elderly, and to ante-natal and post-natal services. The facilities provided should be of a high standard and should guarantee confidentiality.

Traveller specific services in the primary health care area, requiring equipment that is not easily transportable, should be provided on an outreach basis through the designation of special Traveller clinics at an existing health centre. This approach would be particularly important in areas such as dental care. It would also ensure high standards in Traveller specific services.

The practice of designating particular Public Health Nurses to have a Traveller specific brief should be expanded. Recruitment for this brief should be by way of interview to ensure suitability. Training should be provided to successful candidates in intercultural methods.

ER.12 In general hospital services, provision should be made for outreach paediatric and obstetric clinics for Travellers. Special provision should also be made for improved liaison between general hospital and general practitioner services where, for example, after care could be provided increasingly by general practitioners rather than by out-patient clinics.

ER.13 In special hospital services, provision should be made for community psychiatric outreach services to deal with issues of mental health in the Traveller community.

ER.14 **(a)** The Department of Health should commission an in-depth analysis by independent experts of issues related to consanguinity in the Irish context, taking account of WHO work in this area.

(b) Given that Travellers predominantly marry within their own community, marriage of close relatives is common. Accordingly, a specific genetic counselling service to Travellers is required to address any risks associated with this.

148

ER.15 The provision of Traveller specific services recommended in the preceding recommendations should be subject to ongoing evaluation. This evaluation should measure the impact of the particular service, assess the continuing need for the particular service and ensure that the service is complementary to mainstream provision and has not resulted in any segregation.

ER.16 A regular conference of service providers and Traveller organisations should be organised by the Department of Health to facilitate the transfer of experiences of Traveller specific services between health boards.

ER.17 Traveller organisations have an important contribution to make in the targeting and in the appropriate delivery of health services to the Traveller community. This role can be considerably enhanced through support from the health boards. In particular, health boards should:

-   make funding available for Traveller support groups to employ community workers;

-   make resources available to enable Traveller support groups and Senior Traveller Training Centres to include health modules and activities in their training and education initiatives;

-   provide information to Traveller organisations and Senior Traveller Training Centres on Traveller uptake of services, the local conditions and other factors impacting on Traveller health and on the general health status of Travellers, safeguarding confidentiality in respect of such information.

4.2.2   General Practitioner Services

Recommendations

ER.18 The terms of the GMS for General Practitioners should prohibit the refusal to accept people as registered patients solely on the basis that they are Travellers.

ER.19 Where specific practices have a large proportion of Travellers on their lists, an audit and evaluation of drug utilisation by such practices should be conducted with the regional General Practitioner Unit to establish if there is an impact on their drugs bill and to analyse any high prescription rates. If it is found that this has an impact on the drugs costs of such practices, a special allowance should be introduced in the drugs payment scheme.

ER.20 For the additional outreach services recommended in Recommendation ER.12, special fees and allowances should be drawn up under the terms of the GMS.

ER.21 A simplified system of renewing and amending Traveller medical cards, in an expeditious manner that does not require detailed form filling on the part of the Traveller, should be introduced. The validity of medical cards held by Travellers should be extended to a minimum of three years. Simplified procedures should be put in place for General Practitioners to receive payment for Traveller patients who move into their area or who are in temporary residence there.

4.2.3 Health Promotion Education
Recommendations

ER.22 The Health Promotion Unit in the Department of Health, in partnership with relevant Traveller organisations, should draw up a policy for health promotion and education for Travellers. This should be provided in all health board regions and should:

- aim to restore Travellers' confidence in their ability to distinguish and to cope with minor illnesses;

- prioritise child health, breast feeding, the role of preventative and after-care services and the care of the aged;

- be based around personal skills development in order to support Travellers in appropriately meeting the many challenges in their lives and should not merely focus on lifestyle behaviour.

Lifestyle health education should give due recognition to the constraints on Travellers' circumstances, should resource the community to make informed choices and also provide access to the findings of relevant research including that recommended in ER.14 above.

ER.23 Health promotion work, with the general public, should inform people of the impact which the living circumstances and discrimination against Travellers have on Traveller health status. This should be done through a number of approaches such as:

- use of materials on these issues in school health education and lifeskills courses;

- use of mass media campaigns by the Health Promotion Unit.

Travellers and Traveller organisations should be involved in the preparation of materials for this work.

ER.24 All health professionals should receive training on the circumstances, culture of, and discrimination practised against Travellers, as part of their training. Service providers in frequent contact with Travellers should receive more in-depth training in intercultural and anti-discrimination practices. This training should also include a focus on Travellers' perspectives on health and illness. Travellers and Traveller organisations should be resourced to play an active role in this training and education.

4.3 General
Recommendation

ER.25 The Department of Social Welfare should address the difficulties in respect of access to the carer's allowance that arise from Traveller families in multiple dwellings.

150

5. Traveller Children Involved in Street Begging

5.1 This sub-section deals with unaccompanied Traveller children involved in street begging and door to door begging.

5.2 While the problem does not arise only in the Traveller community, it is the case that a small number of Traveller families put their teenaged and infant children onto the streets to beg. This occurs mainly in the larger cities and tourist towns and usually during the Summer and Christmas seasons. While sometimes an adult (usually the mother) might accompany an infant, very often the older children are unaccompanied.

5.3 Children who beg are exposed to various serious dangers. They are at risk to abduction and abuse. They are out on the streets for hours in all sorts of weather, subject to verbal abuse and conflict. In addition, children placed on the streets are exposed to influences such as drug abuse and child prostitution. These children may be regarded as abandoned and neglected for the duration of the day's begging. The general public should not provide money to children who beg, but should re-direct financial and other support to the main agencies which assist vulnerable families.

5.4 Present legislative provisions do not deal adequately with the problem of child begging. It is an offence under Section 14 of the 1908 Children's Act to cause or procure a minor to beg. However, these children would be further punished if it was decided to consider placing them in care as being neglected solely for this reason.

5.5 The 1991 Child Care Act does not specifically legislate for this problem apart, for example, from making it an offence to knowingly sell solvents to minors where there is reason to believe that the substance will be deliberately inhaled. The School Attendance Act, while in effect limiting begging times, cannot in itself resolve the problem of child begging.

5.6 Recommendations to Deal with Child Begging

The following recommendations are made by the Task Force in order to deal with the problem of child begging:

Recommendations

ER.26 Adequate support facilities, including day care centres for children involved in begging, should be provided by the relevant statutory authorities.

ER.27 Where the problem of child begging exists, an Outreach Worker should be appointed in major urban areas by the relevant statutory authorities, to work with vulnerable Traveller children and their families, in conjunction with the social work teams already in place. Adequate resources should be provided by the relevant statutory authorities for this purpose.

ER.28 In order to deter begging by unaccompanied children, Section 14 of the Childrens' Act 1908, which makes it an offence on the part of parents to cause or procure their children to beg or to be involved in petty theft, should be updated to a level where the penalties are an effective deterrent, including the power to confiscate any monies proven to be procured from such activity.

ER.29   The relevant provisions of the Child Care Act 1991 should be implemented to assist the relevant statutory authorities in removing children involved in begging to a suitable place.

6.   The Health Board Social Work Service to the Traveller Community

6.1   The primary focus of the Health Board Social Work Service is family and child care. In practice, this means supporting families where the children are to any extent neglected or at risk. Traveller families are extended this service when it is perceived that their children could be neglected or at risk.

6.2   In practice, day to day health board and local authority services that Travellers require are co-ordinated. The health board team only intervenes to specifically support child care and do so initially through the family.

6.3   Some issues for consideration arise out of this arrangement. For instance, traditionally the local authority social worker monitored Traveller child care and the health board only intervened to put Traveller children into care. The 1991 Child Care Act places child care exclusively as the responsibility of the health boards and this includes Traveller children.

6.4   There was a serious concern that the standards used for assessing child care in the Traveller community may not have been compatible with general health board standards and the implementation of the 1991 Child Care Act is expected to resolve this.

6.5   It should be noted that within the Traveller community, there is a tendency for young children to take on more adult roles and responsibilities than is the case with children in the 'Settled' community.

6.6   There is then a two-fold challenge which must be met by the health board social worker teams in the case of the Traveller community, namely, to ensure that reasonable standards of child care are demanded and provided, while at the same time ensuring that there is sensitivity to childcare practices within that community.

6.7   Recommendations

ER.30   Social workers in health boards who may have responsibility for Traveller children, should receive in-service training both in understanding Traveller culture and in developing skills to interculturally assess children's needs and neglect where it exists.

ER.31   Traveller mobility means that families may move out of the remit of a particular health board social work team. As Traveller mobility is common, it is recommended that effective formal co-ordination is put in place to trace families with children at risk within health boards and between health boards.

ER.32 Health board social workers whose Traveller case moves away, should be obliged to trace the family's whereabouts through the local authority social worker service and then fully inform the appropriate health board social worker in the new area of residence. Similar procedures should also be applied to families who move out of the jurisdiction.

ER.33 Where a Traveller family comes to the attention of a health board social work team and subsequently moves away before the case is closed, regardless of its significance, that case should not be deemed closed without notifying the appropriate social worker in the new area where the Traveller family locates.

References

1.   Report of the Commission on Itinerancy, Stationery Office, Dublin 1963.

2.   Report of the Travelling People Review Body, Stationery Office, Dublin, 1983

3.   "Shaping a Healthier Future", A Strategy for effective healthcare in the 1990's: Department of Health: Stationery Office, Dublin 1994.

4.   Patricia McCarthy and Assoc. and Centre for Health Promotion Studies, UCG, Health Service Provision for the Travelling Community in Ireland: Dublin, 1995.

5.   Barry Joseph and Daly Leslie: The Travellers Health Status Study - Census of Travelling People: Health Research Board, Dublin 1988.

6.   Barry Joseph, Herity Bernadette and Solan Joseph: The Travellers Health Status Study: Vital Statistics of Travelling People (1987) Health Research Board: Dublin 1989.

7.   Townsend, P. and Davidson, Nick (eds.) Inequalities in Health/The Black Report 1982 and the Health Divide: Penguin Books, U.K. 1988.

8.   Ginnety P, The Health of Travellers; Based on a Research Study with Travellers in Belfast: EHSSB, Belfast, 1993.

8a.   Interim Progress Report of the Task Force on the Travelling Community, Dublin 1994.

9.   National Aboriginal Health Strategy Working Party: A National Aboriginal Health Strategy: Commonwealth Department of Aboriginal Affairs, Canberra 1989.

Section F: Education and Training

1.   **General Principles and Broad Objectives for Traveller Education**

1.1   As indicated in its Interim Progress Report (Ref. 1), the Task Force notes and agrees ith the general principles for the education of children with special education needs which are set out in the Report of the Special Education Review Committee, (Ref. 2). In particular, the Task Force supports the Committee's assertions that:

-      *"All children, including those with special educational needs, have a right to an appropriate education. The Committee is in agreement with the principle put forward in the Primary School Curriculum, Teacher's Handbook . . . i.e., "each child . . . . deserves to be . . . . provided with the kind and variety of opportunities which will enable him to develop his natural powers at his own rate to his fullest capacity"*

-      *"The needs of the individual child should be the paramount consideration when decisions are being made concerning the provision of special education for that child."*

1.2   In addition, the Task Force believes that the following fundamental principles and broad objectives should underlie and be applied in the development and provision of education services at all levels (pre-school, primary, second-level, third-level and adult) to Travellers:

-      Equality of opportunity must exist so as to ensure that Travellers shall have access to all forms of education.

-      The principle of anti-discrimination should inform all education provision.

-      Acknowledgement of, and respect for, cultural diversity and multi-ethnicity should inform all education provision.

-      The principle of affirmative action should be applied to Travellers in education.

-      Rule 10 of the rules for National Schools, which states that *"no child may be refused admission to a national school on account of the social position of its parents, nor may any pupil be kept apart from the other pupils on the grounds of social distinction"*, should be applied to all schools, at primary and second levels.

-      There should be full parental involvement in decision making and in the development of education provision for their children.

-      The principle of integration should be applied save in exceptional circumstances.

1.3   All of these fundamental principals and broad objectives form the basis of the various recommendations in respect of access by Travellers to the education system, and their treatment within that system, which are included in this Section on Traveller education.

2. Issues of Concern to All Education Sectors

2.1 Introduction

2.1.1 Certain key issues which impact on education provision for Travellers are of concern to all education sectors but, in particular, in the case of Traveller children, to the pre-school, primary and second-level sectors.

2.1.2 In this section of the Report, the Task Force examines four such key issues namely:

(i) School attendance
(ii) Parental involvement
(iii) Traveller nomadism
(iv) Intercultural education

and, where appropriate, makes a number of recommendations to deal with problems which have been identified by the Task Force in its examination and analysis of the subjects concerned.

2.2 School Attendance

2.2.1 It is important to emphasise the rights of Traveller children to appropriate and adequate education.

2.2.2 Despite a significant improvement in recent years, lack of regular school attendance is a problem within the Traveller community.

2.2.3 The Task Force makes the following recommendations to assist in dealing with low school attendance levels among Traveller children.

Recommendations

FR.1 The Visiting Teacher Service has an important role to play in encouraging Traveller parents to ensure that their children participate in the education system, particularly at pre-school, primary and second levels. This role should be supported and, where necessary, adequately resourced by the relevant statutory authorities.

FR.2 The Task Force endorses the recommendations contained in the Department of Education Working Group Report entitled "School Attendance/Truancy Report", (Ref. 3). It is, however, important in applying these recommendations to Travellers that they are placed firmly and sensitively in the context of the human rights of the child.

FR.3 As a model of good practice, the Task Force strongly supports the integrated effort being adopted between the visiting teacher, the Gardaí and others at community level in Galway, to encourage school attendance and recommends that this approach be adopted as a model elsewhere.

FR.4 Present legislation needs to be reinforced to enable the integrated approach referred to in FR.3 above to have general application. Arrangements should be made by the relevant statutory authorities to have the necessary legislative changes introduced as a matter of urgency.

2.3 Parental Involvement

2.3.1 Traveller parents have a fundamental role to play in the educational development of their children. It is the view of the Task Force that Traveller parents must be encouraged and assisted in undertaking this role and it is with this objective in mind, that we make the following comments and recommendations which apply equally at pre-school, primary and second levels of the education system. It should be noted that a number of comments and recommendations on parental involvement are also included in other parts of this section.

2.3.2 The visiting teacher has an important contribution to make in facilitating the involvement of Traveller parents in the education of their children. However, there can be a danger that the visiting teacher can take over some of the tasks that would allow Traveller parents develop relationships with those teaching their children. Enrolment provides one example. The role of the Visiting Teacher Service is dealt with in detail further on in this section and includes recommendations for the expansion of this Service.

Recommendations

FR.5 Traveller parents should be facilitated to enrol their own children in schools rather than this being done by the visiting teacher. The lack of this initial contact can set the scene for poor future involvement.

FR.6 Attention needs to be given to developing a range of ways which would permit ongoing direct contact between teachers and Traveller parents. There can be direct contact when problems arise, but in some instances, these problems can end up being dealt with through the visiting teacher. Traveller parents should be particularly targeted so as to encourage their involvement in open days or similar events before problems arise.

FR.7 The lack of direct communication is evident in the low level of knowledge that can be displayed by Traveller parents as to what is happening to or being done for their children in school. The method of communication between parent and school must, however, be accessible. The note sent home in the child's school bag is not sufficient for various reasons, including where literacy is a problem or where the terminology is not understood. The visiting teacher should also be informed where problems arise in the education of a Traveller child so as to encourage the parents to communicate with the teacher. Other appropriate channels through which this communication might be encouraged, could also be explored, where necessary.

FR.8 Levels of literacy and lack of experience or knowledge in some school subjects on the part of Traveller parents can be a source of embarrassment and a barrier to communication with teachers. Access to adult education has an important contribution to make to Traveller parental involvement. This issue is dealt with in more detail in the part of this section called Adult Education.

FR.9 Homework programmes have an important contribution to make to parental involvement, but can, in some instances, involve a further removal of Traveller parents. There should be some linked follow up with parents of children on these programmes. Where possible, people on these programmes should be from the Traveller community; the supervisors of the programmes should encourage parents to become involved; adequate training of those who deliver the programmes should be a prerequisite to ensure sensitivity to Traveller culture.

FR.10 There is a lack of information among Traveller parents on how schools are administered and there is an absence of Traveller parents playing roles within the school. Travellers playing roles within the school as committee members or being employed as childcare assistants and classroom assistants would contribute to addressing this information gap.

FR.11 Traveller parents should be encouraged to join Boards of Management and other parent bodies. The National Parents Council should also include Traveller representatives among its membership. In addition, Boards of Management should formulate policies on issues related to Traveller children only after consultation with Traveller interests.

FR.12 Creative ways of bringing Travellers into the planning and administration of the education system should be explored.

2.4 Traveller Nomadism

2.4.1 Nomadism continues to be a significant feature of the Traveller way of life. There is a clash between this aspect of the Traveller way of life and the way in which the present education system is organised. The education system was designed with 'Settled' people in mind. However, with some alteration it could begin to cater more adequately for those who are mobile.

2.4.2 With this in mind, the Task Force makes the following recommendations:

Recommendations

FR.13 The use of different books in different schools is a barrier to Traveller mobility. Movement from one area to another requires the purchase of a new set of books. Some form of book exchange system needs to be put in place to reduce the financial burden on the parents of children who change schools.

FR.14 It should be recognised that strict enrolment cut-off dates have a particularly negative impact on Traveller children moving from one area to another. This can also result in Traveller children missing out on school when they first move into an area as the family is required to prove its intention to stay before the child is admitted. Whether a child is in a mainstream or a special class, flexibility in enrolment dates for children who are moving from one area to another needs to be introduced and should be resourced and supported by the Department of Education.

FR.15 Visiting teacher support has an important contribution to make in facilitating entry into the new school from the child's perspective and the school's perspective.

However, this should be done in a manner that supports direct contact between the Traveller parents and the school teachers.

FR.16   The children of occupational Travellers in other European countries are benefiting from the development of resources to facilitate distance learning. There is a need to explore this in order to find out how Irish Travellers could benefit from this approach. This task could be undertaken by the proposed Traveller Education Service.

2.5   **Intercultural Education: Implications for Curriculum Development and Teacher Training**

A.   **Intercultural Education**

2.5.1   **Education and Social Exclusion in the European Context**

As Ireland is becoming more and more integrated into the European Union and as decision-making at European level impacts more directly on developments in Ireland, it is important that education is examined in this wider context.

A broad range of initiatives such as COMETT, PETRA, ERASMUS and LINGUA have promoted greater exchanges and co-operation between institutions of education in the Member States. Two additional programmes LEONARDO and SOCRATES will further develop this. The SOCRATES programme refers explicitly to measures for the children of Gypsies/Travellers. Other Community Initiative Programmes such as NOW, HORIZON and Youthstart provide new training opportunities for socially excluded groups.

Articles 126 and 127 of the Maastricht Treaty establish a general objective to contribute to the development of quality education and training. The essential aim of European action on education and training is to enable all European citizens to reach their full potential and display initiative and creativity so that they can participate fully in society. Education and training are seen as being of crucial importance in combating social exclusion and unemployment.

2.5.2   **Education and Respect for Diversity**

The European Commission Green Paper on Education, (Ref. 4) stated that:

"respecting different cultural and ethnic identities, and combating all forms of chauvinism and xenophobia are essential components of action in the field of education".

The European Parliament Committee of Inquiry on Racism and Xenophobia (Ref. 5) published its findings in 1991. This Committee set out to address one of the major social and political problems of our time and saw its task as contributing to a peaceful and democratic Europe in which there would be respect for fundamental rights and the rejection of all forms of discrimination. The Report points out that the campaign against racism and xenophobia cannot simply be left to Governments and EU institutions but that a range of groups, institutions and individuals must take on that responsibility. To highlight the seriousness of the situation the Committee recommended that 1995 should be designated European Year of Racial Harmony.

The Report also drew attention to the role and importance of education *"in combating and preventing racism and xenophobia"*. It focuses specifically on the situation of Gypsies and Travellers and calls for the full implementation of the resolution of the European Council of Ministers of Education of May, 1989. In its country by country analysis it draws attention to the plight of Travellers stating that they are *"... the single most discriminated against ethnic group ..."* in Ireland.

With the establishment of an intercultural education budget line at European Union level (1990) new possibilities opened up. This budget was designed for measures targeted at migrants, occupational Travellers, Travellers and Gypsies. In 1992 the Department of Education began to draw down funds under this budget line to promote intercultural education in Ireland.

2.5.3 Different Educational Responses to Multiculturalism

The concept of intercultural education is new in Ireland. Because of the widespread perception of Ireland as a fairly homogeneous society the need to cater for diverse cultures and ethnic groups has not been high on the educational agenda. In contrast, in Britain and many other European countries as well as the United States there have been debates and developments about education systems moving from models of assimilation, to integration and cultural pluralism.

The assimilationist approach viewed ethnic diversity as divisive, conflictual and tended to assume that minority groups were deficient, deprived and lacking in cultural capital. The assimilationist approach promoted the absorption of minorities into the dominant culture in the belief that the socialisation of all into a shared value system was necessary for progress. The integration approach acknowledged the need for economic and social support for minorities in order for these to integrate into society. However, the emphasis was still on the integration of minorities with the dominant culture in order to create a homogeneous society. The expectation of teachers and schools was that it was up to minorities to change and adapt in order to succeed, without any real demand for change in the education system itself, apart from the need for more awareness and tolerance. These approaches have been criticised for being patronising and dismissive of other cultures and for being racist.

The cultural pluralism approach went further and acknowledged the need for broadening the content of the curriculum and for addressing the specific needs of minorities. It set out to change negative attitudes and practices of the majority population. While benefits from multicultural education have been recognised, it has however been criticised for ignoring pupils in schools where there are no minorities and for not adequately addressing issues of power and racism.

Against this background it is not surprising that there are different reactions to the concept of intercultural education. Some fear that it may have some of the shortcomings of previous educational approaches. Others may use the language of interculturalism while following the practices associated with these earlier approaches. It is important therefore to examine how those promoting it use the term.

2.5.4 Intercultural Education in Europe

The following extract from Intercultural Education in Europe, (Ref. 6) is how the European Commission explores the concept of intercultural education:

"Intercultural education aims to develop understanding among pupils and teachers from different cultural and ethnic origins. The goal is the integration of these different origins; it is not their assimilation into a uniform culture. Activities include promoting the study of different cultures and their structures and evolution, developing the ability of different groups to communicate with each other, and developing the ability to gain insight into cultural difference".

Another Commission Report on the Education of Migrants' Children in the European Union (1994), (Ref. 7) adds some other elements and describes intercultural education as:

"a set of educational practices designed to encourage mutual respect and understanding among all pupils, regardless of their cultural, linguistic, ethnic or religious background. Without glossing over the differences or even conflicts between cultures, the approach aims at helping pupils, through the study of cultures, to discover the factors that unite and differentiate humankind, to appreciate its richness and diversity, to develop the capacity to discover their own humanity in any culture (their own as well as that of others), to gain a sympathetic and critical understanding of cultures and finally to learn, making their own informed choices".

It acknowledges the contribution of Gypsies and Travellers to the socio-cultural fabric of Europe and stresses the need for preventative measures to overcome early school leaving and to combat under-achievement. Relevant curriculum and well trained teachers can go a long way to address these issues.

2.5.5 Intercultural Education and Travellers

The Irish Traveller Movement published a policy document called Education and Travellers, (Ref. 8) calling for intercultural education in all education and training systems. It stated that:

"Intercultural education implies an education that promotes interaction and understanding among and between different cultures and ethnic groups on the assumption that ethnic diversity can enrich society".

The Report of the Special Education Review Committee, (op. cit, 2) stated that:

"schools should adopt an inclusive, intercultural approach to curriculum development so as to ensure that their School Plan, class programmes and teaching

160

materials reflect a positive attitude towards the special customs, traditions and lifestyle of minority groups, including the children of Travellers".

In September, 1993 the Department of Education submitted its Report on the Implementation of the EC Resolution (89/C/53/02) on School Provision for Travellers, (Ref. 9) to the European Commission. The Report described the progress being made to pursue an intercultural approach in the education system.

In its submission to the Task Force the Association of Teachers of Travelling People (ATTP), (Ref. 10) made the following demand:

"It is essential for the Department of Education and other relevant agencies to invest the time, expertise and finance, needed to ensure that the quality and suitability of educational provision for Irish Travellers meets their needs. In a multi-cultural society it is also essential that the education system is intercultural and anti-racist and committed to equal opportunities for everyone. For change to be effective and far-reaching, reform must be approached in a holistic manner".

Intercultural education was given another endorsement in Ireland when the Department of Education organised and hosted a major international conference with the title *Intercultural Education - Irish Perspectives* in Dublin Castle in May 1994. At the official opening the Minister for Education, Niamh Bhreathnach, T.D., (Ref. 11) made the following points:

"Recognition and acceptance of differing cultures and lifestyles in our midst must inform decisions on the provision of education. In such decisions, attention must be focused on the development of mutual understanding and tolerance and on the right of each child to an education based on the sum of cultures in his/her community and in his/her particular learning needs".

Referring to the importance of Traveller education the Minister acknowledged the need for appropriate curriculum and adequate in-service training for teachers.

"The education of children of the Traveller community continues to require significant development and resources...We need school curricula which address and respect the cultures of Travellers, migrant and refugee children as well as that of the general population. The preparation and in-career development of teachers must equip them for the education of such a diverse school population".

The Task Force welcomes the commitment contained in the Green Paper Education For A Changing World, (Ref. 12) which states:

"Further action is premised on the principle of full participation in school life by all traveller children. This implies integration - on a phased basis where necessary - into ordinary classes while respecting the unique culture of travellers".

The Department of Education Guidelines contained in The Education of Traveller Children in National Schools, (Ref. 13) state that:

"The School Plan will include a suitable curriculum for the Traveller children in the school, which will be devised through consultations involving the principal, the class teachers, the special teacher for Travellers, the visiting teacher for Traveller education and the school inspectors".

B.   Curriculum

2.5.6   In the context of European integration and the greater mobility of people, the curriculum in education and training institutes needs to be intercultural in its content and in its perspectives.

2.5.7   An intercultural curriculum would need to cover the following principles:

–   The experiences of minority groups, especially Travellers in the Irish context, should be presented in accurate and sensitive ways which show that society is not homogeneous or monocultural. The richness of cultural diversity should be made known in the visuals, examples and information offered to pupils.

–   The content of texts should be monitored to avoid ethnocentric and racist interpretations and to ensure that respect for other cultures is promoted.

–   The curriculum should be designed to help students acquire the knowledge, values and skills they need to contribute to social change in a multicultural context and not just accept existing ideologies and practices.

–   It is not sufficient to merely add some data about Travellers and other minorities to the existing curriculum. In order to integrate information about minority groups into the total curriculum there is need for more substantial and innovative curriculum reform.

–   Focusing solely on exotic customs and practices of Travellers and other minority groups is likely to reinforce misconceptions and negative stereotypes rather than developing cultural sensitivity and understanding. An intercultural module which focuses on broader equality and human rights issues and which contains an anti-racist dimension is recommended.

–   An intercultural curriculum should focus not only on the tangible and material elements of minority cultures but also on the intangible aspects of culture such as values, perspectives and world views.

–   Information should be provided which helps students to appreciate and learn that all human beings have common needs and characteristics but that these take different forms of expression cross-culturally.

–   Intercultural curriculum should not be viewed as a study of minority ethnic groups, rather, it should also involve examining majority ethnic groups. Otherwise there is a danger of the dominant group viewing cultural studies as a study of 'them' and other mainstream studies such as history and geography as a study of 'us'. Differences should be acknowledged; difference should be seen as relational and not as deviant.

– Subjects such as history should be approached from diverse ethnic perspectives rather than primarily or exclusively from the point of view of mainstream historians, artists and writers. Oral history and folk history can be of value in providing these diverse perspectives.

– Research shows that negative and racist attitudes are formed at a very early age. The curriculum needs to address this with a specific programme of instruction in the earlier years of education. Efforts to counter negative attitudes and stereotypes need to be sustained and must permeate the entire curriculum.

– The curriculum should not alienate students from their own ethnic attachments but should help them to clarify their identities and make them aware of other cultures and alternatives.

– An intercultural curriculum needs to give attention not only to psychological and cultural dimensions but also to socio-political economic concerns.

2.5.8 In developing such an intercultural curriculum the Task Force makes the following recommendations:

Recommendations

FR.17 In order to implement a curriculum along the lines suggested in this section, there is need for a comprehensive Traveller Education Service in the Department of Education as recommended by the INTO, the ITM, the EC Intercultural Education Project, the ATTP and in this section under Traveller Education Service. Such a service would have responsibility not only for monitoring the curriculum but also for ensuring greater integration and coherence between all the key personnel and organisations involved in Traveller education and training such as: the National Education Officer, the inspectorate, the Visiting Teachers, the ATTP, Traveller parents, National Traveller organisations, NATC and other relevant bodies.

FR.18 The Department of Education should commission the design of an intercultural/ anti-racist programme (with videos, tapes, materials and games) to be used in national schools and second-level schools, at both junior and senior levels in each case. This would require the setting up of a steering committee involving school psychologists, special teachers, inspectorate and visiting teachers for Travellers, and the involvement of the National Parents Council, teacher unions, representatives from national Traveller organisations and other minority group organisations, on the lines of that used to form the Child Abuse Prevention Programme in 1991. Funding for such an initiative could be shared between the Department of Equality and Law Reform, the Department of Education and the National Lottery.

FR.19 Resources and materials are needed to implement an intercultural, anti-racist curriculum and these should be developed for all pupils. However, such resources are ineffective in the hands of teachers or trainers who have limited understanding and, in some instances, negative attitudes towards Travellers and other minorities. Staff development programmes are necessary therefore and should include administrators, counsellors and other ancillary members involved in education and training schemes.

FR.20 A pilot action programme should be initiated in a number of national schools to implement such a curriculum and to develop a programme for general use in national schools.

FR.21 Changes in text books and teaching materials designed to promote interculturalism and anti-racism should be supported by school organisation and administration procedures and in the drawing up of school plans. There is a need for policies for combating prejudice and anti-Traveller incidents in schools and other education and training institutions.

FR.22 The Department of Education should ensure that Regulations for Publishers should contain guidelines in relation to promoting such a curriculum and only books that comply with the Regulations should be recommended for use in schools.

FR.23 An information pack which could be made available to schools, parents' associations and other relevant bodies should be produced in order to increase awareness of interculturalism in the curriculum.

C. Teacher Training

2.5.9 In the Programme for Competitiveness and Work, (Ref. 14) it is stated that particular provision will be made for *"undertaking a major expansion in in-service training at all levels for teachers to include a specific programme in respect of teachers of disadvantaged pupils"*. It is important that such in-service training be broadened to include the commitment contained in the Green Paper on Education (op. cit, 12) namely that:

"The Department will take up with the Colleges of Education the matter of providing a module on travellers and traveller culture in the pre-service education of teachers. It will also follow-up on the inservice needs of teachers..."

2.5.10 The INTO (Ref. 15) likewise recommends that:

"Courses for use in pre-service and in-service education should be developed in consultation with Traveller bodies and teachers of Travellers; such courses should cover the following areas: Traveller culture, intercultural education, anti-racism and home/school liaison.

Pre-service and in-service education for all teachers should include modules on Traveller culture, in order to support teachers in providing the intercultural environment which is a pre-requisite for true integration".

2.5.11 Teachers are the key agents for change in schools. It is of the utmost importance that teachers are equipped to transmit democratic values and have the knowledge and skills to implement an intercultural and anti-racist curriculum.

2.5.12   Teachers like everybody else have their own beliefs, values, political views, moral codes, hopes and dreams. A teacher's values and perspectives interact with what he/she teaches and this influences how information is communicated to students.

2.5.13   Pre-service as well as in-service courses are important so that teachers can reflect on the challenges of interculturalism and anti-racism. There is also the reality that reflection based on years of action is productive and instructive. Teachers involved in concrete situations are often very open to new insights and learning to improve their practice. In-service training is therefore most important.

Recommendations

FR.24   Training courses should assist teachers to acquire:

- a reflective and clearer understanding of their own cultural heritage and social status and how these relate to others and how these fit with the professional responsibility for the educational and social development of pupils;

- a critical knowledge of multicultural society, and an understanding of the causes and effects of prejudice, racism and xenophobia and other negative attitudes which contribute to discrimination;

- a positive attitude towards cultural diversity;

- pedagogical skills to counteract prejudice, racism and xenophobia to devise teaching strategies and activities which will facilitate academic achievement in the context of cultural diversity;

- democratic values and attitudes towards minority ethnic groups;

- an ability to see and understand the other's point of view;

- knowledge of the curricular and teaching implications of cultural diversity;

- an awareness of equality and anti-discrimination laws and regulations in the State.

FR.25   In-service training, in order to be effective, should be participative, involving not just lectures, but the presentation of diverse experiences, visits, exposure trips, guest speakers, multimedia materials, combined with inputs, analysis and fresh information.

FR.26   Intercultural education should be included in the training programmes of all student teachers, such as higher diploma courses in all universities, teacher training colleges and regional technical colleges.

FR.27   Travellers and Traveller organisations should be resourced to ensure that they can have a significant role in the pre-service and in-service training process.

3. Traveller Education Service

3.1 General

3.1.1 The Task Force agrees with the statement in the INTO Report "Travellers in Education", (op. cit, 15) in relation to education provision for Travellers that, *"over the years a variety of forms of provision and support has emerged, often in an ad-hoc manner, with little evidence of overall policy framework or direction"*.

3.1.2 The Task Force also endorses the view put forward in the Report of the Department of Education Working Group on Post-Primary Education for Traveller Children, (Ref. 16), hereafter referred to as the 1992 Department Working Group Report, that one of the reasons for the failure to make substantial progress in second-level education for Travellers is the lack of a co-ordinated approach and the division of responsibility for Traveller education provision between a number of different sections in the Department of Education.

3.1.3 The 1992 Department Working Group Report (op. cit, 16) notes that there are six different sections within the Department of Education dealing with funding for Traveller education in addition to the involvement of the Inspectorate and the Psychological Service.

Recommendation

FR.28 In order to facilitate a more co-ordinated, structured and comprehensive approach to Traveller education, the Task Force recommends the establishment without delay of a Traveller Education Service under the aegis of the Department of Education.

The Task Force notes that similar recommendations to this effect are included in the INTO Report "Travellers in Education", (op. cit, 15), in the EC Intercultural Education Project Report: "The Education of Children of Gypsies and Travellers" (1993), (Ref. 17) in the Department Working Group Report (op. cit, 16) and also in a number of submissions received by the Task Force.

Structure of Traveller Education Service (TES)

Recommendation

FR.29 The TES should comprise

(i) A Traveller Education Unit in the Department of Education under the direction of an Assistant Secretary with necessary support staff drawn from both general service and departmental grades (such as Inspectors and representatives of the Psychological Service). This Unit should also comprise the National Education Officer for Travellers and the National Co-ordinator for Traveller Training Centres.

(ii) An Advisory Committee to advise the Traveller Education Unit in its work. This Committee should be appointed by the Minister for Education and include staff and management representatives from the pre-school, primary, second-level, adult education and third-level areas, Traveller parents, Traveller organisations, ATTP, NATC and others with relevant expertise or experience in Traveller education.

FR.30 The work of the Special Education Section of the Department of Education in relation to pre-school and primary educational provision for Travellers should continue but a similar Section should be established to deal with second-level educational provision for Travellers.

FR.31 An examination needs to be carried out by the Department of Education with a view to establishing new Departmental structures for dealing with adult and third-level education for Travellers.

FR.32 The National Education Officer for Travellers should report on a regular basis to the TES. The National Education Officer will continue to have an important role to play within the framework set out for the Traveller Education Service. In view of the major changes which the Task Force is recommending in the area of Traveller Education, it is also recommended that the National Education Officer for Travellers, should be supported by two assistants to deal with educational services for Traveller children at primary and post-primary levels, respectively.

Role and Terms of Reference of the Traveller Education Service

Recommendation

FR.33 Within the Department of Education, the primary focus of the Traveller Education Service should be on policy and strategy development in respect of educational provision for Travellers and monitoring their implementation to ensure that policy/strategy is accomplished. The delivery of services should be the responsibility of other existing agencies.

With a view to achieving a co-ordinated and comprehensive approach to Traveller education, the TES should:

(i) Have overall responsibility for the development of Traveller education and co-ordinate the activities of the various sections within the Department of Education dealing with the educational needs of Travellers including the Special Education Section at primary level and the proposed new section to deal with second-level education.

(ii) Draw up, within one year of its formation, a statement of policy in relation to Traveller education which would include medium term plans for all areas of educational provision for Travellers and the staff involved, including special classes, special schools and the Visiting Teacher Service.

(iii) Oversee the implementation of the various recommendations in the Report of the Task Force dealing with educational provision for members of the Traveller community.

(iv) Ensure coherence and consistency in the delivery of educational services for Travellers at all levels.

(v) Establish a consultation process with all interested groups and particularly with Travellers and relevant Traveller organisations.

(vi) Draw up a comprehensive operational strategy for the education of Travellers based on the statement of policy referred to previously. Without neglecting any other aspect of this policy, special urgency should be given in this strategy to resourcing a major increase in the participation rate of Traveller children in mainstream second-level education.

(vii) Facilitate and monitor the execution of this strategy, including the establishment of clear targets to ensure that it is executed with maximum efficiency and speed from pre-school to third level. Review the policy and strategy on an annual basis in the light of experience and of the need to develop further resources for Traveller education.

(viii) Ensure the allocation of the resources necessary to implement the policy on Traveller education set out by the Task Force.

(ix) Promote a major in-service development programme for teachers at primary and post-primary levels on the scale of the Child Abuse Prevention Programme in 1991, which consisted of one in-service day for every teacher in the country.

(x) Commission the training colleges and University education institutions to design and include Intercultural Education modules in all courses for trainee teachers on a compulsory basis.

(xi) Turn into practice the principles in relation to intercultural education, outlined elsewhere in this section, in relation to educational provision and promote an intercultural approach and positive learning environment for Travellers at all levels of education and training.

(xii) Promote curriculum development in intercultural education and the development of appropriate intercultural text books and teaching aids, all of which should be inclusive of Traveller culture. The achievement of this recommendation may require the setting up of a steering committee.

(xiii) Publish guidelines on second-level education for Travellers in accordance with the policy set out by the Task Force.

(xiv) Review the activities of special schools and seek to apply experiences learnt by them to the mainstream education sector.

(xv) Undertake, as a matter of priority, an in-depth analysis (including a qualitative evaluation of attainment) into the reasons for the failure of the present primary education system for many Traveller children (See FR.50).

(xvi)   Undertake a liaison function between visiting teachers to keep them up to date on educational practices and to ensure that they are adequately resourced.

(xvii)   Ensure that adequate liaison arrangements and back-up resources exist for those Traveller children whose families are mobile so that such mobility does not interfere with their educational provision.

(xviii)   Ensure that there is transparency and accountability in relation to the expenditure of monies on all aspects of Traveller education.

(xix)   Develop a comprehensive management structure for all Traveller pre-schools (See FR.46).

(xx)   Carry out a review of the use by second-level schools of standardised intelligence tests for Traveller children prior to or following admission to such schools.

(xxi)   Monitor the development and size of the Visiting Teacher Service to ensure that it has sufficient resources and draw up guidelines for use by the managers of that Service. (See also Visiting Teacher Service in this section).

4.   Pre-School Education

4.1   Introduction

4.1.1   The provision of pre-school education for Traveller children is recognised as having had an important beneficial influence since the pre-school scheme for Travellers was first introduced. The social deprivation suffered by many Traveller children means, in particular, that early education provision is of paramount importance.

4.1.2   The steady development in this area is reflected in the increase in the number of pre-school facilities in the last decade: (See Table F1)

Table F1: **Development of Pre-School Facilities 1984 - 1994**
18 in 1984 41 in 1988 53 in 1993 56 in 1994

4.1.3   The number of pre-schools for Traveller children is broken down countrywide in Table F2 as follows:

Table F2: Number of Pre-Schools for Traveller Children*	
County	**Number**
Carlow	1
Cavan	1
Clare	3
Cork	5
Donegal	1
Dublin	14
Galway	7
Kildare	2
Kilkenny	1
Laois	2
Limerick	2
Longford	1
Louth	2
Mayo	3
Meath	2
Offaly	2
Tipperary	1
Waterford	2
Wexford	2
Wicklow	2
Total	56

*Numbers applicable on 24 November, 1994

4.1.4 The Department of Education grant aids the fifty-six pre-schools listed above which have an enrolment of approximately 660 Traveller children.

4.1.5 The Department of Education provides grants for the purchase of equipment in pre-schools and also defrays ninety-eight per cent of the costs pertaining to tuition and operation of transport. In some areas, the health boards provide grants for child care assistants and for health and hygiene facilities.

4.1.6 Staffing of Pre-Schools:* There are forty-four teachers employed in pre-schools for Traveller children and Table F3 gives details of their qualifications:

Table F3: Qualifications of Pre-School Staff	
Trained Teachers	7
Montessori	13
University Degrees	6
Special Course or Diploma	11
Leaving Certificate	7

Thirty-seven child care workers, under the aegis of the local health authorities, are employed in twenty-eight of the pre-schools. There are also a small number of pre-schools funded either by the local health board or by voluntary organisations which cater for Traveller children, among others.

(*Source: Guidelines for Education of Traveller Children in National Schools (op. cit, 14).

4.2 Comment on Present Situation

4.2.1 Special pre-schools for Traveller children can have a very positive role in introducing small children to a new environment and can act as a bridge in preparing these children for integration at primary level. Where it is not possible to have such pre-schools, every effort should be made to include Travellers in other pre-schools.

4.2.2 There are no guidelines for practice or curriculum in respect of pre-schools issued by the Department of Education. This results in widespread variation from one location to the next and also has implications for the overall quality of service provided to the children and also, in the long run, for the effectiveness of the programmes offered.

The fact that there are no legal registration requirements or guidelines for Traveller pre-schools, particularly in areas such as health, safety, welfare and education, also leads to a situation in which the quality of pre-schools can vary considerably from area to area.

4.2.3 There is little in-service training or support for the staff providing the services and many, coming as they do with varied background training, feel quite isolated. Without specific and well designed training in this area, staff may not in fact provide the services most appropriate to the population of children being catered for.

4.2.4 Funding for pre-school services is very poor and the conditions of service for the staff are not in line with their colleagues in the primary education sector. Good quality, effective pre-school provision is costly but research indicates that the benefits, in the long run, are well worth the initial cost. Funding services inefficiently is actually counter productive because it leads to expectations which will not be met unless the service is of a high quality.

4.2.5 Traveller pre-schools are managed by a variety of individuals and voluntary committees, many of which have limited experience of early childhood education. The voluntary committee structure can at times make it difficult to offer the kind of regular support needed by pre-school staff. Pre-school staff as well as often being isolated, also tend to have responsibility for adminstrative and maintenance tasks. At present, accommodation, including rent expenses and maintenance costs of pre-schools, is provided by local voluntary committees without any capital assistance being furnished by the Department of Education. This often results in sub-standard accommodation.

4.3 Taking into account the Government's commitment in their policy agreement entitled "A Government of Renewal" (Ref. 18) which includes as a priority the *"further expansion of pre-school facilities, with the ultimate aim of an integrated* *professional national system linked to the primary school system"*, the Task Force makes the following recommendations in respect of the development of pre-school education for Traveller children:

Recommendations

FR.34 It is widely acknowledged that Traveller children who attend pre-schools are better prepared for primary school. The Task Force considers, therefore, that a comprehensive pre-school service should be provided for all Traveller children. This service should be available to each Traveller child for a period of up to two years before entering primary school and should be staffed by personnel qualified for this age group and be supported by local management structures. Prior to this extension taking place, however, an external evaluation of existing pre-school provision should be undertaken to see what improvements in the system are required.

FR.35 At the present time, there is no standard programme or national policy on pre-school education in Ireland. Such a national policy and programme needs to be developed and co-ordinated by the Department of Education throughout the country. The Department of Education should also provide guidelines on such issues as enrolment procedures, hours of class contact/parent contact, transport, health and safety, ratios, curriculum, procedures for dealing with children at risk, general programmes for early childhood education, children with special needs, parental involvement, minimum requirements for accommodation and in-service training. All of these would form an essential element in the future development of the pre-school education service.

FR.36 The Department of Education should take over responsibility for pre-school provision for Traveller children. In addition, within the pre-school area, there is need for the development of a co-ordinated inter-departmental and inter-agency approach (to include: voluntary and statutory bodies including teachers, social workers, childcare workers, youth workers, community workers, public health nurses, speech therapists and psychologists).

FR.37 The existing provision of pre-schools for Traveller children should be maintained and expanded in line with demand. The Task Force notes the Government's commitment to develop a system of pre-schools in disadvantaged areas and considers that the range of supports currently provided for Traveller children should be reviewed in this context.

FR.38 Travellers should be trained and employed in pre-schools as teachers and childcare assistants. In Section G on the Traveller Economy, the Task Force identifies strategies by which this can be effectively achieved.

FR39 Child care assistants should be appointed to all pre-schools for Travellers.

FR.40 The Department of Education, through the Visiting Teacher Service, should promote the development and maintenance of close links between pre-schools for Travellers and local primary schools to ensure more effective Traveller pupil participation.

FR.41   Consultation with and involvement of parents and Traveller organisations should be encouraged and developed.

FR.42   Personnel working in pre-schools should have early education/childcare training and have a child centred approach and training to ensure an understanding of Traveller culture and the specific needs of Traveller children.

FR.43   School transport has had a major impact on attendance levels at schools for Traveller children. Increased funding needs to be provided by the relevant statutory bodies in the area of school transport and, in particular, grants should be provided to voluntary groups for the purchase of buses.

FR.44   The mobile Pre-School Service for Travellers provided by Barnardos is commended. The Traveller Education Service should be requested to examine the need for and feasibility of extending this service.

FR.45   Where necessary, the attendance of Traveller children at local community play groups and pre-schools should be resourced by the Department of Health where there is no Traveller pre-school in the area concerned.

FR.46   At present a variety of management/administrative arrangements are in place in existing pre-schools. It is recommended that the Department of Education through the Traveller Education Service develop a comprehensive management structure for all Traveller pre-schools.

FR.47   The full salaries and PRSI contributions, as appropriate, of teaching staff in pre-schools should be resourced on the same basis as teachers in the primary education sector.

FR.48   Capitation grants should be provided on the same basis as the Department of Education Pre-School Pilot Project to cover accommodation, maintenance costs and rent.

FR.49   The provision of Traveller specific pre-schools should not preclude Traveller parents from choosing to send their children to integrated pre-schools.

5.   Primary Education

5.1   Background

5.1.1   According to the Report of the Special Education Review Committee (op. cit, 2) there are approximately 5,000 Traveller children of primary school age in the State.

5.1.2   Primary education provision for Traveller children takes three forms; in special schools, in special classes or in ordinary classes, in mainstream education.

5.1.3   It is also estimated that approximately 4,200 Traveller children attend primary schools, about 1,800 of which are full-time in ordinary classes while the remaining 2,400 attend the special teacher for Travellers. There are also four special schools for Traveller children, with an aggregate enrolment of about 260 pupils. This compares with the situation in 1963 when the Commission on Itinerancy (Ref. 19) published its report, where only 114 Traveller children were regularly attending primary schools.

5.1.4 In the case of special primary education, the four special schools catering specifically for Traveller children are as follows:

1. St. Columba's Special School, Great Strand Street, Dublin 1;
2. St. Thomas', Clonshaugh, Dublin 5;
3. St. Kieran's, Bray, Co. Wicklow;
4. St. Brigid's Special School, Galway City.

5.1.5 St. Thomas's and St. Brigid's cater for Travellers in the twelve to fifteen years age group. St Kieran's caters for children in the four to thirteen plus age group. St. Columba's caters for Traveller children from particularly deprived backgrounds and in view of these circumstances has a more favourable pupil teacher ratio of 10:1. The pupil teacher ratio applied to the other special schools is 15:1.

5.1.6 There are 200 special classes for Traveller children attached to ordinary national schools. The pupil teacher ratio is 15:1, although many classes are operating at more favourable ratios than this.

These classes may operate in one of the following ways:

– to include the pupils within a special class setting;

– to operate on a withdrawal basis (that is, integrate the pupils into an ordinary class but to withdraw them for special tuition as necessary);

– a combination of above (that is, where some children remain in special class full-time while others rotate between ordinary and special class).

5.1.7 A special class teacher is provided regardless of which system is used. It is the policy of the Department of Education to have Traveller children integrated into mainstream education where possible. In this context, approval for the establishment of special classes is given on condition that the children should progress into the mainstream classes as soon as they are considered to be ready.

5.1.8 Traveller children are also integrated into mainstream primary education by enrolling in ordinary classes in national schools. In this regard, it should be noted that Rule 10 of the Rules for National Schools states that no child may be refused admission to a national school on account of the social position of his/her parents, nor may any pupil be kept apart from the other pupils on the grounds of social distinction.

5.1.9 School transport, where necessary, is provided for Traveller children. This is organised at local level by voluntary committees and the Department of Education grant-aids ninety-eight per cent of the running costs.

5.1.10 A special capitation grant per child per annum is payable in respect of Traveller children enrolled in special classes/schools. This amounts to £130 for pupils under twelve years and £316 for pupils aged twelve years and over. This compares with the ordinary capitation grant of £38 per pupil.

5.2   Department of Education - Guidelines

5.2.1   In 1994, the Department of Education published guidelines entitled "The Education of Traveller children in National Schools - Guidelines" (op. cit, 13) which has to be seen as an important document in relation to the education of Traveller children at primary level.

5.2.2   These guidelines emphasize that *"Primary education for travelling children should seek to provide them with attitudes, skills and knowledge which will help them to understand the world in which they live and the interdependence of groups and communities. They should be helped to recognise and value aspects of travellers' culture and the culture of the settled community, within a context which emphasises that which is common to both cultures"*.

5.2.3   Recognising the importance of integrating Traveller children in mainstream classes, the guidelines point out that where *"full integration is not appropriate, and where there is a Special Teacher for Travellers,"* a number of intermediate stages are recommended namely;

"(a)   the traveller child will be placed in a mainstream class and will spend appropriate periods of the school day with a Special Teacher for Travellers;

(b)   the traveller child, placed in a mainstream class, will spend appropriate periods in the special class for traveller children under the care of the Special Teacher for Travellers;

(c)   where it is clear that the traveller child, for a variety of reasons, is not ready for placement in a mainstream class, (s)/he will be placed in the special class for traveller children under the full-time care of the Special Teacher for Travellers until placement in a mainstream class is deemed appropriate. It would not be in the interest of a traveller child that (s)/he be retained in a special class for the duration of his/her primary education."

5.2.4   The guidelines also recommend that:

–   decisions on appropriate placement of Traveller children should result from discussions involving the relevant education authorities (such as teachers and visiting teachers) and parents;

–   the *"curriculum which the school devises for the traveller children on its roll will seek to promote their physical, emotional, social, intellectual, moral and spiritual development and to provide each traveller child with the kind and variety of opportunities, stimulation and fulfilment which will enable him/her to develop at his/her own rate and to his/her fullest capacity"*;

–   *"Every school will have a policy on the integration of traveller children in the school and this policy will be clearly expressed in the School Plan. The School Plan will include a suitable curriculum for the traveller children in the school, which will be devised through consultations involving the principal, the class teachers, the Special Teacher for Travellers, the visiting teacher for Traveller education and the school inspectors"*;

- *"The educational progress of each traveller child will be monitored in the same manner"* as other children;

- the school should keep *"a comprehensive record of the child's attendance, placement, achievement and progress"* with the adoption of a "School Record Card" for this purpose. A "Family Record Card" to facilitate class placement in the case of Traveller children who are transferring schools, is also recommended;

- the maintenance of adequate liaison arrangements between schools and the families of Traveller children and other support groups through the Visiting Teacher Service and the National Education Officer for Travellers.

5.2.5   The Guidelines also deal with practical issues such as primary school accommodation, attendance and timetabling, school supports (such as: staff, grants and transport) discipline and the preparation of Traveller children for entry into further education.

5.3   Comment on Present Position

5.3.1   As pointed out in the report of the Special Education Review Committee, (op. cit, 2) from *"very small beginnings in the 1960's, significant progress has been made in the provision of education for children of the traveller community"*. In particular, at primary level, the Visiting Teacher Service (VTS) established in 1980, has made a significant contribution to the increase in the number of Traveller children in education. The work of the VTS is described elsewhere in this section. Nevertheless, the amount of work which still needs to be done in relation to the development of the present level of education provision for Traveller children at primary level is significant.

5.3.2   As indicated in paragraphs 5.1.1 and 5.1.3 there are approximately 5,000 Traveller children of primary school age in the State, with approximately 4,200 involved in pre-school or primary education. Accordingly, there still remains a substantial number of Traveller children who do not attend primary school. In addition, those who are normally enrolled can be erratic attenders, particularly at certain times of the year which gives rise to learning difficulties for the children in question.

5.3.3   While Rule 10 of the Rules for National Schools states that no child may be refused admission to a national school on account of the social position of its parents nor may any pupil be kept apart from other pupils on the grounds of social distinction, the Visiting Teacher Service regularly encounters resistance from management authorities when trying to enrol Travellers' children in schools. In many cases, schools have refused (and still continue to do so) to enrol these children. This has led to a call to the Department of Education that Boards of Management should have explicit policies concerning the enrolment of pupils, in particular the enrolment of Traveller children.

5.3.4 Access to education, also continues to present major problems for large numbers of Traveller children. This can be particularly evident from time to time in large urban areas where substantial numbers of families move into an area. Often local schools are unable, or unwilling, to accept the children. There are also many individual instances where school authorities have refused to enrol children or where they make enrolment so difficult that parents choose not to enrol their children at all when they are living in particular areas.

5.3.5 School attendance of Travellers has been much improved by the provision of the school transport service for Traveller children. This transport system is able to exercise a large degree of flexibility and can facilitate children whose parents move within specific limited areas. Traveller children who have been fully integrated within mainstream classrooms are not, however, entitled to this service. This anomaly can create endless problems for Travellers living in the same site or in particular areas.

5.3.6 The poor performance of many Traveller children in primary school deeply concerns many Travellers, and their teachers: they share the belief that successful primary schooling is the pre-requisite for any productive engagement with second-level. No survey of terminal attainment levels of Traveller children in primary school has been carried out, but teacher opinion is that many underachieve and are at least three years behind the norm in the core subjects, and that poor attendance, though a problem in many cases, is not a sufficient explanation. Many are very disappointed at the outcome of primary schooling for their children, and this at least adds to their reluctance to continue into second level.

5.3.7 Traveller parents are not significantly involved in the schooling of their children, other than through visiting teacher/class teacher contacts to encourage enrolment and attendance. Such contact can be intense and frequent where the child is in separate provision, such as the Junior Training Centres: however, few, if any, are involved in the process of planning and providing appropriate schooling through membership of Boards of Management or parents' organisations. In 'Issues of Concern to all Education Sectors' elsewhere in this section, the Task Force addresses the issue of parental involvement in the education of their children.

5.3.8 Supports of all kinds are clearly under-supplied: some schools do not have the services of a remedial or special needs teacher; the psychological service is small in size. In common with all sectors of pupils, Travellers need adequate support in all these areas. Material supports for Travellers are better in some areas, such as transport services. Financial supports for books and uniforms, are inadequate for Travellers, as for other disadvantaged pupils. The use of different text books by primary schools is also a problem for those Traveller children who change schools due to the nomadic nature of the Traveller way of life. Movement from one area to another requires the purchase of a new set of books for those children.

5.3.9 The curriculum at primary level is monocultural, presuming a homogeneous society. As a result, Travellers frequently find no mention of themselves in school programmes or materials - or at best a mention of them as a problem (or as not a problem) in religious or social studies. This provides little space for developing a healthy sense of identity in the Traveller child, and in addition, it leaves the 'Settled' child possibly confirmed in ignorance and prejudice.

5.3.10 The curriculum at primary level is now more child-centred and there is a greater awareness of the need for "Educating for Life". The Green Paper supported the aim of broadening the curriculum and of educating young people for life. This involves the development of critical thinking, of self-management, of self expression and of relating effectively to others.

5.3.11 In response to a widely acknowledged need, there has been an increase in recent years in in-service training for teachers. This has been facilitated by the National Education Officer for Travellers in co-operation with the regional inspectors and with the assistance of Traveller support groups. The Task Force welcomes this development and calls for its expansion along the lines set out in 'Issues of Concern to all Education Sectors' on intercultural education.

5.4 Various organisations such as the INTO, ITM, ATTP, and the Blackrock Teachers Centre, have made recommendations in recent years in relation to the improvement of primary education provision for Travellers. The Task Force has considered these carefully in drawing up its Report, and the recommendations which follow in relation to primary education endorse many of these recommendations in an integrated manner.

Evaluation of Present System

Recommendation

FR.50 While it is recognised by the Task Force that problems associated with the underachievement of children who have undertaken primary education are not unique to children from the Traveller community, the problem of poor performance of many Traveller children is of concern especially considering the level of resources invested in the education of such children. Accordingly, while it is the view of the Task Force that many of our recommendations in relation to primary level schooling will assist in addressing the problem of underachievement, the Task Force recommends that an in-depth analysis be carried out (including a qualitative evaluation of attainment) into the reasons for the failure of the present primary education system for many Traveller children. The Task Force further recommends that this survey should be carried out, as a matter of priority, by the proposed Traveller Education Service.

Equality of Opportunity and Access

Recommendations

FR.51 Agreed procedures should be established, as a matter of urgency, to ensure that Traveller children have equal access to the educational provision best suited to their individual needs, taking parents' wishes into account. Every School Plan should include a statement of policy on access and equality of opportunity to Traveller children.

178

FR.52 Where Traveller children are at present in a particular location, enrolment arrangements in the local school should not be restricted to any particular date.

FR.53 Following enrolment, Traveller children who need them, should have immediate access to all the necessary support services, including resource teachers, (either on a full-time or part-time basis), visiting teacher service, social and psychological services and essential ancillary staff, particularly classroom assistants or child care workers.

FR.54 School authorities and, in particular, principal teachers, should have the authority to demand the provision of all the necessary resources, support services and ancillary staff to cater for the individual needs of Traveller children. Appropriate levels of provision should be available, irrespective of the number of Traveller children enrolled in individual schools.

Resources and Funding
Recommendations

FR.55 Substantial additional resources should be invested in supporting Traveller children at primary level, to ensure a level of attainment and personal development which would enable them to gain truly equal access to second level education.

FR.56 As an essential prerequisite for successful integrated education, realistic grants should be made towards cost of transport, books, uniforms, and material expenses.

FR.57 The higher rate of capitation grant should be paid in respect of all Traveller children enrolled in national schools regardless of the type of educational provision being made for them.

FR.58 In recognising the transient lifestyle of many nomadic Traveller families, the Department of Education should ensure that flexible arrangements are in place to enable schools to receive additional capitation funding in respect of Traveller children who are enrolled after September 30th.

FR.59 On the first appointment of special class or Traveller resource teachers, once off grants should be paid to the schools concerned to cover the purchase of items such as books, equipment and art materials.

FR.60 In order to address the problems faced by those Traveller children who change schools because of the nomadic way of life of their families, a Traveller book exchange system needs to be put in place and resources also need to be provided to primary schools to enable them to purchase new text books for these children. Every effort should be made to ensure that such children are fully integrated in their new schools as quickly as possible.

Guidelines for Education of Traveller Children in National Schools
Recommendation

FR.61 The Department of Education has issued a copy of its document "The Education of Traveller Children in National Schools - Guidelines" (op. cit, 13), to all primary level schools. The Task Force recommends that the Department should now issue a Circular:

(i)   instructing teachers to implement their provisions in day to day teaching practice;

(ii)   clearly stating that, as a matter of policy, Boards of Management are obliged to guarantee similar rights of enrolment to Traveller children as those which apply to children of the 'Settled' community.

School Timetable

Recommendation

FR.62   The school timetable (both daily arrival and departure times) should be the same for all children including those of Traveller families.

Special School Provision

The Task Force would not envisage the need to expand the Special School Service for Traveller children. These schools should be looked upon as pilot schools from which lessons are learnt and experiences gained for use by the remainder of the school system.

Recommendation

FR.63   The pupil teacher ratio in special schools - except where additional special needs justify a lower ratio - should immediately be set at that applying to special classes.

School Placement, Staffing and Integration

Recommendations

FR.64   Except in special circumstances, integration of Traveller children at primary level should be mandatory within an intercultural and anti-racist framework. This would enhance participation and educational achievement and would contribute to greater access to second-level education.

FR.65   It is recommended that a regular review be carried out of Traveller children in special classes to ensure that their educational needs are being met and that they are not retained in such classes if they are ready for integration into mainstream classes. This review should be carried out by the school principal and class teachers in consultation with the parents and the visiting teacher.

FR.66   Where problems in relation to individual Traveller children are identified, initial educational provision for those children should take account of reports from pre-schools, psychological assessments, where carried out, and recommendations from the visiting teachers and parents.

FR.67   Only in cases of special educational need which have been identified in consultation with the visiting teachers or parents, should there be a requirement for provision in special classes. Even in such cases, placement should be regarded as temporary and subject to review by the Department of Education Inspectorate on an annual basis. The objective should be to have all Traveller children integrated by sixth standard so as to facilitate their progression to second level.

FR.68   Special classes for Traveller children should be seen as a transitional resource in the process towards integration. Cultural, social, emotional and academic support should be offered to Traveller children on a withdrawal basis where necessary.

FR.69   The assessment of a child's attainment level, particularly that relating to language competency, should be based on tests which are clear of cultural bias.

FR.70   Traveller children, on enrolment, should be assigned to the classes which more closely relate to their chronological age irrespective of the short term provision being made for them within the school. Due regard should be taken, however, of the level of attainment and educational disadvantage of the children. While special provision should be made for such children in the circumstances outlined previously, and for the main core subjects (for example Maths and English), Traveller children should be fully integrated with other children for school activities such as sport.

FR.71   Only in exceptional circumstances should Traveller children be retained in primary school after their twelfth/thirteenth year.

FR.72   The pupil/teacher ratio in special classes for Travellers or, for the appointment of Traveller resource teachers, should be reduced from its current level of 15:1 to 10:1.

FR.73   Special Additional Assistants who are appointed to work with Travellers in schools, should be designated Traveller resource teachers.

FR.74   All schools should plan a programme of action designed to ensure that Traveller and 'Settled' pupils are integrated.

Culture and Curriculum

Recommendations

FR.75   The Task Force supports the recommendation of the Special Education Review Committee, (op. cit, 2) that:

"Schools should adopt an inclusive, intercultural approach to curriculum development so as to ensure that their School Plan, class programmes and teaching materials reflect a positive attitude towards the special customs, traditions and lifestyle of minority groups, including the children of Travellers."

The Department of Education, in consultation with the National Council for Curriculum Assessment, should ensure that Travellers and their lifestyle are reflected in an integrated way in all aspects of the primary level curriculum. The way of life and culture of Travellers and other minorities should be reflected in materials in an intercultural way.

FR.76 Flexible structures and curriculum options should be explored in the curriculum for all pupils Travellers should be included as a group with a distinct culture within and integral to Irish society.

Resources and materials needed to implement an intercultural, anti-racist curriculum (which includes Travellers) should be developed for all children.

FR.77 The Department of Education should commission the NCCA to ensure that in developing the primary curriculum, Travellers are explicitly targeted. This is particularly important in designing "Education for Life" and equality measures.

Teacher Training and Other Support Services

Recommendations

FR.78 Training for all primary level teachers and allied professionals such as speech therapists, psychologists and welfare staff should be informed by and transmit intercultural and anti-racist principles and practice, and should present Travellers as a group with a distinct culture.

Teacher training colleges should also include modules on Traveller issues in their core curriculum and further training should be provided for those who have responsibility for the education of Travellers.

FR.79 As earlier recommended in this Report, the Department of Education should provide a comprehensive teacher in-service programme on Traveller education for all teachers. The Task Force supports the recommendation of the Special Education Review Committee (op. cit, 2) that:

"to raise the level of awareness among teachers of the attitudes, values, customs and lifestyle of minority groups, including Travellers, both pre-service and in-service teacher training courses should incorporate modules on intercultural education".

FR.80 Based on teacher vigilance and the concerns of parents, any Traveller children who are experiencing learning difficulties should have access to a psychological service at primary level. A standard psychological test, appropriate to Traveller children, should be designed and used for this purpose.

FR.81 Where required, Traveller children, including children from transient families, should have access to speech therapists.

School Record Card and Transfer of Information

Recommendations

FR.82 The Task Force welcomes the sample "Family Record Card" and "School Record Card" contained in the Department of Education document "The Education of Traveller Children in National Schools - Guidelines" (op. cit, 13). A comprehensive school record system needs to be developed in recognition of the nomadic lifestyle of Travellers. This record system should ensure the speedy transfer of information on individual pupil attainment between schools. Whenever a "School Record Card" is issued in respect of a Traveller child, a copy should be given to the child's parents.

FR.83 The school record card should be designed to enable the educational progress of children of transient families to be documented. A suitable network should be established to ensure that the transfer of information to schools on the enrolment of pupils is carried out. In view of Traveller mobility across the border with Northern Ireland, such a network should have a North/South dimension; a data base should be provided in the proposed Traveller Education Service to facilitate the transfer of information between schools.

School Transport

Recommendations

FR.84 The Department of Education currently pays ninety-eight per cent of the running costs of approved special transport systems. Full transport costs (including capital costs) should be borne by the Department of Education.

FR.85 Traveller children, who are fully integrated in mainstream schools, do not always have access to an appropriate school transport system. Traveller children, irrespective of whether they are placed in mainstream classes or in special classes, should have access to a school transport system, when necessary.

Special Education Centres

Recommendation

FR.86 In relation to Primary educational provision for Travellers in Special Education Centres (such as detention centres and centres for people with disabilities), the general recommendations in this section would also apply in relation to such issues as access, equipment, teacher training, intercultural education and literacy.

Homework Projects

Recommendation

FR.87 All Travellers should have access to properly resourced homework projects. Where necessary, the Traveller resource teacher should play a role in organising these. The Department of Education should grant aid the provision of teachers for these homework projects.

6.   Second-Level Education

6(a)1   General

6(a)1.1 It should be noted that in this part of the Report, the Task Force has had to rely on statistical data from various sources all of which does not co-relate.

6(a)1.2 In the past thirty years in Ireland there has been a significant improvement in both the standard of and access to second-level education for the general population of young people. However, this improvement has had little or no impact on the Traveller population in Ireland during this time.

A range of special initiatives for Travellers introduced in the primary education sector in recent years has benefited many children. However, only a small minority of Traveller children have transferred successfully to second-level schools and very few of these have completed a full second-level education.

In 1988, 640 Traveller children between the ages of twelve and fifteen years were still attending National schools (Department of Education Survey) (Ref. 20). The Department of Education Working Group on Post-Primary Education of Traveller Children (op. cit, 16), which was set up in 1991, estimated that eighty per cent of Traveller children in the twelve to fifteen year old age group did not attend any school in the 1989/90 school year. An Ad Hoc Group of the Association of Chief Executive Officers of certain Vocational Education Committees reported (1993), (Ref. 21) that only approximately 100 Traveller children aged twelve to fifteen years were attending mainstream second-level schools out of the estimated 2000 children eligible to do so. The majority of Traveller children who attend second-level schools leave within their first two years. These figures clearly demonstrate that the second-level educational needs of Traveller children, though very critical, are not being met and that positive action is urgently required to redress this situation.

6(a)2. Factors Affecting Participation at Second Level

6(a)2.1 Many complex factors contribute to the low rate of participation of Traveller children in second-level education, ranging from health and accommodation to cultural needs of Travellers. The Report of the Department of Education Working Group on Post-Primary Education for Traveller Children (op. cit, 16) identifies the following reasons why Traveller children do not attend second-level schools or why those who do so fail to persevere in second-level education:

- insufficient level of achievement at primary level;
- curriculum not perceived as relevant to vocational and cultural aspirations of Traveller community;
- Traveller children attending mainstream schools do not at present have their distinctive lifestyle and culture validated in their formal education;
- lack of continuity between child-centred approach of first-level schools and more subject-focused curriculum, available at second level;
- lack of support services (such as remedial education and outreach programmes);
- low degree of parental involvement;
- transport difficulties;
- unsuitable conditions for home study;
- lack of mutual understanding by Traveller and settled pupils;
- standardised tests frequently used by schools either prior to or following admission can be quite unsuitable for use with Traveller children, such as standardised intelligence tests;

- where special provision within mainstream education exists it can lead to social isolation and curricular discontinuity between Traveller and 'Settled' pupils: access to full participation in the curriculum can also be restricted for Traveller children;
- the degree of nomadism engaged in by any particular family has crucial implications for the enrolment and meaningful participation in education of the children concerned;
- prejudice;
- fear of some parents that education will lead to their children rejecting the Traveller culture and way of life.

Other important reasons identified by the Task Force are:

- failure to equip teachers for the particular educational needs of Travellers through pre-service and in-service training programmes;
- the high cost of second-level education for low-income Traveller families;
- the assumption of adult responsibilities at an early age by young Travellers, leading to their increased involvement in the domestic and economic activities of the family;
- Traveller pupils experience discrimination in some schools;
- lack of value placed by some Traveller parents on academic achievements which are seen as unrelated to practical needs;
- low expectations of the education system by Travellers themselves.

6(a)3   Curriculum Development

6(a)3.1   The National Council for Curriculum and Assessment (NCCA) in its policy statements and recommendations to the Minister for Education, on issues arising from the publication of the Green Paper on Education, (Ref. 22) draws attention to the need for provision for disadvantaged pupils at post-primary level. *"Within the overall aims, principles and curriculum framework of the Junior Certificate, it is recognised that particular considerations of equity, differentiation and flexibility are required in catering for pupils with specific disadvantages. Such pupils include early school-leavers, young travellers and pupils with particular physical or learning disabilities. National recognition of school programmes for disadvantaged pupils will be provided within the Junior Certificate"*.

6(a)3.2   The NCCA identified the development of civic, social and political education as an important component of the post-primary curriculum, especially at Junior Cycle (i.e. young people in the age range of twelve to fifteen years approximately). The NCCA also specified young Travellers as a group *"for whom the regular school programme is culturally inappropriate"* and for whom *"other curriculum and assessment approaches are required"*.

6(a)4.   Principles Specific to Second-Level Educational Provision

6(a)4.1   In addition to the general principles and broad objectives which should underlie educational provision for Travellers set out at the start of this section, the Task

Force wishes to emphasise the following principles which it considers are specific to second level education:

- A Traveller has the same right of access to second-level schools as any other person.

- As an interim measure, the completion of the Junior Certificate course should be the minimum objective for all Travellers.

- Traveller parents have the right and the obligation to send their children to school for the full period of compulsory education, (from age six to fifteen years).

- Access to mainstream education, with additional support as appropriate, should be the norm for Travellers. Only in exceptional cases, based on special educational need, should separate provision be made and such provision should be regularly reviewed. Likewise, ancillary and extra-curricular activities should be provided in an integrated manner.

- All forms of discrimination against Travellers in educational provision at second level should be eliminated. This principle should not prevent Travellers from benefiting from positive action in this regard.

- All second-level schools, irrespective of the enrolment of any Travellers in the school, should promote tolerance and mutual respect among young people through a pro-active educational programme which challenges racism, prejudice and discrimination towards minority groups, including Travellers.

6(a)4.2 In the lead up to the Education Act which is expected to follow the White Paper on Education, provision should be made in legislation to ensure that these principles inform all educational provision for Travellers.

6(a)4.3 The Task Force also endorses, the principle/recommendation set out in the Report of the ASTI Standing Committee, (Ref. 23) to the Department of Education that:

"The post-primary curriculum and school materials must be philosophically informed by an approach which presents the reality of a multi-cultural society. A respect for cultural diversity and for different lifestyles must become a feature of our education system. In the last decade, enormous advances have been made in eliminating sexist stereotyping and negative images of women from school materials. A similar effort should be made to confront the generalised negative representations of Travellers' and to encourage greater spirit of tolerance among young people towards minority groups in our society".

6(a)5. Recommendations

FR.88 The Task Force considered the Report of the Department of Education Working Group on Post-Primary Education for Traveller Children, (op. cit, 16) and endorses the implementation of the following recommendations from that Report:

*"14.2   There should be continuous evaluation of the provision being made for
         Traveller children at primary level.*

*14.3   The Visiting Teacher Service for Traveller children should be extended to
         the post-primary sector.*

*14.5   The making of arrangements for the transfer of Traveller children to post-
         primary schools should be commenced at the beginning of the school year
         in which they are due to finish their primary education.*

*14.9   Schools should exercise a particular sensitivity in relation to the use of
         standardised tests for Traveller children.*

*14.11   The receiving post-primary school should make a special effort to
         acknowledge and respect the Travellers' distinctive culture and identity.*

*14.13   Traveller children should be integrated with the remainder of the pupils in
         so far as this is possible.*

*14.25   The question of certification and assessment for pupils who would not
         attempt or achieve success in the Junior Certificate Examination should be
         referred to the Assessment Committee of the NCCA.*

*14.27   Teachers directly involved with Traveller children will require an extensive
         programme of in-service education. All practising teachers should be provided
         with in-service training relating to the general area of Traveller education.*

*14.28   Co-operation with the United Kingdom on Traveller education should be
         pursued in certain specified areas.*

*14.32   A formal system of co-ordination between the different sections of the
         Department dealing with Travellers should be set up."*

The Task Force has varying degrees of disagreement with the other recommendations
in the 1992 Working Group Report chiefly for the following reasons:

–   In several recommendations there appears to be an assumption that every
     Traveller student has remedial needs. The Task Force is aware of the harm
     which can result from personnel in the education services having low
     expectations of Traveller children.

–   Some of the recommendations, and points made in the body of the Report,
     might result in a segregationist policy towards Travellers. Travellers in
     general, abhor the experience and the negative results of segregationist
     policies in former and in some current, primary school provision for
     Travellers. Care must be taken not to repeat these at second level.

–   Some recommendations, especially those relating to the curriculum, fail in
     some instances to note that the measures proposed should be culturally
     appropriate or, in other instances, to acknowledge the importance of adopting
     an intercultural approach.

187

         –   The Task Force has endeavoured to incorporate what it considered valuable in these recommendations in its own recommendations.

FR.89   At the beginning of the final year in primary schools, arrangements for the transfer of Traveller children to second-level schools should commence. It is recommended that the visiting teacher should meet with teenage Travellers themselves, have discussions with Traveller parents over a significant length of time and create links (i) between Travellers and post-primary schools, and (ii) between national schools and post-primary schools.

FR.90   Through a comprehensive intercultural approach, the school ethos, curriculum and teaching materials should reflect respect for cultural difference, particularly those cultures relevant to the pupils, including Traveller culture, and enable students to appreciate the richness of cultural diversity.

FR.91   Second-level schools should draw up a School Plan which should include a policy on Traveller education and measures to overcome prejudice. The Department of Education should facilitate this process by issuing guidelines on the preparation of the School Plan. The formulation, implementation and review of the Plan should be the responsibility of the school principal on behalf of the Board of Management. The day-to-day implementation of the plan in relation to Travellers should be the responsibility of the resource teacher, where such a post has been allocated. (see FR.92 below)

FR.92   As a matter of urgency, the Department of Education should allocate ex-quota resource teachers to second-level schools which enrol Travellers. Where the number of Travellers enrolled in a group of neighbouring schools is sufficient to justify the allocation of a resource teacher, a resource teacher should be shared between those schools. A pupil teacher ratio of 8:1 is suggested.

FR.93   The resource teacher for Travellers should be responsible for facilitating the full social and educational integration of Traveller pupils into the school system.

FR.94   The resource teacher for Travellers in liaison with the Visiting Teacher Service should advise the teaching staff on Traveller resource materials relevant to the curriculum and on in-service courses on Traveller education.

FR.95   All Travellers do not share the same educational needs and, while special provisions may be required to meet the varied educational needs, access to mainstream provision must be regarded as the norm for Travellers. Traveller pupils must not be segregated.

FR.96   Traveller children should not be stereotyped as low academic achievers. Only when special educational needs have been identified should more information than is normal be transferred from primary to second-level schools in the case of individual Travellers. Schools should exercise particular caution in the use for Traveller children of tests of intellectual functioning which have not been refined to take account of the specific culture of Travellers.

FR.97 All Travellers should have access to properly resourced homework projects. Where necessary, the Traveller resource teacher should play a role in organising these. The Department of Education should grant aid the provision of teachers for these homework projects.

FR.98 The Department of Education should publish guidelines on second-level education for Travellers based on the principles set out in this Report.

FR.99 In relation to second-level educational provision for Travellers in Special Education Centres, the general recommendations in this section should apply in relation to such issues as access, equipment, teacher training, intercultural education and literacy.

Many Traveller children suffer from the same financial difficulties as children from disadvantaged backgrounds, but the degree of disadvantage while not insurmountable, is often greater due to the absence of a school-going network. A general example of possible costs to be faced by families at second level is included at Appendix F(I) of this section.

FR.100 In order to assist in reducing the financial burden imposed on Traveller families at second level, the Task Force recommends that:

    (i) Child benefit levels should reflect and respond to times of particular financial difficulty in school life.

    (ii) A realistic school clothing and footwear grant and school books allowance be provided for Traveller pupils.

    (iii) Greater communication between School Principals, Community Welfare Officers and voluntary groups should take place in order to co-ordinate help for families with full respect for the privacy of these families.

    (iv) Families should be fully informed of schooling costs and their rights fully explained to them.

FR.101 The Department of Education should commission the NCCA to develop the Junior Certificate School Programme to cater for the needs of Travellers. In particular, the civic, social, political, environmental education dimension of the Junior Cycle opens up new possibilities which should be availed of in the context of the preparation of young people for their roles as citizens.

FR.102 The Department of Education should commission the NCCA to develop the curriculum at Senior Cycle level in continuity and progression from the Junior Certificate in ways which are relevant and appropriate for Travellers.

6. **Junior Training Centres (JTC's)**

6(b)1. The transition of Traveller children from primary to second level education raises problems which are still largely unresolved. Between the ages of twelve and fifteen years, there are an estimated 2,000 to 2,400 children. Of these some 1,400 to 1,600 do not continue their education. Junior Training Centres (JTCs) are said to cater for about 300 children. However, actual daily attendances are markedly less. Some children are retained in primary schools. A remaining 100 are in other post-primary schools. Recommendations for the future must therefore start from the lack of take up of second-level mainsteam education provision by the great majority of this age group.

6(b)2. The goal to be striven for is clear. Every Traveller child must have a complete education, at a minimum, from the age of six to the age of fifteen years. Education in mainstream second-level schools for all Travellers must be the aim. This has implications for the role and future of Junior Training Centres.

6(b)3. While the Junior Training Centres provide for only a small number of Travellers it is relevant to note that they cater for more Travellers in the twelve to fifteen age group than do mainstream schools. The Junior Training Centres enjoy certain advantages such as a low teacher-pupil ratio, and a flexible curriculum that allows a variety of learning experiences. The Junior Training Centres have provided a safety net for the failure of the mainstream service to attract Travellers in this age group.

6(b)4. Set alongside these advantages however, there are a number of issues that give cause for concern:

- the quality of buildings and facilities is uneven;
- the financial provision for centres can be inadequate;
- the absence of an organised progressive curriculum common to the centres results in uneven quality of provision.

The Junior Training Centres appear to exist within a policy vacuum. There is a lack of common goals and strategies to inform the work of the centres. Further, there is the real danger that their existence removes the pressure on the mainstream providers to adapt to the needs of Travellers.

6(b)5. The strategy that has informed the work of the Task Force is based on the inclusion of Travellers within the mainstream education system and the necessary adaptation of that system to accommodate the particular needs of Travellers.

6(b)6. **Recommendations**

FR.103 The Task Force recommends that no further Junior Training Centres should be established, and that the existing JTC's, with the exception of those at primary level, should be taken over by the Vocational Education Committees on the basis of the agreement which the CEO's in the areas where these Centres are located have established with the Department of Education, regarding management structures, staffing, capital provision and non-pay and pay provision. (See Appendix F(2) of this section). These VEC's should be given responsibility for the ultimate phasing out of Junior Training Centres at the most appropriate speed. The speed of this transition will be determined by the successful application of the Task Force recommendations in relation to second level education. Capital costs associated with this transition period should be additional to the existing budget of the VEC's.

Immediate measures should be taken by the VEC's to ensure improvement in the quality of the curriculum and of teaching where this may be required.

The Traveller Education Service of the Department of Education should monitor the policy set out here for Junior Training Centres.

FR.104 This does not exempt other schools from improving their provision for Traveller education. All Travellers must have equality of access to all mainstream second-level schools.

FR.105 The resourcing of the Task Force policy for the improvement of mainstream second-level educational provision, particularly in relation to visiting teachers, resource teachers and the creation of an intercultural educational environment for Traveller education, must be urgently addressed.

7. Visiting Teacher Service (VTS)

7.1 General

7.1.1 As acknowledged by the Department of Education (Ref. 24) (in Circular 20/88), few initiatives in the area of Traveller education have been as successful as the appointment of visiting teachers.

7.1.2 The Visiting Teacher Service (VTS) was introduced in 1980 and is currently available in Dublin, Cork, Limerick, Galway, Wexford, Kerry and Tipperary.

7.1.3 The main objectives of the VTS, as set out in the Department of Education Guidelines entitled "Education of Traveller Children in National Schools" (op. cit, 13) are:

–   Identification of the educational needs of Traveller children in the region.

–   Assisting with the planning and establishment of education provision by:

    *   consulting with Traveller families;

    *   providing relevant information, names, numbers and location of children to relevant authorities;

    *   assisting with the setting up of pre-schools and special classes;

    *   identifying transport needs and the other back-up services in consultation with the Department of Education.

–   Ensuring optimal use of existing educational facilities and provisions by:

    *   monitoring numbers of children by school visits;
    *   checking attendance;
    *   advising as to appropriate placement for pupils in consultation with other professionals;
    *   ensuring transfer of relevant information from one visiting teacher to another when families move within visiting teacher areas;
    *   recording information;
    *   monitoring transport arrangements;

*   issuing school record cards to transient families to facilitate future enrolment of children in schools.

7.2   Present Size of Visiting Teacher Service

The Visiting Teacher Service has twelve existing posts, eleven of which are filled at present. The locations of existing posts are set out in Table F4 as follows:

Table F4: Distribution of Visiting Teacher Service	
Dublin	5
Cork	1
Limerick	1
Galway	1
Kerry	1
Wexford	1
Tipperary	1
Laois/Offaly	One post to be filled

7.3   Expansion of Visiting Teacher Service

7.3.1   Numerous reports published over recent years have identified the expansion of the Visiting Teacher Service as an important element in the development of education services for Traveller children.

7.3.2   The Irish National Teachers Organisation in a Report entitled "Travellers in Education", (op. cit, 15) called for the VTS to *"be extended on a county by county basis to cover all counties"* with a proposed ratio of one visiting teacher to every one hundred Traveller families. Recommendations for the expansion of the VTS were also included in the Report of the Travelling People Review Body, (Ref. 25), the Report of the Primary Education Review Body, (Ref. 26) and in the Report of the Special Education Review Committee (op. cit, 2)

7.3.3   It is also noted that in the Green Paper "Education for a Changing World" (op. cit, 12), the Department of Education provides a commitment that as "additional teaching posts become available in the future", it will "allocate further posts of visiting teacher".

7.3.4   It should be noted that in the part of this section which deals with the Traveller Economy, the Task Force recommends the adoption of a policy of Traveller recruitment to the public service which would include a rolling programme for recruitment to certain identified posts including the post of Visiting Teacher Assistant. The recruitment of Visiting Teacher Assistants from among the Traveller community would make an important contribution to the Visiting Teacher Service in terms of background knowledge and experience.

7.4   The following recommendations are made by the Task Force in relation to the role, development and expansion of the Visiting Teacher Service:

Recommendations

FR.106 In view of the positive impact which the VTS has had in areas where visiting teachers have been appointed, it is recommended that the number of such teachers should be immediately increased by the Department of Education in line with the ratio of one visiting teacher to every one hundred Traveller families as proposed by the INTO in its Report entitled "Travellers in Education" (op. cit, 15).

Based on this ratio and subject to other factors influencing the allocation of visiting teachers being taken into account, such as: distances to be travelled, the number of schools involved, and the size of Traveller families in each area of a teacher's responsibility, it is recommended that the number of visiting teachers be increased to thirty-nine, possibly on the basis set out in Table F5 below. We note the commitment of the Minister for Education to increase the size of the Visiting Teacher Service to thirty-two and, with due regard to the recommendations on the VTS contained in this Report, request that this be implemented as a matter of urgency.

FR.107 Traveller families should have to deal with one visiting teacher only whether their children are attending primary or second-level schools. This would enable a bond of trust to develop as the basis for a good constructive working relationship between the visiting teacher and individual families.

Accordingly, as proposed in Recommendation 14.3 of the Report of the Department of Education Working Group on Post Primary Education for Traveller Children (op. cit, 16) it is recommended that the Visiting Teacher Service for Traveller pupils should be extended to the post-primary sector. Individual visiting teachers should be responsible for pupils of both primary and post-primary school age in their area and operate in an integrated service embracing both sectors. Qualified primary and second-level teachers should be eligible to apply for positions in the service and a suitable balance between teachers from both sectors should be maintained in recruitment to the VTS.

FR.108 As indicated in recommendation FR.106 above, the resources allocated to each VTS area should reflect its geographical size, the total number of Traveller families and the number of schools in that area.

FR.109 Due to the isolated nature of the VTS, provision should also be made to enable the teachers concerned to meet, on a more regular basis, with the National Education Officer for Travellers, with VTS management and with the proposed Traveller Education Service in the Department of Education to discuss issues of common concern.

FR.110 In situations where large numbers of Traveller families move into a particular area, a visiting teacher, or an additional visiting teacher, should be appointed on a temporary basis without delay to arrange educational provision and support for the children.

FR.111 A number of 'supply' teachers should be appointed in order to provide substitute cover for all recognised absences of existing visiting teachers, such as sick leave and maternity leave. The pilot Supply Panel Project operating in a number of national schools in Ballymun/Finglas, North Mayo and Limerick City provides a useful model of substitute cover.

FR.112 The managers of the Visiting Teacher Service should be given clear guidelines, which should be drawn up by the proposed Traveller Education Service, regarding the question of equal access for visiting teachers, including the responsibility and authority to ensure that such guidelines are being implemented. This should apply at both primary and post-primary levels with a suitable mechanism being put in place to ensure that any problems are resolved with particular reference to difficulties arising in the area of cross-sector (primary and second-level) access by visiting teachers.

FR.113 The Task Force endorses the role of the Visiting Teacher Service as set out in the Department of Education Guidelines entitled "The Education of Traveller Children in National Schools" (op. cit, 13). The Task Force, however, recommends that the current Visiting Teacher Service should be expanded into an education service which can meet, in a co-ordinated way, all the educational needs of Traveller families in any given area. Central to the visiting teachers' role should be ensuring that each school catchment area has an explicit policy and mechanism formulated to ensure that all schools in the catchment make provision for the special educational needs of Travellers and seek to accommodate them. As recommended in 'Issues of Concern to All Education Sectors' elsewhere in this section, the role of the Visiting Teacher Service should not be seen as a substitute for parental involvement in the education of their children.

FR.114 The visiting teacher in co-operation with the parents should ensure that Traveller children are enrolled in adequate time to commence their second-level education in the school of their choice.

FR.115 In the case of Traveller children who are perceived to be apprehensive about entry to a second-level school, the visiting teacher should ensure that appropriate measures are implemented to facilitate the successful transfer of these children to second level education. This process requires identification of the inhibiting factors and development of measures to overcome these in consultation with the children concerned, their parents and the relevant teachers in primary and second-level schools.

FR.116 The Task Force recommends that appropriate measures be put in place to ensure that teachers in the Visiting Teacher Service do not suffer from 'burnout'.

TABLE F5

Possible Allocation of Visiting Teachers

County Councils	Traveller Families (1994)(a)*	Visiting Teachers (b)*
Carlow Kilkenny	58 47	1
Cavan Monaghan	50 47	1
Clare	90	1
Cork	159	2
Donegal	83	1
Dublin - Fingal	194	2
Dublin - South	270	3
Dun Laoghaire-Rathdown	90	1
Galway	285	3
Kerry	182	2
Kildare Wicklow	39 68	1
Laois Offaly	80 123	2
Leitrim Roscommon Sligo	22 35 41	1
Limerick County	149	2 (with Borough)
Longford	120	1
Louth	128	1
Mayo	114	1
Meath	124	1
Tipperary N.R. Tipperary S.R.	94 71	2
Waterford	31	1 (with Borough)
Westmeath	126	1
Wexford	150	1
County Boroughs	**Traveller Families (1994)(a)**	**Visiting Teachers (b)**
Cork	180	2
Dublin	335	3
Galway	164	2
Limerick	61	2 (with County)
Waterford	68	1 (with County)
Total	**3878**	**39**

Notes re Table F5

This suggested breakdown is based on the 1994 Annual Count of Traveller Families, carried out by the Department of the Environment.

(a) *Numbers include settled families and those residing on the roadside.

(b) *Based on a ratio of one visiting teacher to every one hundred Traveller families. Figures generally rounded to the nearest 100.

8. Third-Level Education

8.1 General

8.1.1 At the present time third-level education is not a possibility for the vast majority of Travellers. There are many reasons for this, but the main reason has to do with the poor performance of Travellers in primary and second-level schools. Given that access to third-level education is determined to a large extent by high levels of achievement in second-level schools, it is not surprising that very few Travellers go on to third level.

8.1.2 It is possible that some Travellers have gone on to third level without being identified as Travellers. There is no data available in support of this, but it is known that a small number of Travellers have completed courses in Regional Technical Colleges (such as Galway) and in St. Patrick's College, Maynooth. (See Crickley, (Ref. 27)).

"While the number involved is very small, it is nevertheless significant, considering what has been stated above about primary and post-primary levels. What is important about these courses is that the Travellers referred to have identified themselves as Travellers and have subsequently become active in work within the Traveller community. This is particularly true of Maynooth College, where the professional two-year training course in Community and Youth Work was made accessible to Travellers over four successive cycles. There are probably a number of other Travellers who have gone on to third level but who have been invisible because of the pressure to assimilate and to hide their Traveller identity".

8.2 Challenges and Obstacles

8.2.1 Travellers who complete second-level education, and go on to further education, gain from that experience but, without ongoing support, risk losing their Traveller identity and being set apart from their families and friends.

8.2.2 The general principles set out in 'General Principles and Broad Objectives' of this section, and the issues raised on intercultural education should also be considered in relation to third-level education provision in order to ensure that courses are sensitive and relevant to Travellers participating in such courses.

8.2.3 The financial costs of further education are also prohibitive for most Traveller families and those who have availed of third-level education have only been able to do so because of voluntary support and grants which were made available.

8.3   Recommendations

FR.117   In the long-term, it is essential that more Travellers progress through the mainstream system and gain access to third-level education in the normal way. In the short term, it is possible for more Travellers to benefit from third-level education. Universities and other third-level and post second-level institutes should be encouraged to take positive action in this regard.

FR.118   The Department of Education should encourage Traveller participation in third-level education by targeting Travellers through the Higher Education Grants Scheme and by ensuring that grants are adequate to cover the costs involved.

FR.119   A national trust should be established, with Government support and private sector sponsorship, to facilitate and encourage Travellers to avail of third-level education.

FR.120   The TES should identify where Travellers have gained access to and successfully completed third-level courses in order to derive lessons for the future.

9(a)   Adult Education

9(a)1   General

9(a)1.1   The Report of the Commission on Adult Education (1983), (Ref. 28) has described adult education as including:

"all systematic learning by adults which contributes to their development as individuals and as members of the community and of society, apart from full-time instruction received by persons as part of their uninterrupted initial education and training. It may be formal education which takes place in institutions e.g. training centres, schools, colleges, institutes and universities; or non-formal education, which is any other systematic form of learning, including self-directed learning".

This broad definition includes a wide range of different forms of education which are known as ongoing learning, in-service development and second chance education.

9(a)1.2   That there is a general lack of data in relation to adult education is widely known (such as: types of courses, profile of participants and the extent and nature of the service provided by voluntary bodies). To compound this information gap, the Department of Education does not have any reports or publications with information on Travellers in adult education.

9(a)1.3   The dearth of information is all the more serious given the importance of adult education as referred to in the Green Paper on Education, (op. cit, 12) and in numerous publications, especially in the Report of the Commission on Adult Education, (op. cit, 28). Adult education is still regarded as an optional extra rather than as an integrated part of the formal system of education. In comparison with the rest of the education system, adult education is very under-resourced, much of the funding is sporadic, there is insufficient long-term planning, and there is no coherent policy for development.

Some grants are available for adult education but these are fairly limited, and there is also an over heavy reliance on volunteers, part-time and temporary workers.

9(a)2.   Inequality

9(a)2.1   Professor Clancy (Ref. 29) refers to the *"stubborn persistence of marked social inequalities"* in the Irish education system and points out that *"the more prestigious the sector and field of study, the greater the social inequality in participation levels"*. Inequalities in the mainstream education system have also been highlighted by Breen, (Ref. 30), Whelan, (Ref. 31), Drudy and Lynch, (Ref. 32) and others. Their research demonstrates that the children of higher professionals, employers, managers, big farmers, salaried employees and intermediate non-manual workers are over-represented in higher education. In contrast the children of non-manual, skilled, semi-skilled, and unskilled and other agricultural workers are under-represented. Travellers are not referred to at all but it does not require further research to prove that the vast majority of Travellers leave school early and do not participate in second or third-level education.

9(a)2.2   These inequalities in higher education do not disappear in the adult education sphere even though it is often seen as targeting the 'disadvantaged' and as providing second-chance education. However as the Report of the Commission on Adult Education (op. cit, 28) showed, seventy-four per cent of adults did not participate in any form of adult education and, of those who did, most had a positive experience of schooling. Some analysts have concluded from this that, instead of eliminating inequalities adult education may therefore reinforce them. Even though women are over-represented in adult education it is estimated that it is middle-class rather than working-class women who are the main beneficiaries (Drudy and Lynch, op. cit, 32).

9(a)2.3   Access to adult education is a problem for many Travellers, just as it is in other areas of education. The main barriers to adult education are: lack of resources, inadequate information and guidance, difficult entry requirements, lack of childcare facilities, inappropriate curriculum, inflexibility of structures, lack of funds for books, materials and transport and having to forego necessary earnings in order to participate in courses.

9(a)2.4   The Green Paper (op. cit, 12) refers to *"people who left the education system prematurely because of lack of motivation or interest in the programmes available to them. For many people, lack of confidence and motivation, rather than limitation in provision, may prove the major barrier to participation"*. Such an explanation is criticised because it shifts the focus away from the system and individualises the problem: *"Liberal equal opportunities policies create the image that the reason people do not participate in education is that they are not interested; lack of participation is defined as an individual problem rather than a structural one, with all the implications for public policy. There can be no real equality of opportunity in education without equality in peoples' economic, political and personal circumstances, otherwise, there are simply too many barriers for those without resources to pass through"* (op. cit, 32).

9(a)3   Statutory and Voluntary Bodies

9(a)3.1   Adult education has been and still is closely linked to social movements such as the trades unions, rural development, religious projects, and the women's movement. Likewise adult education for Travellers is closely related to the emergence of a Traveller movement.

9(a)3.2   Voluntary organisations have played a major role in most of these movements and have thereby contributed to the richness and variety of adult education provision.

9(a)3.3   While much of the conventional adult education courses available cannot be associated with progressive social change there are links between adult education and various social movements. In some cases this has contributed to the emergence of a number of key principles for adult education such as critical reflection, empowerment and emancipation. Paulo Freire's "Pedagogy of the Oppressed", (Ref. 33) and its critique of the banking system of education influenced some forms of adult education and highlights the potential of literacy training for overcoming *"the culture of silence"* and for facilitating social change.

9(a)3.4   Statutory agencies, FÁS and especially the Vocational Educational Committees have contributed greatly to the development of adult education. Community and comprehensive schools provide a wide range of adult education opportunities. Nevertheless there is a lack of integration, lack of accreditation, lack of long-term planning and a lack of a coherent policy for developing adult education. In addition, there is little or no attempt by these agencies to target adult Travellers.

9(a)4.   Literacy

9(a)4.1   Literacy problems are often referred to in discussions about adult education although the extent and the nature of the problems are not fully known. In order to obtain more information on the situation a national survey of literacy has been commissioned by the Department of Education. According to the Report of the Travelling People Review Body (op. cit, 25) *"virtually all (adult Travellers) are illiterate and inumerate"*. While more and more younger Travellers are becoming literate, there is still a major challenge for those involved in the delivery of adult education to cater for those Travellers who cannot read or write. Illiteracy is still a major barrier in allowing adult Travellers to participate fully in society and to Traveller participation in adult education programmes.

9(a)4.2   The Green Paper on Education (op. cit, 12) acknowledges the seriousness of illiteracy and quotes from the OECD, Adult Illiteracy and Economic Performance (1992) which shows that people who are functionally illiterate *"are unable to participate fully in the economic and civic life of today's advanced nations"*. The Adult Literacy and Community Education Scheme (ALCES), which is operated through the Vocational Education Committees, provides literacy and basic education tuition free of charge or at a nominal cost but relies on volunteer tutors. The Green Paper states that: *"The ALCES will be continued and developed to meet the needs of those who lack basic literacy skills ... the semi-voluntary, community based service offered through the VEC's will be maintained and strengthened..."*

9(a)4.3 Under Article 42 of the Constitution of Ireland, (Ref. 34), the State acknowledges that the primary and natural educator of the child is the family. The School Attendance Act (1926) compels parents to fulfil their obligation in a particular way. Traveller parents are not always in a position to fulfil their duties because of illiteracy, as well as other forms of disadvantage and they need support to do so.

9(a)5.   Accreditation

9(a)5.1 People who leave school without academic credentials have less chance of finding paid employment and of progressing within the labour market than those with such credentials. In the context of widespread and high unemployment many people see adult education as another chance to acquire the educational credentials which they lack. This raises the issue of accreditation of adult education courses. At present there is no comprehensive system of credit transfers or a recognition of prior learning, neither is there a co-ordinated system of accreditation of courses.

9(a)5.2 A warning against credentials for their own sake is given by Drudy and Lynch (op. cit, 32):

"Offering people certificates, diplomas, and the like, often based on short courses that are not formally recognised by established accrediting bodies (indeed not recognised by the very authorities that provide them) seem to be an insult to the people who take the courses, and a waste of limited resources".

9(a)6.   Recommendations

FR.121 The importance of adult education should be reflected in the status attributed to adult education within the whole system and in the allocation of resources. The TES should examine current adult education provision in order to ensure that it addresses inequality issues and has the capacity to address the educational needs of Travellers.

FR.122 The values and ideals associated with progressive forms of adult education should be cultivated and the richness of the varied provision should be encouraged. There is need for long-term planning and greater co-operation between statutory and voluntary sectors in order to arrive at a more coherent national policy and a statement of practice on adult education. Such a policy should draw on the experience and insights of Traveller organisations involved in the provision of adult education.

FR.123 There is a need to tackle the many disincentives and barriers which prevent Travellers from participating in adult education. A pro-active approach is needed and adequate information and guidance should be designed for and targeted at Travellers. Entry requirements and structures should be sufficiently flexible to facilitate access and there is a need for resources to cover materials and expenses as well as childcare facilities.

FR.124 As well as making adult education courses more accessible for Travellers there is also a need to resource courses specifically designed for and targeted at adult Travellers in order to address their educational needs. Such resourcing should also be transparent so as to clearly benefit adult Travellers.

FR.125   Accreditation of adult education courses, including prior learning, should be given careful consideration so that established accrediting bodies are involved and progression is possible, but also to ensure that educational credentials do not become another obstacle to Traveller involvement.

FR.126   Illiteracy is still a major issue in the adult Traveller population and a key factor contributing to their social exclusion. The Department of Education and the VEC's should allocate more resources and personnel to tackle this issue in a comprehensive way and to build on the existing initiatives of voluntary organisations. Special literacy programmes for Travellers should be developed by each VEC with full-time organisers to enable Travellers to access existing literacy schemes. Courses should be specifically designed for Travellers and should include one-to-one as well as group tuition as provided under the Adult Literacy and Community Education Scheme.

FR.127   As indicated in 'Issues of Concern to All Education Sectors' the involvement of Traveller parents in the education of their children is essential for progress. Specific education should be available for Traveller parents to enable them to provide the best support for their children. In this regard, the Task Force endorses the recommendation of the Department of Education Working Group on Post-Primary Education for Traveller Children (op. cit, 16) which states:

"The Adult Education Section of the Department distributes about £1,000,000 each year to Vocational Education Committees for Adult Literacy and Community Education. Sports Section distributes £225,000 per year to Vocational Education Committees under the Special Projects for the Less Advantaged Grant Scheme. We recommend that, in the local allocation of these funds, VEC's give top priority to the financing of courses/activities aimed at Traveller parents. The objective of these courses/activities would be to facilitate Traveller parents in appreciating the benefits of education for their children and to encourage them to give full support to their children's attendance at school up to the compulsory school leaving age and beyond".

9(b)   Youth Work

9(b)1.   Introduction - Context for Youth Work with Travellers

9(b)1.1   Youth work and youth services for Travellers are of particular importance given the possibilities for informal education they could offer to young people who may not have had adequate formal education experiences. It is important to locate the provision of youth services for Travellers against the background of the development to date of the whole youth service nationally.

9(b)1.2   There are a number of key Government reports which set out to develop a national youth policy: A Policy for Youth and Sport (Bruton Report), Department of Education, (Ref. 35): the Final Report of the Task Force on Child Care Services , Department of Health, (Ref. 36); Development of Youth Work Services (O'Sullivan Report) Department of Education, (Ref. 37); Final Report of the National Youth Policy Committee (Costello Report) Department of Labour, (Ref. 38); In Partnership with Youth: the National Youth Policy, Department of Labour, (Ref. 39); The Green Paper, Education For A Changing World (op. cit, 12).

The Department of Education commissioned an evaluation of youth work which resulted in a report A Review of Youth Work Practice in Community-Based Projects, by D. Treacy, (Ref. 40). The Irish Government passed the Child Care Act in 1991 and also ratified the UN Convention on the Rights of the Child in 1992.

In addition, there are numerous reports from voluntary youth organisations such as the National Youth Council of Ireland Draft Policy: The Youth Service and Disadvantaged Youth, (Ref. 41). There was also the Report of the Consultative Group on the Development of Youth Work, (Ref. 42) in response to the Green Paper on Education and the NYCI Towards the Development of a Comprehensive Youth Service, (Ref. 43). However, there is still no legislative basis for youth services and responsibilities are shared by different Departments: Education, Health, Enterprise and Employment, Social Welfare, Environment and Justice. The new programme of the Government "A Government of Renewal" (op. cit, 18) contains a commitment to *"prepare a Youth Service Act to provide a statutory basis for developing youth work in Ireland"*.

9(b)1.3 Since 1988 most of the funding for youth services has come from the National Lottery. This resulted initially in a huge increase in the amount of money provided from about £4m to £10m per year. It also gave rise to insecurity because of the lack of long-term commitment and separation from exchequer funding.

9(b)1.4 The bulk of this funding is divided between mainstream voluntary youth services and special services and projects with disadvantaged groups. Remaining funds are granted to local voluntary youth councils and special services such as youth information centres and youth exchange.

9(b)1.5 Mainstream youth services include uniformed organisations and youth clubs. These youth services are primarily geared to provide leisure, recreational and cultural activities during after-school hours, at week-ends and during summer holidays.

9(b)1.6 Special services and projects with disadvantaged groups include community based projects in disadvantaged areas, drop-in centres, young homeless projects, young Travellers, neighbourhood youth projects and information and advice centres.

9(b) 2. What Youth Work Means

9(b)2.1 The primary task of youth work according to the Final Report of the National Youth Policy Committee (op. cit. 38) is *"to offer young people, on the basis of their voluntary involvement, developmental and educational experiences which will equip them to play an active part in our democratic society as well as meet their own developmental needs"* ... *"through a challenging programme of social education ... which assists the young person to be an active and critical participant in society and social development"*. The Green Paper on education describes youth work as *"informal education"*.

9(b)2.2 The Report (op. cit, 38) outlined some of the core values needed for this task:

"Youth work must empower young people and enable them to emerge from the enveloping state of dependence... Young people must know, feel and believe that

they have some control over their situations in the sense of having ability to influence intentionally what happens to them and their community. The ability of young people to assess alternatives and choose the most appropriate one in any given situation, is central to our views of social education " .

9(b)2.3 Youth work as an educational process, according to the 1984 Costello Report is expected to *"play a key role in enabling young people to analyse society and in motivating and helping them to develop the skills and capabilities to become involved in affecting change"*.

9(b)3.   Definition and Elements of Youth Work

9(b)3.1 The Costello Report (op, cit, 38) has formed the basis of the most widely held definition of youth work of the main youth work organisations in Ireland as is evident in the Report of the Consultative Group on the Development of Youth Work (op. cit, 42). The Group, relying heavily on the Costello Report stated that: *"Youth work is a planned systematic educational process which assists and enhances the personal and social development of young people, is carried out primarily by voluntary groups and organisations"*. Youth work is seen therefore as taking place outside the formal school curriculum and as involving experiential learning. It is associated with leisure and recreation but also with addressing issues of inequality and disadvantage.

9(b)3.2 It is generally accepted that the key elements of youth work are its underlying value system, the methods and approaches used, the content of the programme, and the structures for participation.

9(b)3.3 In accordance with the Costello Report (op.cit, 38) the core values of youth work should be as follows:

–   enabling young people to make choices;
–   providing support for young people to reach their full potential as free and dignified individuals;
–   creating the conditions for the development of critical thinking, social analysis, and clarified values and attitudes, informed by a sense of social justice;
–   ensuring the involvement of adults and young people in partnership.

9(b)3.4 The methods and approaches used in youth work should:

–   ensure that young people themselves are involved in setting the pace and the agenda;
–   encourage young people to recognise and develop their own talents and capacities;
–   challenge young people to take responsibility for their values, actions and behaviour;
–   cooperate with other groups such as the families and communities of the young people;
–   recognise and respect the needs and interests of different groups of young people.

9(b)3.5 The youth work process, involving informal education based on a specific set of values, distinguishes the practice of youth work from commercial leisure provision. The content of youth work programmes depends on the situation as well as on the age and composition of the target youth population. But, in order for youth activities to contribute to the learning process, there is a need for ongoing review and art evaluation. Youth work programmes may include the following:

- recreational events (such as: sport art and games) which encourage personal growth and development;
- addressing issues of concern (such as: discrimination, inequality, poverty and lack of facilities);
- cultural exchanges and visits;
- developing a spiritual dimension to the lives of the youth;
- fostering healthy interpersonal relationships.

9(b)3.6 The structures needed for youth work should promote participation and involvement of young people themselves. This involves dealing constructively and creatively with issues of authority and power, goal-setting, fund-raising and accountability, developing and passing on skills and knowledge.

9(b)4. Diversity in Delivery

9(b)4.1 Given the age structure of the Irish population, with its relatively high number of young people, as well as the strength of the voluntary sector overall, it is not surprising that there are numerous organisations and groups involved in the delivery of different types of youth services in Ireland. These organisations include national and regional organisations, community-based initiatives, local groups and councils.

9(b)5. Department of Education

9(b)5.1 While mainstream youth work in the State is dominated by voluntary effort organised through diverse voluntary agencies, the Department of Education, particularly through the Youth Affairs Section and the Vocational Education Committees, is also a major player in promoting policy development and in providing funding for youth work organisations. In 1988, the Department of Education set up a grant scheme to promote youth work with young people from disadvantaged communities. This initiative was in response to the growing poverty and inequality and the marginalisation of the disadvantaged from the mainstream youth services.

9(b)5.2 The Green Paper (op. cit, 12) refers to the importance of youth work *"in responding to the needs of young people who are perceived to be disadvantaged because of such factors as unemployment, social isolation, substance abuse, homelessness and the inadequate take-up of formal education and training opportunities ... youth workers can build on the main features of effective youth work to counteract the experience of alienation, to restore a sense of self-esteem and to support positive action to develop potential. Return to the formal education or training system is an important objective"*.

9(b)6. Youth Work and Travellers

9(b)6.1   The role and importance of youth work in response to the needs of young Travellers is obvious given the striking age structure of Travellers, and the serious gaps in the provision and take-up of education. Youth work with Travellers should not be seen as a substitute for formal education but as an important complement to it.

9(b)6.2   The educational needs of Travellers highlighted elsewhere in this section combined with the lack of recreational and leisure facilities add to the overall social exclusion of young Travellers. These circumstances make the need for a good quality youth service for Travellers all the more urgent.

9(b)6.3   Youth work with Travellers should aim to enable young people to become active participants in their own communities and in the wider society, and to work towards breaking cycles of poverty and exclusion.

9(b)6.4   Youth work should assist in the development of individual and collective self-esteem through services which are based on standards of excellence, are non-judgemental, accepting, culturally appropriate, encouraging and yet challenging.

9(b)6.5   The Costello Report (1984) recommended that the national youth service should specifically include Travellers and that specially trained youth workers should be available to assist with local youth work activities.

9(b)6.6   The White Paper "In Partnership with Youth: the National Youth Policy", (op. cit, 39) had a section on young Travellers which referred to the many disadvantages they experience related to accommodation, education and training, employment, health, and inadequate services. The report stated that *"the Government acknowledge that the lack of adequate education is the greatest single barrier to the progress of young Travellers in society"*. In addition to emphasising the need for *"the integrating of Traveller education into the general education system"*, it stressed that *"youth services are as important for young Travellers as they are for other young people"*. It also committed the Government to enabling local youth service boards *"to support the provision of appropriate additional youth services for young Travellers, including the employment of full-time youth workers"*.

9(b)6.7   The existing youth service with Travellers comprises:

-   mainstream youth organisations which include a focus on Travellers in their work with the disadvantaged or have special Traveller projects;
-   specialist organisations which provide youth work programmes designed specifically for and/or with Travellers;
-   the youth activities established through the National Lottery, delivered through the National Association of Training Centres using the senior training centres as the focus.

In addition to the youth services provided by mainstream youth organisations there are a range of projects for Travellers which have developed in an ad hoc way which include the following:

- St Brigid's Welfare Centre, Waterford;
- Education and Social Project, Hillside, Galway;
- Fairgreen Crafts Co-op Project, Galway;
- Education Committee for Travellers Pre-school Project, Galway;
- Emergency Programme for Young Travellers at Risk, Galway;
- Travellers Training and Education Committee, Tullamore, Co. Offaly;
- Personal and Social Development Programme for Young Travellers at St Mary's CBS Tralee, Co. Kerry
- Roscommon and Mayo Projects;
- Special Programmes for Young Travellers in New Ross and Bunclody, Co. Wexford;
- Special Programmes for Young Travellers, Cashel, Co. Tipperary;
- Travellers' Committee Youth Project, Navan, Co. Meath;
- St Angela's Convent Hygiene and Nutrition Programme; Castlebar, Co. Mayo;
- Youth Work Project, Dublin Travellers Education and Development Group, (Pavee Point), Dublin;
- Sub-Committee for Youth Affairs, Dublin Committee for Travelling People, Dublin;
- Trudder House After Care Programme, Dublin Committee for Travelling People, Co. Wicklow;
- Youth Services, National Association of Training Centres.

There is a need to ensure that these services are in line with the principles and standards which are outlined elsewhere in this section.

9(b)7. Recommendations

FR.128 The Task Force welcomes the commitment in the Green Paper on Education (op. cit, 12) to:

- develop a comprehensive integrated youth work service across the country;
- target resources for disadvantaged people;
- improve mechanisms for grant-aiding;
- agree mechanisms for monitoring and evaluating youth work;
- identify criteria of excellence.

It is important, however, that Traveller youth are given explicit mention in youth service provision and not just assume that the "disadvantaged" category will automatically ensure that the needs of Travellers are adequately and appropriately addressed. This means explicit targeting of resources for appropriate Traveller projects, and appropriate inclusion of Travellers. It also involves clear monitoring and evaluation mechanisms.

FR.129 The Department of Education should:

- ensure that youth work with Travellers is based on an analysis of the needs of Travellers. In order to achieve this the Department should commission a review of existing provision, identify gaps in the service, and formulate guidelines for policy and standardisation of support services;

–   promote the development of a clearer understanding of youth work with Travellers based on a set of values and principles which have been identified as prerequisites for good practice;

–   ensure that youth work projects should be required to operate from within a written Code of Practice which reflects the principles and values of youth work including respect for Traveller identity and a recognition of the special needs of Travellers.

Organisations involved in the delivery of youth services to Travellers should be funded on the basis of their capacity to deliver a good quality service in accordance with the process and values outlined in this section.

FR.130   The Department of Education should consolidate youth work practice by providing grants for a three year period, subject to fulfilment of annual contractual requirements, including evidence of satisfactory progress and financial accountability. Funding should be provided to cover salaries of youth workers and programme activities. Under the present system it is very difficult or impossible for voluntary organisations to pay wage increases because insurance premiums and programme funding have to be taken from the same grant allocation.

FR.131   The European Youth Campaign against Racism, Xenophobia, Intolerance and Anti-semitism organised by the Council of Europe, the UNESCO International Year of Tolerance, and the EU Year of Racial Harmony make 1995 an opportune year for ensuring that youth work addresses the issue of discrimination, and, in particular, racism. This opportunity should be grasped to ensure that young Travellers are accepted, included and treated as equal citizens in Irish society and that youth organisations are aware of the implications for youth work practice.

FR.132   There is need to give recognition to the value and contribution of youth work. The Task Force welcomes therefore the commitment in the Government programme "A Government of Renewal" (op. cit. 18) to provide a statutory basis for youth work in Ireland. The primary role of youth work as informal education would thereby be reinforced in this process. However, it is especially important for Travellers that the priority role of youth work as informal education is reinforced in this process. The Education Act which is expected to follow the White Paper should link the youth service to the relevant education authorities.

FR.133   The Department of Education with the other relevant Departments should ensure that an integrated inter-departmental approach is achieved between youth work, childcare, sports and recreation, home/school links, the Juvenile Liaison Scheme, literacy and other adult education schemes. This integrated approach should be reflected in structures at national and local level.

FR.134   An effective and appropriate youth service with Travellers should be based on a social education model containing such values as: respect, co-operation, participation, consultation, responsibility, empowerment and equality. Youth work with Travellers should avoid any connotations of a rescue mission for the deprived or a top down social control approach.

FR.135 Funding should be provided to cover salaries of youth workers and also programme activities.

FR.136 (a) It is essential that training for youth workers is provided and adequately resourced. Such training, to include pre-service and in-service, would ensure a professional approach whether workers are unpaid volunteers or paid workers.

(b) In order to sensitise and develop a better understanding of Travellers' needs and concerns, in-service training programmes should be a requirement of all youth projects and organisations. Such programmes should be designed to assist youth workers and youth organisations to develop an intercultural approach and to promote good relations with Travellers.

FR.137 Special efforts on the basis of positive action should be made to resource Travellers to acquire the training necessary to become youth workers. It should be noted that in Section G on the Traveller Economy, youth workers are included among the identified posts for public service employment for Travellers.

FR.138 There is an ongoing danger that young Travellers may be targeted in disadvantaged youth projects but in practice not included or very marginally present in mainstream youth organisations. Therefore, integrated youth projects in receipt of funding for work with young Travellers should specify actions and objectives in their proposed programmes and provide explicit information about results in order to ensure accountability.

FR.139 The special youth work needs of Travellers should be met by a community based service supported and managed by a local voluntary committee in partnership with the Vocational Education Committees. Such local committees should foster a community youth work approach as recommended in the various reports referred to in this section.

FR.140 Young Travellers are not a homogenous group and it is important that the different needs of young men and young women are acknowledged. It is also important that youth work as informal education challenges sex-stereotyping and promotes respect and responsibility between the sexes.

9(c) **Senior Traveller Training Centres**

9(c)1. **Background**

9(c)1.1 There are twenty-eight Senior Traveller Training Centres located in nineteen counties in the State. The first Centre was opened in Ennis in 1974. Thirteen more were opened within another decade and the remaining fourteen were established within a further few years.

9(c)1.2 The administration of these Centres is the joint responsibility of the Department of Education, through the V.E.C.'s, and FÁS. They are managed locally through community based management committees, which include the Chief Executive Officer of the V.E.C., the FÁS External Training Manager, or his/her representative, representatives of Travellers and Traveller organisations and representatives of interested groups in the local 'Settled' community.

9(c)1.3 Each year approximately 600 Travellers participate in the forty-eight week training programme provided in these Centres. The ages of these Travellers generally range from fifteen to twenty-five years and in recent years there has been an increasing number of Travellers who are over twenty-five years attending these Centres. This contrasts with the low participation of Travellers in mainstream training centres. Some Senior Traveller Training Centres have lists of Travellers awaiting entry to their programmes. Other Senior Traveller Training Centres have at various times provided for the participation of 'Settled' trainees in their training programmes.

9(c)1.4 There are various reasons why Travellers find these Centres attractive, apart from the training allowance, which they could receive in mainstream training centres but which does not attract them there. Travellers find Senior Traveller Training Centres secure and supportive. This results from a combination of factors such as the attitude of staff, the predominance of Travellers in the Centre, the trainee-centred method of instruction and even the scale of the physical environment.

Many find the emphasis on practical work attractive. In some Centres the valuing and celebration of Traveller culture increases Travellers' self-esteem and this enhances the attractiveness of the Centres. Many, particularly the older Travellers, appreciate the opportunity to acquire an education which they did not receive in their earlier years. The predominantly practical training programme, together with the training allowance is seen as more attractive than school to the adult status which Travellers acquire much earlier than their 'Settled' counterparts. In contrast with schools, which cost money, training centres are a source of family income.

9(c)1.5 Originally Senior Traveller Training Centres were established as another means of integrating Travellers into the 'Settled' community. Their original aim was to prepare Travellers to secure regular full-time employment in the mainstream labour market.

To qualify for funding each Centre had to achieve over eighty per cent placement of trainees in employment at the end of their forty-eight weeks of training. The industrial training authority was assigned responsibility for a substantial part of the training programme. The Department of Education was responsible for the remainder: literacy and numeracy. Eighty per cent of the training programme consisted of vocational skills training and approximately twenty per cent was devoted to literacy and numeracy. The vocational skills programme usually included industrial sewing, woodwork, welding and metalwork, typing and a variety of crafts. However, because of limitations of staffing it was not generally possible to match these subjects to the interests and aptitudes of individual trainees, nor were subjects necessarily related to perceived employment opportunities in the Traveller Training Centre location.

This original programme had a major impact on establishing the ethos of these Centres and, despite later efforts to develop a more relevant programme, this has persisted in many ways to the present time. It is evident with hindsight that the original aim of securing full-time employment for the majority of trainee Travellers was both unrealistic and inappropriate considering the general prejudice which existed towards Travellers in a rapidly decreasing employment market, the fact that there continues to exist in the Traveller culture a preference to enter into the Traveller economy and particularly the fact that the period of training allowed to achieve this aim was much too short.

9(c)1.6 The Travelling People Review Body Report (op. cit, 25) recognised the need to broaden the training programme in Senior Traveller Training Centres in order to meet the needs of Travellers. The Report stated that *"While the objective of these Training Centres is to prepare for employment, it is recognised that the need for Centres arose primarily from the educational deprivation of the young Traveller"*. For this reason the Review Body considered that the Department of Education, with its responsibility for providing education and its experience in vocational education and training programmes, was the appropriate Department to which State responsibility for training programmes should be assigned. This recommendation was never implemented and its merit continues to be debated. The fact that this debate has not been resolved has impeded the necessary development of the Senior Traveller Training Centre programme.

9(c)1.7.1 In 1984 a reassessment of the training programme was carried out in the preparation of a Code of Practice for these Centres by the National Association of Travellers Training Centres (NATC) (Ref. 44) and the State agencies involved in the provision of this service.

The Code states that *"the over-riding goal of Training Centres for Travellers is to help them to develop their full potential, to break the cycle of illiteracy and deprivation in which they are trapped and to enable them to become, as soon as possible, self-reliant and self-supporting members of society"*.

The Code recognised the need to enable Travellers *"to discover and attain their own aspirations"* and to give them the freedom to make real choices about their future way of life. The Code noted the importance of complementing technical skills training with personal development, but the education as distinct from the training aspect of the programme was still described in terms of literacy and numeracy. Self-employment, described as *"work-activities"* which young Travellers might take up on leaving the Centre, was also acknowledged as a valid objective of training, but the primary emphasis remained on preparation for future full-time paid employment.

9(c)1.7.2 The new training aims and objectives set out in the 1984 Code of Practice were a significant advance on the original programme for Traveller Training Centres but they have remained largely an unattainable ideal because the necessary resources were not provided to achieve them.

9(c)1.7.3 The Code failed to acknowledge that for the greater majority of Travellers entering the programme the forty-eight weeks provided to achieve these objectives were very inadequate. It provides little more than an induction in which pre-training takes place. This has been a constant source of frustration to both the staff and trainees, who find it demoralising to have to abandon the training programme at that point.

210

9(c)1.7.4 In 1989, representatives of FÁS and the Department of Education, at the instigation of NATC, prepared a second year programme for these Centres. However, the piloting of this programme in seven selected Centres was postponed indefinitely pending a decision on whether FÁS or the Department of Education should have the sole responsibility for the administration of Senior Traveller Training Centres. This matter has not yet been resolved.

9(c)1.7.5 The full achievement of the changes proposed in the 1984 Code of Practice was also hindered by the failure to facilitate the type of staff development necessary to achieve them. The Code set out a new training methodology based on an AnCO training programme for early school leavers. This methodology was not suitable to the needs of trainees. It presupposed a level of self-knowledge and maturity which the majority of trainees did not have.

9(c)2. Achievements of Training Centres

9(c)2.1 Senior Traveller Training Centres could obviously have achieved more if they had been resourced differently in the past decade, nonetheless their achievements have not been insignificant. These Centres have contributed significantly to the development of local leadership and consciousness raising among Travellers.

They have provided the encouragement and inspiration for emerging local Traveller leadership in various parts of the country. Traveller Training Centres have enabled many Travellers to acquire a basic education which has compensated somewhat for the incredible shortfall in education that many experienced through primary school. The majority of the Travellers who have attended Senior Traveller Training Centres are parents of the current generation of primary school Traveller children. Their training experience encourages them to value and foster the education of these children.

9(c)2.2 In recent years there has been an increasing recognition of the importance of offering training in Senior Traveller Training Centres from the perspective of Travellers' distinct culture. Increasingly Traveller Training Centres are encouraging and developing Traveller leadership, independence and self-reliance by training in a context of pride in their own culture.

9(c)2.3 In recent years, Traveller Training Centres have been involved in enterprises which employ Travellers. A Traveller co-operative in Galway city, which produces flags and banners was developed through the local Traveller Training Centre. Currently Traveller enterprises in fashion knitwear, industrial clothing, sulkie fabrication, car valeting, laundry services, jewellery making and patchwork quilting are being developed through Traveller Training Centres. Another Traveller has developed a bridal dress outlet through the skill she acquired in the Traveller Training Centre. The editor of the National Traveller magazine, "The Voice of the Traveller", is a former Traveller Training Centre trainee. Two Traveller teachers in Training Centres were formerly trainees in Traveller Training Centres.

9(c)2.4 Despite the fact that the limitation on the time available for training generally restricts the education and training offered to a very basic level, several Travellers who were interested in employment, have secured regular steady employment through the Traveller Training Centres. This number, however, is small relative to the total number of participants in these Centres.

9(c)2.5 In addition to their training role, most Senior Traveller Training Centres also serve as valuable resource centres within the local Traveller community. They provide information on Traveller issues, such as: legal entitlements, actions against discrimination, Traveller publications, networking with regional and national Traveller organisations, and information on Traveller social activities in other locations. These Centres also promote local community youth development programmes and in many locations the development of local community youth leaders. There are currently eleven such community youth leaders and it is planned to increase this to eighteen in the coming year.

9(c)2.6 In a small number of Traveller Training Centres weaknesses have been identified by the Task Force and by the NEXUS Research Co-operative research project commissioned by the Task Force (Ref. 45) such as failure to recognise cultural identity, gender stereotyping, quality of training and inadequate management practices. Such weaknesses must be clearly identified and action taken to overcome them.

9(c)3.   Future Development

9(c)3.1 The development of Senior Traveller Training Centres should be based on the following principles:

- Senior Traveller Training Centres are not and should not be developed as an alternative second-level education system to the mainstream provision but rather as a form of adult and second chance education for a community where young people are considered adult at an early age.

- All Travellers have a right to education and training which is culturally appropriate to them and which responds to their needs.

- Every individual Traveller has the right to be literate and numerate, to have a minimum basic education and to have the resources and length of training time required to provide this.

- All Travellers have a right to the provision of training to a nationally certified quality standard of training which carries national currency.

- Every training programme in Senior Traveller Training Centres, and the ethos of these Centres, must aim at developing self-reliance, independence and pride in their identity.

- There must be sufficient flexibility in the administrative regulations for Traveller Training Centres so as to ensure that the training system meets the needs of the individuals whom it serves.

9(c)4.   Training Administration

9(c)4.1   The Traveller community has a distinct culture which is expressed through social and economic activities in a way which is different to that of the 'Settled' community. The aim, or purpose, of Senior Traveller Training Centres should be to promote the development of human resources within the adult Traveller community so as to enable this community to develop its own cultural, social and economic well-being as an integral part of Irish society. Therefore it would be more accurate to describe these Centres as Traveller Development Centres, rather than Training Centres, which will better reflect what happens there.

9(c)4.2   The development of Senior Traveller Training Centres throughout the country has been uneven. It has usually been proportionate to the resourcefulness of the Centre director and staff. It is obvious to most directors that these Centres need serious development if they are to be enabled to fully achieve the purpose which they should serve. The people working in these Centres have significant experience which could contribute to their development in a way which would make them more relevant to the real needs of Travellers, but there is no adequate mechanism at a national level to monitor the performance, analyse the needs and promote the development of these Centres. The National Association of Traveller Centres (NATC) is trying to fulfil this function but it has not the resources to do it adequately.

9(c)4.3   NATC represents the management and staff in Senior Traveller Training Centres. Its functions include negotiating with statutory bodies and development of the curriculum of Centres in response to the needs of Travellers. This function has been endorsed in the past by the State agencies involved in the provision of this training service. However, because there are two State bodies involved, viz. the Department of Education and FÁS, and because there is no clearly established structure for joint consultation between these and NATC, the development of these Centres is not being promoted efficiently. Another factor contributing to this has been the lack of a National Co-Ordinator for Travellers' Training Centres. As far back as 1983, the Travelling People Review Body Report (op. cit, 25) pointed to the need for a formal structure for co-ordination at national level:

"The training centres have suffered severely in the past from lack of co-ordination of planning and funding at national level. The Review Body proposes the establishment of a Central Co-ordinating Committee to determine policy at national level, undertake long-term planning and co-ordinate applications for......" funding.

The situation has been further complicated by the uncertainty in recent years as to whether the national administration of these Centres should be the sole responsibility of the Department of Education or the Department of Enterprise and Employment through FÁS. There is clearly merit in having both bodies involved but also the disadvantage that inefficiency can result from divided responsibility.

9(c)4.4   It was noted above that the Report of the Travelling People Review Body, (op.cit,25) recommended that, because of its responsibility for providing education in the Centres and its experience in vocational education, the Department of Education should have sole responsibility.

213

9(c)4.5 There are inherent difficulties in organising the development of these Centres where eighty-four per cent of the staff are employees of the Department of Education and the monitoring and development of the Centres' programmes is largely the responsibility of FÁS. The aim set out above for these Centres could be achieved more efficiently and effectively were their full administration placed under one Government Department.

9(c)4.6 The longer term development of Senior Traveller Training Centres may not be best served by over dependence for funding on European Union sources. For the most part the State has incurred minimal expenditure on the education of the adult Traveller community, which these Centres should serve. Therefore they should be funded more directly by the Department of Education in line with the mainstream services of that Department.

9(c)4.7 As human resource development centres promoting the cultural and social development of the Traveller community, these Centres would be better located under the direct administration of the Department of Education. The Department of Enterprise and Employment through FÁS should continue to have responsibility for assisting with the work of the Centres in promoting the economic development of this community.

9(c)5. National Co-ordinator

9(c)5.1 The development of Senior Traveller Training Centres was assisted through the National Co-Ordinator for Travellers' Education. When this post was vacated several years ago the development of these Centres suffered for want of a person at national level with the authority and resources to monitor the performance, analyse the needs and promote the development of these Centres, similar to the Department of Education National Co-ordinator for the Youthreach Programme. It is necessary that this work be carried out on a national level because these Training Centres serve the needs of a small community of people which is located in various parts of the country. Many of these Centres are remote from each other and they could benefit greatly from a national co-ordination service which would disseminate good practice and promote good standards. There is no official in the Department of Education to whom this function is currently entrusted.

9(c)6 Recommendations

FR.141 **(a)** The Department of Education should be assigned responsibility for the full administration of Senior Traveller Training Centres in accordance with the policy for these Centres set out by this Task Force. This recommendation is made on the basis that it will have no negative implications in relation to the funding of the Centres and of training allowances, including the provision of EU funding.

(b) It is important that FÁS continue to accept responsibility for promoting and resourcing the development of the employment and enterprise needs of the Traveller community at regional level. This should include the appointment of FÁS representatives to local Traveller Training Centre Management Committees. Such representatives should advise the Centres on resources available through FÁS for promoting this development and promote the progression of trainees from Traveller Training Centres to mainline training courses in FÁS Training Centres, whenever this is the desired option of such trainees.

FR.142 The Department of Education should appoint a National Co-ordinator to promote the development and monitor the performance of Senior Traveller Training Centres. The person appointed should have a clear commitment to Travellers' development, and knowledge of the development of Traveller Training Centres and proven management and facilitation skills.

FR.143 The National Association of Traveller Training Centres should have the authority to advise the Department of Education and FÁS on the running of Senior Traveller Training Centres. This should include representation on the Advisory Group of the TES.

FR.144 The Code of Practice for Senior Traveller Training Centres should be revised in accordance with the policy set out by the Task Force through consultation between the Department of Education, FÁS and NATC.

9(c)7. Management Committees

9(c)7.1 Management Committees of Traveller Training Centres should be re-organised in line with the Task Force policy for these Centres as follows:

9(c)7.2 **Membership:** Each Training Centre will have a community based Management Committee consisting of the following members:

– One representative of each of the following:

- V.E.C. (either the C.E.O. or a member);
- FÁS;
- the Health Board Community Care Department;
- the local authority;
- local Department of Social Welfare
- a Traveller organisation.

Each Management Committee will contain:

- a minimum of two Travellers;
- the Centre Director;
- a Centre Staff Representative;
- a trainee representative;
- four representatives of the local community (such as Chamber of Commerce, Trades Unions and Rotary).

All members shall have a clear commitment to the social, cultural and economic well-being of the Traveller community.

9(c)7.3 **Officers:** Officers shall be elected from the Committee and shall hold office for two years. No officer shall be re-elected to the same office for more than two terms consecutively.

The officers of the Management Committee shall be Chairperson, Assistant Chairperson, Secretary, Assistant Secretary, Treasurer and Assistant Treasurer.

9(c)7.4 **Role of Management Committee:** The Management Committee shall provide effective management of the local Centre in accordance with the policy set out by the Task Force. The Committee shall prepare an annual Centre plan which shall include budget requirements.

The National Co-ordinator, the appointment of whom is proposed above and in FR.142, shall inform the Management Committee of the annual financial allocation to the Centre. This allocation shall reflect the budgetary requirements set out by the Committee.

9(c)7.5 **Duties of the Management Committee**

The duties of the Management Committee shall include:

–   Preparation of annual Centre Plan and budget.
–   Mobilisation of external community resources.
–   Ensuring high quality standards in the following:

*   an environment conducive to a high quality programme and safety standards;
*   a programme conducive to the development of the social, cultural and economic well-being of the Traveller community;
*   appointment of all staff, who shall have disposition, skills or expertise to ensure delivery of a quality programme;
*   in-service training of staff to meet the ongoing development needs of the Centre.
*   placement of trainees.
*   ensuring the active participation in the National Association of Traveller Training Centres through the elected representatives of Management Committees.

9(c)7.6 **Review of Management Committees**

It shall be the responsibility of the National Co-ordinator to review the composition and function of all Management Committees to ensure that they operate according to the policy set out by the Task Force.

9(c)8. **Traveller Participation in Development Processes**

9(c)8.1 Traveller participation is essential for the successful development of Training Centre policy both nationally and locally because the programmes offered in these Centres must meet the distinct cultural and development needs of Travellers.

9(c)8.2 It is only through full participation in policy-making that Travellers can establish their independence and right to self-determination.

9(c)8.3 The Code of Practice for Training Centres (op. cit, 44) provides for Traveller membership of local Management Committees. The extent of this representation of Travellers varies. In some areas it is very good, in some it is non-existent. While it can be difficult, especially in smaller Traveller communities, to get Travellers to join management committees, it is imperative that every effort be made to achieve this effectively. Training Centres, through the training programme, should develop trainees' confidence and skills to participate meaningfully in democratic processes.

9(c)9. The Training Programme

9(c)9.1 The training programme offered in Senior Traveller Training Centres must be based on a clear analysis of the interests and needs of the participants and it must be culturally appropriate.

Such needs may include:

- education to compensate for earlier educational deprivation;
- education in Traveller culture, history and language and traditional crafts;
- personal development;
- development of the critical capacity for social awareness;
- health education;
- child development and care;
- development of leadership capacity;
- vocational skill training either as an end in itself or as a means to personal development and development of transferable skills;
- development of entrepreneurship and of the Traveller economy (this may range from training in basic business methods to development of an enterprise project).

Clearly such a programme requires a capacity for flexibility in its deliverance.

9(c)10. Duration of Training

9(c)10.1 As noted above, forty-eight weeks is definitely not a sufficient period in which to meet the average training needs of Travellers who enrol in Senior Traveller Training Centres. For most participants this time will merely meet their induction. The average Traveller will require a minimum of three years training in order to compensate him/her adequately for his/her previous educational and social deprivation. Training Centres must have flexibility in this regard.

9(c)10.2 The fact that a longer period of training is available to educationally disadvantaged 'Settled' people on the Youthreach training programme reinforces the belief of many Travellers that they are being discriminated against by State agencies and that the special training provision for them in Senior Traveller Training Centres is no more than a token excuse for a more adequate service.

9(c)10.3 If the duration of training is restricted by the sources of funds, such as EU social funding, this should be changed so that these Centres can be funded directly from the exchequer in line with other mainline education services.

9(c)10.4 Extension of the period of training will require an increase in teaching resources in Centres.

9(c)11   Age of Trainees

9(c)11.1 The Code of Practice for Traveller Training Centres (op. cit, 44) states that *"trainees are normally aged between sixteen and twenty-five years. When deemed necessary by the Management Committee young persons aged fifteen years may be accommodated"*.

9(c)11.2 In recent years most Centres have experienced an increasing demand for admission by Travellers who are over twenty-five years, but for budgetary reasons there have been restrictions on the admission of Travellers in this age group. There should be no upper age limit for admission to Senior Traveller Training Centres. The Travellers, who are over eighteen years, who attend Training Centres are mainly women. Occasionally Traveller men, who are over eighteen years, express interest in attending Training Centres but they are deterred by the effect this might have on their social welfare entitlements.

9(c)11.3 It is important to provide incentives and opportunities for Traveller men to progress their education on a par with Traveller women. The NEXUS Research Co-Operative's "Report of National Study on the Travelling Community" (op. cit, 45) commissioned by this Task Force states: *"Given the traditional power dynamics of Traveller families, where, for instance, the men make the major decisions in relation to movement etc. women with too much education are perceived as a threat, with a direct correlation between level of education and chance of marriage"*. This was expressed succinctly by some women in Location 1 *"girls with too much learning"* might be frowned upon and their chances of *"getting a husband lessened"*.

9(c)11.4 This Report recommends the *"introduction of flexibility of social welfare payments to Travellers to supplement income without penalty (in line with initiatives in regard to the small farming community and the homeless community)"*.

9(c)11.5 As an incentive to Travellers to access programmes which will improve their education and training, allowances for trainees in Traveller Training Centres need to be increased to reflect the true costs of participation and to provide adequate incentives over and above social welfare entitlements.

9(c)11.6 It has been noted elsewhere in this section that the participation of Travellers in formal education, particularly in post-primary education, is extremely low relative to that of the 'Settled' population. As education is one of the major agents of development in any society, action which will seriously promote educational development in the Traveller community should be supported. Role modelling of parents and older siblings has been a significant method of education within traditional Traveller culture. Therefore, incentives to encourage the educational development of older Traveller adults, especially of older male Travellers, should be positively supported. If parents experience the value of education for themselves, they will become better role models for younger Travellers and they will also value better and foster the education of their children.

9(c)11.7 Traveller Training Centres should not be developed as alternative education centres to mainstream second-level schools for Travellers who are qualified to attend mainline schools, and whose development needs can be best provided by such schools.

9(c)11.8 Training Centres are adult and continuing education centres in accordance with the definition of the Report of the Commission on Adult Education, (op. cit, 28):

"Adult Education includes all systematic learning by adults which contributes to their development as individuals and as members of ....society apart from full-time instruction received by persons as part of their uninterrupted initial education and training".

9(c)11.9 In accordance with the principle contained in this definition, there should be a clearly established termination of mainstream school education by Travellers after they have reached the compulsory school attendance age before they are admitted to Senior Traveller Training Centres or to any other State sponsored training programmes. Parents and the visiting teacher should be consulted to establish that this serves the best interest of the person concerned. Admission to Senior Training Centres should be based on seniority. Older Travellers should be admitted before those who have recently terminated their compulsory education.

9(c)12 Training Methodology

9(c)12.1 An appropriate training methodology for Senior Traveller Training Centres should be developed in consultation between NATC and the State agencies responsible for the provision of this service. This methodology should include:

- Induction training which will develop basic education and pre-training skills of participants.

- For those who have acquired basic education and pre-training skills, an effective participative training methodology which will enable the trainees to develop and take responsibility for their own learning.

9(c)13. Training Standards

9(c)13.1 The training programmes offered in Senior Traveller Training Centres should always be of a very high quality. While it is recognised that not all trainees may be able to achieve an equal standard of training, those programmes should be aimed at nationally recognised standards (such as National Council for Vocational Awards standards). The delivery of the programmes should be externally monitored by an approved Assessment and Certification agency. Certification awarded for these programmes should carry national currency for further progression.

9(c)14 Teaching Staff

9(c)14.1 The teaching staff in Senior Traveller Training Centres should demonstrate a capacity to empathise and work with Travellers, and have a recognised professional qualification appropriate to the subjects which they are teaching and a training or teaching qualification. They should receive in-service training in an understanding of Traveller culture and its implications for their work, if they have not already received this. They should not require any other additional qualification than is required for teaching in the special education services of the Department of Education or in the training services of FÁS and the health boards.

9(c)14.2 Existing members of staff, who have proven their commitment and suitability over a period of three years, but who do not possess the relevant professional qualifications, should be assisted in acquiring them through appropriate staff development programmes.

9(c)14.3 There should be a determined pro-active effort by the vocational education committees, which are responsible under the Department of Education for the staffing of Traveller Training Centres, to recruit staff from suitable members of the Traveller community to fill any vacancy which may occur. Such vacancies should also be advertised nationally among the Traveller community.

9(c)14.4 Travellers who have demonstrated their capacity to do the work required in the vacant post should not have to possess all the necessary professional qualifications which would normally be required from members of the 'Settled' community for these posts. While holding these posts they should be resourced to acquire professional qualifications. In order to encourage and provide opportunities for Travellers to access these positions, posts of assistant teachers/instructors should be developed in Senior Traveller Training Centres through Community Employment or other incentive schemes. This should be done within the strategies on the Traveller Economy which provide for special apprenticeships.

9(c)14.5 Future Traveller Training Centre Directors should have a third-level education, or equivalent, and competency in education management.

9(c)14.6 The conditions of employment of staff in Senior Traveller Training Centres fall seriously short of those of staff in similar special education or training centres or in mainline training and education services. Many highly professional members of staff in Traveller Centres have given very dedicated service to Traveller Centres under temporary employment conditions and for remuneration which is substantially less than their colleagues in other similar services. This is not conducive to provision of a good professional service as has been proven by the fact that many of the best teachers and directors have been constrained to leave these Centres because of their conditions of employment.

9(c)14.7 This also reflects a practice of the marginalisation and under-valuing of the Traveller community. The conditions of pay and employment of staff in Senior Traveller Training Centres should be reviewed immediately so as to provide permanent pensionable employment and a pay structure and other conditions of employment which is on parity with staff in other mainline training and education Centres under FÁS and the Departments of Health and Education.

9(c)14.8 Senior Traveller Training Centres must not be used at the expense of existing staff to redeploy teachers, who may become redundant in mainline education services or who may not have the necessary personal qualities for posts in these Centres.

9(c)15   Training Centre Premises and Training Resources

9(c)15.1 The NEXUS Research Co-operative Report on the Travelling Community, (op. cit, 45) notes:

"Our survey showed that in almost all locations, buildings were in very poor condition and resources wholly inadequate to meet the needs of the Travelling population in this area.

This inadequate sub-standard provision only served to reinforce the Travellers belief that they are being discriminated against and being treated as inferior to the settled community. For example, in Locations 6 and 12, the Traveller Workshop was located in part of a school building and through observation and interviews it was apparent that the conditions of these workshops were below the overall standards of the school in terms of general repair and decoration".

This observation is further reinforced by the fact that obsolete equipment which is being replaced in mainline services has often been transferred to Senior Traveller Training Centres.

9(c)15.2 The NEXUS Report recommends that national standards be applied to all Traveller Training Workshop facilities. The Task Force recommends that measures be put in place without delay to bring all Traveller Training Centre premises up to mainline national standards and to make available an adequate level of other resources, such as teaching equipment, in all these Centres.

9(c)16   Training for Enterprise

9(c)16.1 Traditionally self-employment was a key feature of Traveller culture and way of life and the pursuit of enterprise remains very strong among modern Travellers. Training for enterprise development should be offered in every Senior Traveller Training Centre.

9(c)16.2 The State agencies, which provide the Senior Traveller Training Centre service, in conjunction with NATC, should develop a suitable culturally appropriate enterprise training programme for these Centres. Provision should also be made adjacent to these Training Centres for small enterprise units, which will be available to Travellers as incubator units for enterprise development for a limited period of time on a phased rental scale, if appropriate.

9(c)17   Mixed Traveller Training Centres

9(c)17.1 In some locations in the country the Traveller community may not be sufficiently large to require the standard twenty-five training places. In the past in such instances 'Settled' people have been admitted to the training places not required by Travellers provided they have not achieved a second-level educational qualification. This has contributed positively to developing mutual understanding and respect between Traveller and 'Settled' participants. Local Traveller communities have generally welcomed this arrangement as a means of giving such access to a Senior Traveller Training Centre. However, in some instances, some Traveller parents have

221

expressed concern that young 'Settled' offenders referred through the Probation Service have been admitted to these Centres and might influence their children. There has also been some concern that priority may not always have been given to Travellers over 'Settled' people in admitting Travellers to these Centres. These are valid concerns, therefore in Senior Traveller Training Centres:

– Travellers must always be given priority in admission, except where there is evidence of an individual's inability or unwillingness to follow the Centre programme. Where this is disputed the decision should rest with the Management Committee.

– Senior Traveller Training Centres are not geared to cater for the specific needs of young offenders.

– Priority must be given to the cultural needs of Travellers and Traveller development must be the main focus of the Centre programme.

9(c)18   The Code of Practice

9(c)18.1 The Code of Practice for Traveller Training Centres (op. cit 44), which was jointly developed in 1984 by the Department of Education, AnCO, and the National Association of Traveller Training Centres should be revised to bring it into line with the recommendations set out by this Task Force.

9(c)19   Senior Traveller Training Centres

In addition to paragraph 9(c)6 above, the following is a summary of the recommendations set out on Senior Traveller Training Centres.

Recommendations

FR.145 A determined effort should be made to develop full Traveller participation in the Management Committees of Senior Traveller Training Centres.

FR.146 The training programme in every Centre must be based on a clear analysis of Travellers' interests and needs and it must be culturally appropriate to them.

FR.147 A minimum of three years' training should be available to Travellers in Senior Training Centres and teaching resources should be increased appropriately.

FR.148 There should not be an upper age limit on Travellers attending Traveller Training Centres. Older Travellers should be encouraged and facilitated to attend.

FR.149 Mechanisms should be developed to promote progression of trainees from Senior Traveller Training Centres into a range of mainstream and other options.

FR.150 Where mixed Traveller Training Centres are in operation:

(a)   priority should be given to the recruitment of Traveller trainees which should be ensured through a range of flexibilities including:

> (i) holding places for Travellers who are temporarily absent from an area;
>
> (ii) varying the maximum enrolment numbers.
>
> (b) Priority should be given to cultural needs of Traveller trainees.
>
> (c) It should be recognised that these Centres are not geared to the specific needs of young offenders.

FR.151 Allowances for trainees in Traveller Training Centres need to be increased to reflect the true costs of participation and to provide adequate incentives over and above social welfare entitlements.

FR.152 An appropriate training methodology for Senior Traveller Training Centres should be developed.

FR.153 Training programmes offered in Traveller Centres should be to nationally recognised standards which should be externally monitored by an approved certification agency.

FR.154 All teaching staff in Traveller Centres should have a proven ability to empathise and work with Travellers and have recognised professional qualifications.

FR.155 Resources should be available to all Centres for ongoing staff development.

FR.156 There should be a determined pro-active effort to train and recruit Traveller teachers to the staff of Training Centres.

FR.157 Measures should be put in place without delay to bring all Traveller Training Centre premises up to mainstream national standards and to make available an adequate level of other resources, such as teaching equipment, in all these centres.

FR.158 A culturally appropriate enterprise training and development programme should be developed for Senior Traveller Training Centres.

FR.159 All members of staff in the Senior Training Centres should receive in-service training in an understanding of Traveller culture and its implications for their work, if they have not already received such training.

FR.160 Traveller Training Centre Directors should have at least a third-level qualification, or equivalent, and should have competency in education management.

FR.161 The conditions of pay and employment of staff in Senior Traveller Training Centres should be reviewed immediately so as to provide permanent pensionable employment and a pay structure and other conditions of employment which are on parity with staff in other mainstream training and education centres under FÁS and the Departments of Health and Education.

FR.162 Incubator enterprise development units should be provided adjacent to Training Centres, where appropriate.

FR.163 The name of Senior Traveller Training Centres should be changed to Traveller Development Centres.

FR.164 Management Committees should be organised in the Senior Traveller Training Centres in accordance with the policy set out in Section 9(c)7 above.

10. Traveller Education
Collection and Collation of Statistics

10.1. General

10.1.1 In carrying out its examination and analysis of educational provision for Travellers in the State, the Task Force noted the lack of availability of reliable and up to date statistical data on Traveller participation in the education system.

10.1.2 While some statistical data is available in the Department of Education on pre-school and primary educational provision and participation rates in respect of the Traveller community, no detailed statistical information is available about Traveller participation in second-level, adult and third-level education and in Junior and Senior Training Centres.

10.1.3 The availability of up to date and reliable statistics on Traveller participation in the Irish education system at all levels is essential, particularly if progess is to be monitored in relation to the implementation of the recommendations on education provision in the Task Force Report.

10.1.4 There is also a lack of statistical data on Travellers on the basis of gender and this makes it difficult to evaluate the relative participation and outcomes for Traveller boys and girls in the education system.

10.2 Recommendations

FR.165 In order to monitor the progess of Traveller participation in the education system, the Task Force recommends that a detailed examination should be carried out of the systems at present in place in the Department of Education at all education levels, for the collection and collation of statistics on Traveller participation rates. It is particularly essential that this review be carried out at pre-school, primary and second-levels of the education system and take cognisance of the gender make up of Traveller pupils. This examination should be undertaken by an expert statistician who should recommend changes which need to be put in place in the statisical collection system in the Department of Education so as to ensure that detailed statistics on Traveller participation rates are available at all education levels and are updated on an annual basis.

FR.166 When the Report of the expert statistician is available, the necessary resources should be allocated by the Department of Education to ensure that any changes which are required in relation to statistical collection arrangements are implemented.

11 Role of Ombudsman

11.1 Since its establishment, the Office of the Ombudsman has made a significant contribution to the development of public administration in Ireland and has provided a valuable channel to the public for obtaining rectification of grievances in relation to their dealings with the public sector.

11.2 Recommendation

FR.167 The Task Force notes that Vocational Education Committees continue to be excluded from the ambit of the Ombudsman Act 1980 and recommends that the second schedule of that Act be amended to remove the exemptions to Vocational Education Committees.

Appendix F (1)

Possible Costs of Second-Level Education

Many Traveller children suffer from the same financial disadvantages as other children from low income families, but the degree of disadvantage is often greater due to the absence of a school going network. For example:

(i)   School books for the first year, for example, can cost up to £170.00, clothing up to £160.00 and school extras up to £150.00.

(ii)   First year students study a wide variety of subjects each requiring text books which are individually expensive with a short "shelf-life" and subject to frequent change.

(iii)   The School Book Rental Scheme is not organised uniformly and evenly. Throughout Ireland qualifying criteria vary from school to school.

(iv)   School uniforms are cost effective long-term, but create a financial crisis when purchased at the same time (August/September).

(v)   School extras place a constant but unplanable financial drain on parents. Not being able to participate in school sports etc. can increase a sense of alienation.

Appendix F (2)

Education for Travellers aged 12-15

Agreement between Department of Education and ad hoc Group, Association of CEO's of Vocational Education Committees

July 1993

Policy

1.1   The provision in mainstream second-level schools for the special educational needs of travellers is the optimum desirable arrangement.

1.2   All post-primary schools have a responsibility to recognise and meet the educational needs of travellers.

1.3   Many travellers leaving primary school are not in a position to benefit from mainstream second-level provision even with additional support and curricular adjustments.

1.4   Special units to be referred to as Junior Post-Primary Education Centres for Travellers designed specifically for the educational needs of travellers aged 12-15, are an essential requirement in the existing situation in many locations.

1.5   Currently twelve (12) special units exist catering for approximately 300 of the estimated 2,000 traveller children eligible. A further 4-5% of the total are in post-primary schools.

Management Structures for Junior/Secondary Education Centre

A variety of management/administrative arrangements are in place in existing Centres. The following management structure is recommended:

2.1   The Centres to operate as institutions under the Vocational Education Committee with a Board of Management, a Centre Director and approved allocation of staff and non-pay resources.

2.2   **Composition**

The Board to consist of 12 (approximately) persons representative of the following:
CEO/Nominee (1)
VEC/Member (1)
Local Social Caring Agency (1)
Community/Local Representative/Social Worker/Visiting Teacher (2)
Staff Representative (1)
Centre Director [non voting] (1)
Parents (2)

The Board will be free to co-opt additional members to a maximum of twelve (12) in total.

Duties and Functions

2.3   The Board shall be responsible to the Committee for the management of the Centre in all aspects of its operation.

2.4   The Centre Director shall be responsible for the day to day running of the Centre and act as Secretary to the Board.

2.5   The Board shall ensure the preparation and submission to the Vocational Education Committee of an Annual Education Scheme in respect of the Centre before 1st June each year.

2.6   The Board shall ensure for the preparation and submission to the Vocational Education Committee of an Annual Financial Scheme before 1st April each year.

2.7   The Board shall be allocated an annual budget for its scheme by the Vocational Education Committee.

2.8   The Board shall advise the Vocational Education Committee as to the category of teachers that should be appointed within the approved allocation.

2.9   Following consultation with interested groups in the Centre area, the Board shall submit recommendations to the Vocational Education Committee as to the development of the Centre and its facilities.

Procedures

2.10   The members of the Board shall, at their first meeting, elect one of their number as Chairman. If the Chairman shall be absent for any meeting, the members shall before any other business is transacted, choose one of their number to preside at that meeting.

(a) The Board shall have a 3 year term.

(b) The Chairperson of the Board shall not hold office for more than two terms.

(c) Any casual vacancy occuring on the Board shall be filled by a representative of the category represented by the person vacating the Board place.

2.11   The Board shall meet at least once per school term. It may hold such other meetings as may be necessary for the efficient discharge of its functions.

2.12   The quorum shall be four (4) members.

2.13   Seven clear days at least before a meeting of the Board, a notice to attend the meeting, specifying the business proposed to be transacted shall be sent by the Secretary, under his signature, to the usual residence of each member of the Board.

2.14   A meeting of the Board may be convened by any five of its members. In the case of such meetings, the notice of the meeting shall be signed by the five members convening the meeting who shall also notify the Secretary.

2.15   The names of the members present at each meeting of the Board should be recorded in the minutes of that meeting.

2.16   Minutes of all meetings of the Board shall be forwarded within seven days to the Vocational Education Committee for consideration.

Conditions of Service

2.17   Permanent appointments may be made utilising allocations for Junior Post-Primary Education Centres provided such appointments are within the total approved allocation for the VEC concerned. Persons proposed for permanent appointment will be required to meet existing requirements for such appointments.

Where appropriate, Eligible Part-time Teaching Contracts will apply.

2.18   Centre Directors will be offered a contract relating to administrative and teaching duties.

3.0   **School Year**

3.1   **Capital Provision**

It is <u>noted</u> that considerable variation in quality of accommodation exists.

Capital and current non-pay items will be treated separately.

'Capital and Equipment' requirements for Centres will be submitted as "emergency" applications to the Department of Education.

3.2   **Non-Pay Provision**

The Department of Education will provide an additional £200 per pupil enroled in Junior Post-Primary Education Centres to meet instruction related non-pay costs in 1993 as an interim non-pay arrangement. The Department of Education requires that this funding be additional to funds currently provided by VECs to Centres.

3.2.1   Non-pay provision for meals, health services etc., provided in some Centres by Health Boards, Local Authorities or others will be sought from such sources for all Centres.

3.2.2   Existing arrangements re Transport will continue. It is open to other centres who have a requirement to make application to the Special Ed/Transport Sections of the Department.

3.3   **Pay Provisions**

3.3.1   The Department of Education offers to provide Pay Resources to Centres on the following basis:

(i)   PTR at 10:1 on enrolments;
(ii) Plus 12 hrs/wk for 36 weeks towards Administration & Co-ordination;
(iii) Plus a Directors allowance equivalent to an "A" Post Allowance.

3.3.2   Existing allocations will remain for a transition period.

3.3.3   A minimum allocation of 2,500 hours per Centre will be available for start-up purposes for new Centres.

3.3.4   It was noted that there would be no change in the employment status of the eight (8) Primary Teachers currently working in Junior Centres.

3.3.5   It was agreed that (National) co-ordination arrangements would be made by the Centres co-operatively from their own resources.

3.3.6   It was agreed that a common approach re 'Care Staff' from the Health Boards would be pursued by the Ad Hoc Group as a separate matter.

July, 1993.

References

1. Interim Progress Report of Task Force on Travelling Community, Dublin, 1994.

2. Report of the Special Education Review Committee: Department of Education Stationery Office, Dublin, 1993.

3. "School Attendance/Truancy Report",: Department of Education Working Group, Dublin, 1994.

4. Green Paper on the European Dimension of Education: Commission of the European Communities: Brussels COM (93) 457 Final, 1993.

5. European Parliament: Committee of Inquiry on Racism and Xenophobia (Ford Report): Office for Official Publications of the European Communities Luxembourg, 1991.

6. Community of Learning: Intercultural Education in Europe: Commission of the European Communities: Brussels, 1994.

7. Report on the Education of Migrants' Children in the European Union: Commission of the European Communities: Com (94) 80 Final, Brussels, 1994.

8. Education and Travellers: Irish Traveller Movement, Dublin, 1993.

9. Report on the Implementation of the EC Resolution (89/C/153/02) on School Provision for Travellers: Department of Education, Dublin, 1993.

10. Submission to Task Force by Association of Teachers of Travelling People (ATTP) Dublin, 1993.

11. From Speech by Minister for Education, Niamh Bhreathnach, T.D. at Conference entitled Intercultural Education - Irish Perspectives, Dublin Castle, May, 1994.

12. Green Paper: Education for a Changing World: Department of Education, Stationery Office, Dublin, 1992.

13. The Education of Traveller Children in National Schools - Guidelines: Department of Education: Stationery Office, Dublin 1994.

14. Programme for Competitiveness and Work: Government of Ireland: Stationery Office, Dublin, 1994.

15. Travellers in Education: Irish National Teachers Organisation: Dublin, 1992.

16. Report of the Department of Education Working Group on Post-Primary Education for Traveller Children, Department of Education, Dublin, 1992.

17. Kenny Mairin, The Education of Children of Gypsies and Travellers: EC Intercultural Education Project; Blackrock Teachers Centre, 1993.

18. A Government of Renewal - A Policy Agreement between Fine Gael, the Labour Party and Democratic Left, Dublin, 1994.

19. Commission on Itinerancy: Report of the Commission on Itinerancy, Stationery Office, Dublin, 1963.

20. Survey, Primary School Inspectorate, Department of Education, Dublin, 1988.

21. Ad hoc Group of the Association of Chief Executive Officers of certain Vocational Education Committees, 1993.

22. Curriculum and Assessment Policy Towards the New Century: NCCA Policy Statements and Recommendations presented to the Minister for Education on issues arising from the publication of the Government's Green Paper "Education for a Changing World": NCCA, Dublin, 1993.

23. "Guidelines for Responding to the Needs of Travellers' Children at Post-Primary level". Submission by ASTI Standing Committee to Department of Education, ASTI, Dublin, 1991.

24. "Education of Children of Travelling Families", Circular 20/88 issued to Boards of Management and Principal teachers of National Schools, Department of Education, 1988.

25. Report of the Travelling People Review Body, Stationery Office, Dublin, 1983.

26. Report of the Primary Education Review Body, Department of Education, Stationery Office, Dublin, 1990.

27. Crickley, A.: Traveller Participation in the Education System: in Equality of Opportunity in Third-level Education in Ireland (Proceedings of Forum held in UCC in November 1993): National Unit on Equal Opportunities at Third-level, UCC, 1994.

28. "Lifelong Learning", Report of the Commission on Adult Education, Stationery Office, Dublin 1983.

29. Clancy, P., Who Goes to College?, Higher Education Authority, Dublin, 1988.

30. Breen, R, Education and the Labour Market - Work and Unemployment Among Recent Cohorts of Irish School Leavers, Paper No. 119, ESRI, Dublin, 1984.

31. Whelan, CT, and Whelan BJ, "Equality of Opportunity in Irish Schools: A Re-Assessment", Economic and Social Review 16(2), 1985.

32. Drudy, S. & Lynch, K, Schools and Society in Ireland, Gill and MacMillan, Dublin, 1993.

33. Freire, P, Pedagogy of the Oppressed, Penguin, New York, 1972.

34. Bunreacht Na hÉireann, Constitution of Ireland, Stationery Office, Dublin, 1937.

35. A Policy for Youth and Sport (Bruton Report), Department of Education, 1977.

36. Final Report of the Task Force on Child Care Services, Department of Health, 1980.

37. Development of Youth Work Services (O'Sullivan Report), Department of Education, 1980.

38. Final Report of the National Youth Policy Committee (Costello Report) Department of Labour, 1984.

39. "In Partnership with Youth", The National Youth Policy, Department of Labour, 1985.

40. Treacy, David "Youth Work Practice in Community-based Projects: A Report for the Youth Affairs and Adult Education Section of the Department of Education", Department of Eduation, 1994.

41. Draft Policy - The Youth Service and Disadvantaged Youth, National Youth Council of Ireland, 1991.

42. Report of the Consultative Group on the Development of Youth Work, Department of Education, Dublin, 1993.

43. Towards the Development of a Comprehensive Youth Service, National Youth Council of Ireland, 1994.

44. Code of Practice for Senior Traveller Training Centres, compiled by Department of Education, AnCO, Youth Employment Agency and National Association of Training Centres for Travellers, 1984.

45. Nexus Research Co-operative, Report of National Study on the Travelling Community prepared for the Task Force on the Travelling Community, 1995.

Section G: Traveller Economy

1. Introduction to the Traveller Economy

1.1 Background

1.1.1 The phrase 'Traveller Economy' refers not only to the range of activities pursued by some Travellers but also to the particular and distinct manner in which these activities are organised. It is an economy that is often invisible to the external observer. Indeed, there is a perception that Travellers are not engaged in economic activities. This perception is mistaken as economic activities continue to play a major role in the life of Travellers. If developed, the Traveller economy could play a significant role in enabling increased numbers of the Traveller community towards financial independence.

1.1.2 The Traveller economy is a service economy. Trading or dealing is one economic activity which involves a broad and varying range of items from antiques to garden gates to carpets. Recycling is another key economic activity. Scrap metal is collected, sorted and sold on. Door to door collections are made for second hand goods which are repaired and sold at various markets. Old cars are stripped for their parts to be sold. Horse dealing is another important economic activity. In providing various services, the primary market for the Traveller entrepreneur is the 'Settled' community. In addition to the above, there is increasing evidence of trading within the Traveller community.

1.1.3 Alongside these major activities engaged in within the Traveller economy, there exist many other activities which are turned to at the economically opportune moment. These activities vary from area to area and include seasonal farm work, painting and decorating, sharpening garden implements and tarmacadam laying among others. There are still a number of Traveller tinsmiths and flower makers.

1.1.4 A small number of Travellers are employed within the mainstream labour force. Some Travellers have set up small co-operative enterprises. Travellers have worked in a number of sheltered employment projects. Travellers are employed in jobs providing services to their own community. This latter area has been one of recent growth with Travellers gaining employment as youth and community workers, child care assistants in pre-school and other settings, in culture and heritage work, and in health promotion work. The vast majority of these posts have been created in the voluntary sector. Direct employment of Travellers in the state sector does not occur at present except for a small number of local authorities that employ Travellers as site caretakers.

1.1.5 In 1963 the Commission on Itinerancy (Ref. 1) found that *"the majority insofar as they have any business or calling, are dealers and collectors of scrap of all descriptions"* and that *"almost all itinerants avail of any opportunity that presents itself to obtain scrap or waste material of any description that has a saleable value"*.

Horse dealing was also identified as a key economic activity as was seasonal agricultural work where Travellers were seen to have *"recognised skills in dealing with seasonal operations on certain crops such as beet and potatoes"*.

1.1.6 The Commission on Itinerancy reported a 1960 census of Travellers which found that out of 3,167 Travellers over fourteen years of age *"600 claimed to be tinsmiths, 103 claimed to be chimney sweeps, 36 claimed to be flower makers, 30 tinsmiths also claimed to be sweeps"*.

1.1.7 The Report of the Travelling People Review Body, (1983), (Ref. 2) found that *"the majority of the Traveller people are untrained, unskilled and unemployed. They have traditionally been attracted to self-employed activities as these have fitted in best with their travelling way of life"*. This Report also identified that *"the few who are employed are engaged in unskilled or domestic work and, in general, have worked for less than five years"*. The 1983 Report also stated *"the vast majority of Traveller families are in receipt of unemployment assistance and that it is the single most important source of income for most families"*.

1.1.8 A more positive picture emerges where the Report examines the economic activities engaged in by Travellers, finding many *"profitably engaged in trading and in door to door sales, but there is anxiety that their freedom to trade may be hampered by over restrictive application of the terms of the Casual Trading Act, 1980"*. The Report also found that *"traditionally, many have been involved in scrap collection"*, *"many also engage in casual seasonal employment, often in family groups"*, and *"in some areas there is a tradition of army service"*.

1.1.9 Profiles of the Traveller economy in two separate towns were prepared for the Task Force. These confirmed the analysis of a distinct Traveller economy alongside Traveller participation in the mainstream labour force. They demonstrated the importance of trading, recycling and horse dealing in the Traveller economy, alongside a broad variety of positions taken up in the mainstream economy. These profiles also identified a range of constraints on the Traveller economy and on Traveller participation in the mainstream labour force.

1.2   Manner of Organisation

1.2.1 Although the perception is often otherwise, a significant and distinct work ethic exists within the Traveller community. The Traveller culture and way of life values enterprise. What distinguishes the Traveller economy, and what is the basis for referring to a Traveller economy, is the distinct manner in which economic activity is organised. A number of features stand out as central to the Traveller economy, largely independent of whatever particular economic activity is engaged in and largely constant over years past. It is these features that allow Travellers to find their particular niche in a variety of markets and that enable Travellers to make a profit in areas others have found non-viable. As such, an understanding of these features must be an important element in any development strategy focused on the Traveller economy.

1.2.2 Nomadism is one such feature where mobility allows Travellers to access a market large enough to make marginal economic activities viable. The 1963 Commission on Itinerancy, (op. cit, 1) set out an economic classification of Travellers. It found that what was referred to as the *"motor trailer group"*, which travelled the country extensively *"spending only a few days in each place sufficient to cover the area for* *the purposes of their business"*, had the highest income levels. On the other hand it found that the *"group whose travelling is confined to a small area"* had extremely low income levels. This phenomenon continues today where higher income levels are visible within Traveller groups who are most mobile.

A minority of Travellers are now nomadic on a continuous basis. Department of Environment statistics indicate that less than five per cent of the Traveller population are continuously nomadic (i.e. Transient) Traders. However, there is increased Traveller movement between Ireland and other European countries, particularly to Britain. Traveller mobility has also taken new forms as the context within which it occurs changes. It now encompasses Travellers who move out from a fixed base, those who only travel for a certain period in each year, and those who are static for a long period and then move on.

This is paralleled across Europe where the Council of Europe Report "Gypsies and Travellers" (Ref. 3) identified that:

"The range of situations in the matter of nomadism is extensive. Diversity is manifested in means of transport, from the slowest to the swiftest, from the horse drawn caravan to the aeroplane, from the most outmoded to the most sophisticated, from creaking cart to the American trailer. It is manifested in the frequency or rarity of journeying, in journeys of a few days or several months, with or without a return to base, or in regular journeys in connection with work".

and concluded that

"in the past few years there have been important changes which have changed travel. There is less rural nomadism and correlatively more urban-based nomadism".

1.2.3 Another feature of the Traveller economy is its focus on generating income rather than job creation. The Traveller entrepreneur does not usually seek to employ or to be employed. The economy is based on immediate payment in cash for service provided or goods traded. This feature was also evident in the Commission on Itinerancy (op. cit, 1) description of Traveller involvement in agricultural work: *Some farmers were glad to avail of their services, usually on a contract basis for an agreed sum per acre, or for the job. In this way the itinerant was enabled to employ his whole family on the work and work his own hours. The itinerants apparently prefer this type of arrangement to working regular hours for wages"*. While the availability of agricultural work is now quite limited, the Traveller economy continues to operate on the basis of immediate payment in cash for services.

1.2.4 The family is still the basic economic unit of the Traveller economy and self employment continues as a predominant feature. Travellers in self employment can more easily respond to social and cultural demands required of them by their own community, than is possible in a wage labour situation. Young Travellers often serve a valuable apprenticeship in self employment as part of the family unit. Young Travellers achieve entrepreneurial status within their community on beginning to receive a share of the particular deal being made. Partnerships also exist between different family units for economic activity.

1.2.5   The home base of economic activities is another feature of the Traveller economy where workspace and living space are one and the same. This element of the Traveller economy has clear implications for the location of Traveller accommodation depending on the nature and size of the economic activity involved. This was recognised in the Commission on Itinerancy Report, (op. cit, 1) which in its recommendations on Traveller accommodation stated that: *"part of each site should be set aside for the stallage of the itinerants animals and this section should be adequately fenced"* and *"adequate provision should also be made on the site for the stock-in-trade of itinerants and consideration should be given to the provision of separate storage accommodation for each lot"*.

The 1983 Report of the Travelling People Review Body, (op. cit, 2) reflected a similar understanding in recommending: *"The self employed Traveller provides the community with some valuable services and the community should facilitate the continued provision of such services. The provision, by local authorities or businesses, of adequate space and appropriate facilities for scrap dealing or trading is recommended as a worthwhile approach to accommodating Travellers in pursuing their livelihood"*.

The Report made particular reference to the provision of small sheds close to the Travellers' accommodation for light scrap activities while suggesting that heavier scrap should not be accommodated so close to living quarters.

1.2.6   A final feature of the Traveller economy worthy of note is that of flexibility. The ability to respond to market demand by turning to new economic activities with potential for profit is an important attribute of the Traveller entrepreneur.

1.3   European Perspective

1.3.1   The Council of Europe report (op. cit, 3) devotes a section to 'Economic Organisation'. This serves to highlight the many parallels that exist between the Traveller economy and that of similar groups across Europe.

Features identified that are specific to the manner in which Gypsy and Traveller groups organise their economic activities across Europe include *"economic independence"* or self employment, the family group as *"the basic economic unit"*, nomadism, and a service focus where *"all these occupations are conceived as a sale of goods or services to customers who are neither Gypsies nor Travellers. A transaction is always involved. Seeking out a customer, persuading him, bargaining, are important sides of economic activities"*. In relation to the economies of Gypsies and Travellers, the report makes the point that *"What counts most in an occupation is, therefore, the manner in which it can be exercised"*.

Nomadism is another central feature identified where *"journeys confer adaptability, flexibility, and autonomy with a view to maintaining economic independence"* and *"most occupations necessitate movement and extensive prospecting, as a local market is rapidly exhausted"*.

The Report sets out a range of challenges faced by these economies over the past decades: *"The most important changes in the majority of countries took place between 1945 and 1960. This was the time of the drift away from the land, as a result of which habitual customers disappeared" and "There was also the vast increase of mass-produced commodities eliminating many outlets and motorised transport entailing new customs for the nomad, namely more rapid and more frequent journeys, radiating around a fixed or semi-static point".*

1.3.2 The Traveller economy in Ireland has had to adapt to similar challenges since the 1960s. This has meant some economic activities changing as old trades lose their markets and as new markets open up. It has also influenced a change in location as the Traveller moved from a rural setting to an urban setting. However, the manner in which Traveller economic activity is organised has maintained its key features throughout this period of change.

1.4 Responses to the Traveller Economy

1.4.1 The response to the Traveller economy has principally focused on supporting Travellers to secure employment on the mainstream labour market. The Report on the Commission on Itinerancy, (op. cit, 1) recommended: *"It will be of the utmost importance if absorption into the general community is to succeed that as many itinerants as possible should be encouraged and where necessary, assisted, to adapt themselves to the employment patterns of the ordinary population".*

This recommendation did not recognise the potential in the "employment patterns" of the Traveller population. The Report of the Travelling People Review Body, (op. cit, 2) promoted the same strategy but from a slightly different starting point in recommending: *"the traditional self-employed occupations of Travellers should be encouraged. Even though many of the skills involved belong to another era, consideration should be given to the adaptation of such skills for use in modern light industrial employment or in craft and souvenir work" and "with upwards of 2,000 Travellers in the 15 to 25 year age group, it is essential that their employment opportunities be improved radically and rapidly".*

The employment focus meant that there was an emphasis on the economic activities engaged in, rather than the manner in which these activities were organised. The 1983 report also suggested: *"there may still be some jobs for which Travellers are suited, an example being the provision of public services for themselves".*

1.4.2 The lack of emphasis on the distinct manner in which Travellers organise their economic activities is reflected in a failure to consider supports appropriate to the Traveller economy, leading to increasingly restricted space within which it can operate. The Council of Europe report "Gypsies and Travellers", (op. cit, 3) documents this as a Europe wide phenomenon highlighting: "Regulations which hinder the exercise of small trades" and *"restrictive regulations governing camp sites for nomads, which limit or prevent work on the spot, spelling economic failure for those who need to stay there, forcing them to fall back on social security".*

The Report found that this has led to a situation where: *"as a result of multiple constraints, increasing numbers of Gypsies and Travellers are in some places currently operating with steadily diminishing resources. This entails economic competition which breaks the bonds of solidarity, and may result in conflict, particularly when newcomers want to share a territory. The gap between prosperous and poorly-off family groups is widening".*

1.4.3 A significant amount of Traveller economic activity takes place within the informal economy. This can be a source of tension and conflict between the Traveller and 'Settled' communities and can also create situations which are in conflict with the law that serve to further confine Travellers to the margins of Irish society.

Strategies need to be developed that allow this sector of the economy to make its contribution to the broader welfare of society and to ensure that it fulfils required legal obligations. These strategies should sustain the economic activity that is involved, given the two fold role that the informal economy plays in serving to sustain those who are within the informal economy and also to support wealth creation and job creation in the formal economy. They should also make special allowances in relation to particular communities experiencing social exclusion such as the Traveller community.

1.4.4 The Task Force on the Travelling Community is reporting at a time of unprecedented unemployment. The mainstream labour market can only offer very limited opportunity for the Traveller community. Debate on unemployment at national and international level has focused attention on the need to explore new ways of organising work, the potential of the social economy, and the importance of environmental works and recycling. This offers new encouragement to the Traveller economy and presents a challenge to identify relevant and appropriate supports to improve its viability and to expand its potential.

The Council of Europe Report, (op. cit, 3) concludes that the trades of Gypsies and Travellers *"are useful because against the present background of the consumer society, they mean salvaging on a wide scale; the future is unquestionably bright for salvage collectors".*

The EU Commission White Paper on "Growth, Competitiveness, Employment", (Ref. 4) emphasises the importance of the social economy which is described as existing within the *"continuum of possibilities ranging from supply totally protected by public subsidies to totally competitive supply".*

The social economy is further identified as covering local services, improvements in the quality of life, and environmental protection. A number of strategies are suggested in the White Paper in support of the social economy including tax exemptions, public/private partnerships, part work and part income support models, and public expenditure associated with EU environment programmes.

The White Paper also stresses the need for a *"widening of the concept of work, incorporating all forms of paid or partially paid work within a common framework comprising the social economy, intermediate employment enterprises and the informal economy".*

1.5   Policies and Strategies Targeting Indigenous Australians

1.5.1 The Task Force commissioned research into economic and employment development policies in Australia that are targeted on indigenous Australians (Ref.

5) such as Aborigines and Torres Strait Islanders. Given the parallels between Irish Travellers and indigenous Australians, the Australian experience was identified as containing a number of valuable lessons in examining strategies of economic and employment development for the Traveller community.

1.5.2 The 1986 census recorded that six per cent of Aboriginals held formal qualifications in contrast to twenty-six per cent of the non-indigenous population. Employment rates for those aged between fifteen and sixty-four years was thirty-three per cent for Aboriginals and sixty-three per cent for non-indigenous Australians. Australia's indigenous people constitute 1.57 per cent of the population and have higher childhood dependency and larger household size relative to the non-indigenous population.

The parallels with Irish Travellers are clear. Irish Travellers are also a small minority in Ireland, with their own distinct identity, culture and way of life. The distinct demographic patterns are also a feature of the Traveller community as are the major difficulties experienced in terms of access to education and employment.

1.5.3 It is of interest to note that in 1993 the Aboriginal and Torres Strait Islander function was transferred from the Employment, Education and Training portfolio, to the Prime Minister's portfolio. The Minister of Aboriginal and Torres Strait Islander Affairs is designated "Minister Assisting the Prime Minister for Aboriginal Reconciliation".

1.5.4 Government policies for Aboriginal peoples and Torres Strait Islanders have shifted position since the 1960's, from the previous strategy aimed at the integration of indigenous people into urban mainstream labour markets to current policy which aims to promote economic and employment equity on indigenous people's terms. The objectives of Aboriginal Employment Development Policy (AEDP) are identified as the achievement of:

- employment equity with other Australians;
- income equity with other Australians;
- equitable participation in primary, secondary and tertiary education;
- a reduction of Aboriginal welfare dependency to a level commensurate with that of other Australians.

Key strategies within the Aboriginal Employment Development Policy include:

- provision of training and labour market assistance to facilitate access to mainstream employment in the public and private sectors;
- assistance with employment in Aboriginal and Torres Strait Islander controlled enterprises;
- enhancing Aboriginal and Torres Strait Islander control and involvement in the policy and delivery of programmes.

An important aspect of the AEDP was the aim of offering employment opportunities to be located outside mainstream labour markets by cultural choice or by force of circumstances. In the words of the AEDP policy statement:

"Traditional economic activity continues to be a significant feature of Aboriginal lifestyle and culture in many remote areas, but has not been sufficiently recognised as a legitimate form of employment. The Government now recognises these activities as a legitimate form of employment and economic activity". (op. cit. 5)

1.5.5   The centrality of educational attainment to labour force life chances is recognised. Labour market equity is recognised as only achievable if the educational disadvantage of Aboriginal and Torres Strait Islander people is addressed. A separate Aboriginal and Torres Strait Islander education policy has been established. This has four objectives:

–   to ensure Aboriginal involvement in educational decision making;
–   to provide equality of access for Aboriginal people to educational services;
–   to raise the rates of Aboriginal participation in education to those for all Australians;
–   to achieve equitable and appropriate education outcomes for Aboriginal people.

1.5.6   A review of the AEDP was published in 1994. This noted:

–   a significant improvement in the relative employment position of Aboriginal and Torres Strait Islander peoples;
–   the number of indigenous people who are self employed almost doubled;
–   a substantial increase in Aboriginal representation in the community services sector;
–   a significant improvement in public sector employment at Commonwealth level.

However, the conclusion of the review body was that *"the overall employment and economic situation of Aboriginal and Torres Strait Islander peoples remains dire"*. The review called for a renewed commitment to the philosophy and directions of the AEDP, priority emphasis on the private sector, and action to ensure under-performing public sector agencies show results.

1.5.7   The research identified a broad range of relevant Australian programmes. A number of these could usefully be redesigned and applied within the Irish context. These include:

–   A target of two per cent of total public service employment was set for Aboriginal and Torres Strait Islander Peoples. This target was reached in 1991 and subsequent attention focused on career progression.

–   Specific posts within the public service are labelled as 'identified positions'. These are those posts deemed to require a knowledge of Aboriginal and Torres Strait Islander culture and society and an ability to communicate effectively with Aboriginal and Torres Strait Islander people. Identified positions are central to the strategy of increasing the employment of indigenous peoples.

–   Aboriginal Cadetship Programmes allow access to professional careers which require formal qualifications or accretion, by sponsoring full-time study. Cadets are appointed on probation to training officer designations. They attend full-time academic study and participate in a structured programme of practical on-the-job training between periods of formal training.

- The Council for Aboriginal Reconciliation Mining Committee identified a strategy of preferential purchasing by industry from local indigenous communities. This involves encouraging local private sector businesses to purchase goods and services from local community enterprises.

- Strategies in relation to the private sector have not had good results. There is now a recognition of the need for targeted intervention on particular industries. Committees are established comprising representatives from the relevant sector, with Government Agencies and Aboriginal and Torres Strait Islander Commission representation.

- The Community Economic Initiatives Scheme is designed to address the poor capital base of Aboriginal and Torres Strait Islander Communities seeking to set up businesses and in recognition of the need to invest in the income generating capacities of these communities. Capital funding, consultancy support, marketing support and wage subsidies are provided. Of particular interest is the recurrent cost subsidy to meet a gap between annual income and expenditure which is available over a five year period.

- The Community Development Employment Projects Programme was created out of an acknowledgement that employment and enterprise opportunities must be provided wherever indigenous people live and must be sensitive to the needs of these communities. This covers grant assistance to fund employment in community development projects and traditional activities, and grants for training to support community based development.

1.5.8 A number of key issues are identified as continuing to face these programmes. These include:

- the lack of compatible employment opportunities for those Aboriginals who are living traditional lifestyles;
- the need for specific initiatives in respect of the strategic issues raised by poor performance in the private sector;
- the contradiction between income equity objectives and wage levels on Community Development Employment Projects;
- the challenge to focus on career progression within the public sector once employment targets are reached;
- the need for indigenous Australians to be in control of the decisions which affect their economic situation.

2. Trading in the Traveller Economy

2.1 Introduction

2.1.1 Traditionally Irish Travellers traded in the rural agricultural economy. They bought and sold or bartered with the farming community. The Traveller traders have survived economic changes in the rural economy and progressed to exploit niches in modern society by trading, in for instance, antique furniture, farm gates, bed clothing, video and electrical equipment, tyres and carpets.

242

2.1.2   The Report of the Commission on Itinerancy, (op. cit, 1) identified the *"motor trader group"* of forty to sixty families who *"travel the country extensively . . ."* and whose occupations were described as follows: *"Traders and dealers in new mattresses, linoleum, household goods. Purchasers and collectors of old mattresses, feathers, horse-hair, ticks, scrap, rags etc. on a large scale. Some also deal in horses on a large scale"*.

The considerable change since this Report, in the range of goods that Traveller traders deal in, reflects their adaptation to economic changes by their flexibility. The Report of the Travelling People Review Body, (op. cit, 2) points out that: *"There are, however, certain types of work and trading for which they display particular aptitude and in which they have achieved success"*.

However, this Report regarded the extent of trading as small. In outlining Traveller employment it states: *"A small number of others have been successful as traders"*.

2.1.3   Trading is done by selling from the roadside, door-to-door selling or by selling from stalls in the markets. There are two main types of trading namely, Transient Trading which involves selling from the roadside and door-to-door and Market Trading which involves selling from stalls in the casual trading areas.

2.2   Transient Trading

2.2.1   Travellers involved in Transient Trading usually travel in extended family groups, along patriarchal lines. Their overheads are significantly different from 'Settled' business people. While they do not have property costs, and current costs such as for instance employees' wages, electricity and heating, they require quality vans and caravans and significant cash resources to buy and sell in bulk where and when opportunities arise. They also have considerable fuel energy costs. It is generally acknowledged that there are difficulties involved in Transient Traders fully participating in the taxation and social insurance systems as presently structured.

2.2.2   The Annual Count of Traveller Families carried out by the Department of the Environment, (Ref. 6) estimates the number of Traveller families involved in Transient Trading as follows:

Table G(1) Transient Trading			
Year	**Overall Traveller Total**	**Families in Transient Trading**	
		No.	**%**
1991	3,671 families	179	4.8%
1992	3,725 families	181	4.9%
1993	3,806 families	192	5%
1994	3,878 families	205	5.3%

Three main groups based in Rathkeale, Wexford and Sligo form between 141 and 150 of all these families engaged in Transient Trading.

2.2.3   The Transient Traders are a very small part of the overall Traveller population. They trade as extended family groups (from about seven or eight families up to forty families) and it is generally accepted that they are wealthy and successful.

2.2.4   These Traveller Traders have exploited niches in the modern economy such as antique dealing, trading in farm gates and such. Existing groups already dominate the niches identified and it is unlikely that new groups could set up to compete with them. However, they have shown that Transient Trading as currently practised is feasible and profitable. Transient Trading is a model of entrepreneurial skill to encourage extended family groups to identify other niches and exploit them.

To succeed in Transient Trading requires:

  – identifying feasible niches to exploit;
  – significant resources to buy and sell and diversify when opportunities arise;
  – capital to get quality vans and caravans;
  – a large united extended family group for support, division of work and company while moving around;
  – access to parking space and facilities.

2.2.5   The difficulties arising out of roadside parking, especially when large numbers are involved, create conflict and tension with the 'Settled' community. Problems such as nuisance, safety, rubbish and despoliation, trespass on private and public property, toilet and hygiene problems create significant hostility towards these Traveller traders. In this respect it is very important that those involved in Transient Trading would secure parking space and facilities adequate to their needs, at an appropriate payment.

2.3   Market Trading

2.3.1   This is a long tradition in some families, who trade from stalls on market day in the designated casual trading areas. These casual trading areas or markets are in the majority of market towns in rural counties.

2.3.2   It is generally accepted that there is widening interest among both Traveller and 'Settled' communities in this form of trading and car-boot sales, roadside fruit, vegetable and cake stalls and such are increasing in number. The number and size of casual trading areas is not adequate to the growing demand. Only a few Traveller families in each county have licences and stalls.

2.3.3   For most families involved in market trading it is an intermittent source of income, depending on whether markets are good or bad and on how flexible they are in their range of goods for sale. In the winter months bad weather can seriously affect trading. However, unlike the Transient Trading it is more feasible for Travellers to take up Market Trading especially if they were encouraged to do so. This is because Market Traders do not need large cash resources and quality vans and caravans. Equally Market Traders can function as a single family unit.

2.3.4   At present there are considerable obstacles to unemployed Travellers taking up Market Trading, as follows:

* The Casual Trading Licence can be bought from the Department of Enterprise and Employment for £175 for one year. Most unemployed people would have difficulty affording £175 to get a licence.

* This licence is granted, without regard to the availability of permits for spaces on the designated casual trading areas. Thus a Traveller may get a licence but have no access to a casual trading permit for the designated casual trading area. This difficulty is prevalent as there are so few designated casual trading areas and those which exist are small. In its explanatory memorandum to the existing Casual Trading Act, 1980, (Ref. 7) the Department of Enterprise and Employment states: *"Local Authorities are empowered by the Act to designate casual trading areas and, where casual trading areas are designated, it is an offence to engage in casual trading anywhere else in these Local Authorities' areas"*.

  This creates a situation where permits are granted to a limited few, for small designated casual trading areas and others are excluded due to lack of trading spaces even though they may have licences.

* The Report of the Travelling People Review Body, (op. cit, 2) states: *"Many of those who are self-employed are profitably engaged in trading and in door-to-door sales but there is anxiety that their freedom to trade may be hampered by over restrictive application of the terms of the Casual Trading Act, 1980"*.

  Door-to-door selling is not included under the Casual Trading Act.

* The Report of the Travelling People Review Body, (op. cit, 2) recommended:

  "Local Authorities should also facilitate the trading and marketing activities of travellers by designating a number of approved markets in their areas, in keeping with the licensing provision of the Casual Trading Act, 1980."

* The Casual Trading Bill (1994), (Ref. 8) proposes that the local authority will provide casual trading licences and permits and provide designated casual trading areas. However, under Section 4(5)(c) *"A local authority may refuse to grant a casual trading licence to a person if a trading place for the purpose of casual trading is not available"*. This does not oblige local authorities to assess the need/demand for casual trading space. Section (7) of the Bill merely proposes: *"(1) A Local Authority shall, as soon as may be after the commencement of the Act, make bye-laws in relation to the control, regulation, supervision and administration of casual trading in its functional area"*.

* The provision of designated casual trading areas is a reserved function. In providing such facilities the impact of pedestrian and motorised traffic, the impact on residents, local (rate-paying) traders and the availability of nearby toilets are significant issues. Nonetheless, failure to provide adequate space for market trading stifles any potential enterprise for unemployed Travellers and it is at this level that unemployed Travellers can most likely start trading.

2.3.5 Market Trading is generally a low profit intermittent economic activity for Travellers. It is unlikely that many Market Traders could generate an ongoing sufficient income from this activity. The Casual Trading Bill, (1994) proposes that a tax clearance certificate be a prerequisite for getting a licence. While it is accepted that those liable should pay tax, this strategy will present serious difficulties for most of those seeking to trade at this level.

2.3.6 Commercial activities receive a range of supports from the State. Appropriate and adequate supports should be developed for those seeking to enter the field of Market Trading, in a manner similar to the way the State supports other economic activities. These supports should take account of the start-up capital requirements and the flexible and intermittent nature of Market Trading. The support strategies for the social economy proposed in the EU White Paper on "Growth Competitiveness and Employment" (op. cit, 4) could be developed for this purpose.

As there is an increasing interest generally in Market Trading, Travellers can be at a disadvantage in competing with 'Settled' persons for limited numbers of licences and permits. Such licences and permits should be provided in a manner that is accessible to Travellers.

2.3.7 It is useful to take account of the trading activities engaged in by Traveller tenants in the provision of accommodation/facilities.

The Report of the Travelling People Review Body, (op. cit, 2) recommended as follows:

"Adequate facilities should be provided to allow self-employed Travellers to pursue their chosen livelihood. Local Authorities in conjunction with commercial interests should provide facilities to accommodate Travellers engaged in the scrap business, ensuring that such activities do not contribute to environmental damage or despoliation".

As such, provision for Travellers should take account of the trading activities engaged in by Traveller tenants. This will serve to encourage enterprise and equally to ensure that no unsightly stock piles are strewn around halting sites and housing schemes.

2.4 Recommendations

GR.1 Local authorities, in being authorised to licence traders, should provide casual trading space based on a full assessment of requirements and impact on existing consumer services.

GR.2 Where Transient Trading groups require living accommodation, local authorities should allow them to park on transient sites where available for an agreed period.

GR.3 Larger groups, beyond the capacity of a transient site, should be required to secure adequate space to accommodate their own needs, when they are deemed to have adequate resources. It is envisaged that the local authority would advise on orderly movement and parking.

GR.4   Transient Traders should be required to maintain contact with local authorities so that orderly movement and parking can be achieved through co-operation.

GR.5   Travellers should be identified as one target group in the licensing of casual trading given their tradition in this area and given the appropriateness of this activity to the way in which their economy is organised. Licences and pitches should be available in a manner accessible to Travellers.

GR.6   The design and construction of Traveller specific accommodation should include limited storage/workspace. Such space is seen as the first step in the development of trading activity under planned conditions. Where the trading activity develops to the level that the storage space provided is inadequate and therefore unacceptable in a residential environment, the Traveller should be required to relocate the activity to an appropriate location.

GR.7   A range of strategies should be developed by the Department of Enterprise and Employment to support Travellers and others in Market Trading. These strategies should be based on the proposals in the EU White Paper in relation to supporting the social economy.

3.   Recycling in the Traveller Economy

3.1   Traveller Recycyling

3.1.1   Travellers have been involved in recycling for generations. An often narrow interpretation of what recycling involves has contributed to a lack of recognition of Traveller recycling initiatives.

The term recycling covers waste materials:

–   being reused without further processing;
–   being recovered for use in manufacturing the same type of product;
–   being reclaimed for use in the manufacture of a new and different product.

Travellers have occupied a particular niche in the recycling chain - that of sourcing, transporting and segregating the waste materials, which are the initial stages upon which depends the existence of the whole recycling chain. They are also the stages that have been found to be determining factors in the viability of recycling operations.

3.1.2   Travellers recycle a broad range of materials. Scrap metals, both ferrous and non-ferrous, are of primary importance. Car parts are extensively recycled. Furniture, household machinery, clothes and other household goods are another important set of materials recycled.

3.1.3   Travellers source their waste materials from landfill sites, door to door collections and small factories or engineering works. Access to landfill sites can be problematic and even a source of conflict where restrictions are imposed. Access is generally restricted on the grounds of personal and public safety and landfill management. However, limited access is usually facilitated. Door to door collections can be highly

247

organised with printed bills delivered to advise of a forthcoming collection. Such collections can also be organised to precede local authority junk collection schemes.

Scrapped cars are also sourced as part of door to door collections. However, people sometimes leave scrapped cars at Traveller sites and they are also sourced at motor garages. Small factories or engineering works or demolition sites can be a source of scrap metals where the amounts involved would not allow for viable recycling by the factory itself.

3.1.4 Travellers transport waste materials from the source to a storage point by a variety of means. The storage point is usually the halting site or group housing scheme where the Travellers are based. Further segregation and any processing will occur at this point. Processing is minimal. Repairs are made to household goods and scrap metals are cleaned for resale. Copper wire is also stripped through burning, a process which is hazardous to health and damaging to the local environment. This has been a source of complaint from neighbours as has the storage of waste materials as it is presently organised. Storage space is crucial as small amounts of waste materials are sourced and collected until an adequate amount is gathered to make a sale. Storage is also important to deal with price fluctuations in the international scrap metal market.

3.1.5 Waste materials are then sold at the halting site or group housing scheme, at local market stalls, to scrap merchants, or to other Travellers for selling on. Scrap metals that are ferrous eventually find their way to Irish Steel while those that are non-ferrous are exported. Some second-hand materials are sold at market stalls.

3.1.6 Traveller recycling exhibits most of the features described above of the Traveller economy - mobility in sourcing materials, self employment and home base. It can also be an intermittent activity for most Travellers, particularly in the scrap metal area. Collection of the scrap metals can take place intermittently over a long period and onward sale will depend on price fluctuations in the market for these materials.

3.2 Policy Context

3.2.1 The European Union published its Fifth Environmental Action Programme in 1993 (Ref. 9). This identifies priorities in waste management as waste prevention, promotion of recycling and optimisation of final disposal methods for waste which is not recycled. Targets set out in the programme include:

- implementation of waste management plans in Member States;
- stabilisation of the quantities of waste generated;
- recycling of consumer goods;
- development of markets for recycled materials.

A landfill Directive (Ref. 10) has been prepared to regulate and improve landfill operations throughout the EU. Site licensing will be stricter with technical, operational and structural requirements having to be met. This has implications for the design and upgrading of Irish landfill sites as well as for the access of Travellers and others involved in recycling to these sites.

A packaging Directive (Ref. 11) has also been prepared to reduce the environmental impact of packaging waste. The Directive would require Member States to achieve minimum and maximum recovery targets for packaging waste. All of these targets would have to be reached within five years of the Directive's entry into force and will require significantly increased rates of recycling. It is also of significance to note that used tyres and used cars are identified as priority waste streams, that is key items to be recycled, in EU waste management policy. Travellers are involved in both of these areas.

Finally, EU Environmental Action Programmes do not specifically include the recycling activities of Gypsy and Traveller groups. In developing an Irish policy in this area, it would be important to ensure that this contributes to informing EU Environmental Action Programmes.

3.2.2 The Department of the Environment has published "Towards a Recycling Strategy for Ireland", (Ref. 12) a strategy document for recycling domestic and commercial waste. This sets out how the Government will achieve the target of diverting twenty per cent of combined household and commercial waste away from landfill through recycling. The primary focus within this general objective is to meet the five-year recovery rate of twenty-five per cent for packaging materials. Although packaging waste is the central focus, action on other waste streams will also be actively promoted. Batteries, waste oils and motor vehicles will be among the priorities.

The strategy is based on the concept of producer responsibility. However, it also details important roles for central and local government. Central government will produce a waste Bill and will arrange financial support for the development of recycling infrastructure. Local government will assist in the provision of sites and facilities for waste recovery, produce waste management plans, develop facilities to support recycling at landfill sites, and operate a scheme of recycling credits for the benefit of persons involved in the recycling of household waste.

The strategy is defined as *"an evolving one which must remain open to further improvement and refinement"*. In outlining the benefits of recycling the documents make particular mention of the fact that increased recycling will:

"support the activities of voluntary, charitable and other small-scale agencies already engaged in recycling campaign (such as; REHAB, Recycling Campaign, and the Traveller community)".

3.2.3 In the preparation of this waste management strategy the Department of the Environment published a research project entitled "Towards a Recycling Strategy for Ireland" (op. cit, 12). This identifies five major constraints on recycling in Ireland:

— *Technical Barriers* which include contaminants on the reclaimed materials or inherent characteristics of materials which restrict recyclability;
— *Institutional Barriers* which relate to the difficulties in changing people from set and familiar ways of dealing with waste;
— *Convenience Barriers* where recycling demands a greater effort from the public than traditional waste management practices;

      –   *Demographic Barriers* where a low population density means sourcing of adequate quantities for viable recycling requires transportation over long distances;

      –   *Market and Economic Barriers* where Ireland provides a limited market for recycled materials so that much of the material collected must be exported, which adds to the cost and leads to viability problems.

3.2.4   Recycling rates in Ireland are low. The potential for expansion lies principally in the export market although there is scope in the domestic market for expansion of glass and plastic recycling. There is a nineteen per cent recovery rate of waste paper. The majority of our post consumer plastic waste is landfilled or burned. There is a twenty-one per cent recovery rate of glass waste. Volatile prices impede the expansion of scrap metal recovery. Metals have a twenty-four per cent recovery rate at present. While producer responsibility based on "the polluter pays" principle will be of central importance to increasing these recycling rates, it is also clear that central and local Government policy and action will be vital.

3.2.5   The Department of the Environment at present administers a grant scheme to encourage waste recycling projects. Grants are made to projects recycling glass, paper, cans or plastics. Grants cover fifty per cent of capital start-up costs. However, there is a problem in that the structure of these grants does not reflect the manner in which Travellers organise their recycling. The Travellers Resource Warehouse situated in Pavee Point, Dublin is a Traveller project which has received grant aid.

3.2.6   The present policy trends allied to a growing environmental consciousness makes up a favourable context for those involved in recycling. Ironically, they could also create a scenario where Travellers find their niche as recyclers taken over by 'Settled' people. This could be due to 'Settled' people being in a better position to access grant support available or due to policies evolving in a way that does not take fully into account the distinct manner in which Travellers organise their recycling activities.

3.3   The Contribution of Traveller Recycling

3.3.1   Research into Traveller recycling carried out by Environmental Management and Auditing Systems Ltd. published by Pavee Point Publications and entitled "Recycling and the Traveller Economy: Income, Jobs and Wealth Creation, (Ref. 13) found:

      –   at a conservative estimate Travellers source, transport and segregate fifty per cent of all scrap metals;

      –   as such, Travellers recycle 75,000 tonnes of ferrous metals with a final value to the Irish economy of £1.5 million and 13,500 tonnes of non-ferrous metals with a final value to the Irish economy of £6 million. This latter value is in foreign currency as most non-ferrous metal waste is eventually exported;

      –   there are some 400 jobs held by the 'Settled' community in the scrap metal industry. Traveller recycling underpins and sustains these jobs.

3.3.2   The research identified six constraints on Traveller recycling, particularly in relation to scrap metals. These are:

- the fluctuations in market prices for scrap metal;
- restricted access to landfill sites;
- the lack of a statutory policy on recycling and the inappropriate funding structure for recycling schemes;
- the restrictions on storage of waste materials on Traveller halting sites and group housing schemes;
- the difficulties Travellers encounter in getting motor vehicle insurance;
- the lack of recognition of the significance of Traveller recycling.

3.3.3　The research also documents how the distinct features of the Traveller economy allow the Traveller community to overcome the barriers that restrict the viability of recycling initiatives:

- an income based economy revolving around the family unit means that labour is not a fixed cost;
- hand sorting in such a situation becomes viable and overcomes technical barriers due to contaminants on recycled materials;
- Traveller mobility is not a fixed cost but a way of life;
- the flexibility in the Traveller economy reduces the destructive impact of fluctuating prices.

3.4　Recommendations

GR.8　Waste management policy and legislation in Ireland should recognise and encourage Traveller recycling activities and the distinct manner in which they are organised.

GR.9　With the implementation of the packaging directive and the "Recycling for Ireland" (Ref. 14) strategy there will be a broad new range of opportunities for recycling in Ireland. These should be promoted within the social economy sector with a range of strategies put in place to secure their viability in line with the proposals in the EU White Paper on "Growth, Competitiveness, Employment" (op. cit, 4). These would include:

- tax exemptions;
- public/private partnerships;
- part work and part income support models;
- public expenditure associated with EU environment programmes.

Travellers should be one priority target group for these strategies.

GR.10　The Department of the Environment, with the participation of relevant Traveller organisations, should design and develop strategies to support social economy recycling initiatives targeted on the Traveller community.

GR.11　Should a general consultative process be deemed necessary prior to implementation of EU Directives relevant to recycling, relevant Traveller organisations should be included.

GR.12　The implementation of the landfill Directive will require an upgrading of Irish landfill sites and their management structures and procedures. This should be used as an opportunity to develop site designs and procedures that will allow safe access to recyclable materials. The development of baling stations should allow similar access to recyclable materials. This is the approach that is outlined in the "Recycling for Ireland" strategy. This process should not disadvantage Travellers currently involved in recycling.

GR.13   The approach adopted under GR.4 in paragraph 2.4 above for storage of trading materials should also apply in relation to recycling.

GR.14   There is an existing grant scheme to encourage the development of recycling projects. In the light of the "Recycling for Ireland" strategy launched by the Government in 1994 this scheme should be reviewed to take account of the distinct approach of the Traveller community to recycling.

GR.15   Door to door collections of household waste could make an important contribution to the diversion of waste from landfill sites. This area has potential for further development and expansion. Travellers already play a role in this area. Recycling credits schemes as proposed in the "Recycling for Ireland" strategy should include an incentive for Traveller recycling in this area.

GR.16   The local authority should investigate and take advantage of opportunities for the involvement of Travellers and recycling organisations in the arrangement of junk collection schemes in order to maximise the amount of material recycled.

GR.17   The Department of the Environment should support Travellers and Traveller organisations in researching and introducing appropriate and safe technologies for the processing of copper wire waste.

GR.18   The "Recycling for Ireland" strategy states that *"waste management plans of local authorities and the business sector should aim at harnessing and engaging the contribution of community and residents' associations"*. It is important that Travellers and Traveller organisations be consulted in the development of these plans and that regard is taken of Traveller recycling activities.

4.   **Traveller Participation in the Horse Trade**

4.1   **Introduction**

4.1.1   According to research (Ref. 15) commissioned by the Task Force it is estimated that on average one quarter of Traveller families keep horses, and the majority of these deal in horses. This figure varies significantly from area to area.

4.1.2   Traveller participation in the horse trade is at two levels, as the buyers of horses for cultural pastime and as the breeders, users and traders of horses as a specific economic activity.

According to this research Travellers trade in two types of horse, Trotters (faster horses) and Cobs (heavier horses). 'Settled' buyers are most interested in the Trotters. The research indicates that the Trotters average £6,000 - £7,000 for a yearling and up to £11,000 when older. Some Travellers use their own Trotters to race in competition with each other. The main venues for this racing are Kilkenny, Limerick and Cork and the jockey is carried on a light tubular frame called a sulky. It is generally accepted that while the actual prizes are not significant, considerable amounts of money change hands through betting on races. The Trotters are half or three quarter bred, blending the strength of the draught horse (Cob) with the speed of the thoroughbred. Travellers have black and white horses exclusively bred by themselves and just commonly known as Travellers' horses. Cobs are used also as family pets and both 'Settled' people and Travellers buy them, from Travellers, for their children. According to the research, Cobs are sold for prices from £400 upwards.

In the Dublin area, there is evidence of Traveller involvement in the horse meat trade.

4.1.3 For many Travellers and especially those who have horses, the horse fairs are great financial and festive events. Travellers support fairs at Ballinasloe, Smithfield Market, Spancilhill, Maam Cross and Cahirmee (Buttevant), in great numbers. At Ballinasloe horse fair approximately 3,000 horses and ponies are sold annually and it is generally accepted that about one-third of the participants are Travellers. It is disappointing in this regard that Ballinasloe in promoting the fair makes no reference to Travellers and that Ballinasloe has failed to provide accommodation for its group of roadside families permanently parked outside the town for over seven years.

As well as trading in horses many Travellers have stalls at the rural fairs. The fair (especially Ballinasloe) is much more than just a market. Friends and relatives from Ireland and Britain meet there annually, bills are paid and arrangements for marriages are made. Our research suggests that Ballinasloe Fair is one of the highlights in the social calendar for Travellers.

4.2 The Importance of Horses for Travellers

4.2.1 It is generally accepted that having a horse or number of horses confers a status on the Traveller among the community.

4.2.2 There is a financial importance involved in trading horses and many Travellers keep horses so that when they face costly events or bills they can sell the animals to get the extra money needed. For a great many Travellers who have just a few horses this is a means of getting through the expense of weddings, funerals and other major events, rather than a more lucrative business.

4.2.3 Traveller families who have a tradition of keeping horses, regard it as part of their cultural lives and, despite many constraints, could not envisage being without a horse or rearing their children in a childhood without horses.

4.2.4 Caring for their horses provides an important occupation for many Traveller men. They take pride in handing the particular skills involved onto their sons.

It is obvious that this is a proud tradition of great importance culturally and financially to many Travellers. Although it is appreciated within the trade, this is not generally understood by the 'Settled' population. Facilitating Travellers in their keeping of horses contributes to their cultural well-being.

4.3   Constraints

4.3.1   The research, (op. cit, 15) identifies two main constraints for Travellers in keeping horses, namely lack of facilities and harassment arising from this lack of facilities.

4.3.2   At the present moment, the future of some of the traditional fairs is in doubt. Their disappearance would mean a loss not just to the cultural life of the Traveller community, but also the wider community. It is hoped that the difficulties facing local authorities in relation to these fairs can be resolved in a manner that ensures their long term survival.

4.4   Recommendations

GR.19   Where Traveller families keep horses, they should be required to secure adequate grazing areas for their animals. In the urban areas, there can be no requirement on local authorities to provide for this, due to lack of space. In other areas, local authorities have been able to assist in the provision of grazing facilities. This should continue and where possible, be expanded with the support of the relevant Department.

GR.20   Within the training and work schemes provided for Travellers, there should be support in developing their skills at breeding and caring for horses in order to create employment for young Travellers and to ensure the continuation of a tradition that is culturally important to them. This should be explored within FÁS and the VEC's.

5.   Traveller Participation in the Mainstream Labour Force

5.1   Introduction

5.1.1   Traveller participation in the mainstream labour force is very low. Travellers can be identified as a distinct group within the long term unemployed. In June, 1994 a survey was carried out by the National Association of Traveller Training Centres (Ref.16) of Travellers, who had participated over the previous decade in courses run by sixteen Traveller Training Centres which confirmed this low participation rate. The survey demonstrated a level of interest in engaging in the mainstream labour force and a diverse range of experiences of participation in the mainstream labour force.

5.1.2   Reasons advanced in the survey for this low participation rate include:

–   low pay and poor work conditions;
–   need for further training;
–   cultural factors;
–   lack of acceptance by 'Settled' counterparts;
–   lack of support from Traveller community;
–   movement and emigration.

5.1.3 Cultural factors are a significant element in this low participation rate as Travellers enter the Traveller economy in preference to the mainstream labour force. In setting out recommendations to increase Traveller participation in the mainstream labour force it is important to ensure that this is combined with strategies creating a supportive infrastructure for the Traveller economy.

5.1.4 Strategies to increase Traveller participation in the mainstream labour force have to be developed within a scenario characterised by high levels of unemployment. The ESRI Medium-Term Review 1994-2000, (Ref. 17) while forecasting rapid growth for the Irish economy, acknowledges that, without policy changes, Ireland will continue to have one of the highest unemployment rates in the European Union. The National Economic and Social Forum report "Ending Long Term Unemployment", (Ref. 18) stated that *"Ireland suffers from an exceptionally high relative level of long term unemployment and had the highest long-term unemployment rate in the OECD in 1991"*.

5.1.5 In its study of long term unemployment the NESF identifies a number of factors as relevant to long term unemployment. Two of these have an immediate relevance to Travellers:

– *"barriers facing the long term unemployed in finding and accepting jobs"* which *"include factors such as employer reluctance to hire long term unemployed people"*, a reluctance which is magnified when combined with anti-Traveller prejudice.

– *"skills and education levels of the long term unemployed"*. Access to mainstream training and education will be crucial to facilitate Traveller entry into the mainstream labour force. Participation in third level education is important, but in the short term will require special access measures to secure the direct entry of Travellers into third level education and to support their successful conclusion of such studies. Examples of such measures already exist with Travellers receiving Diplomas in Youth and Community Work from St. Patrick's College, Maynooth.

5.1.6 Given the low demand for labour in the Irish economy, in the immediate term, strategies to increase Traveller participation in the mainstream labour force should be focused on the development of Traveller community enterprise within a social economy sector and on the employment of Travellers in the public sector, particularly within those areas providing services to, or in contact with, the Traveller community. Clearly in the longer term the private sector has to play a key role in Travellers being employed within the mainstream labour force. This sector must also be encouraged to play its role in this regard.

5.2 Community Enterprises

5.2.1 Community enterprise has been defined as those enterprises which (Ref. 19):

"generally evolve through the activities of community development organisations, who in their work have identified gaps or deficiencies in services in their area and opportunities for their provision by local people. Their aim is to offer their service or services at suitable cost to the community and to provide moderate employment

with reasonable conditions and levels of security to local people, while generating income to ensure their sustainability".

A key market for many community enterprises is, therefore, the community within which they are located or from whom the employees are drawn. Frequently these are communities suffering social exclusion. Sustainability rather than profit is the main motivation for community enterprises (Ref. 20).

5.2.2 A number of Travellers have accessed the mainstream labour force through community enterprise. Current initiatives trading include a small number of enterprises involved in construction work, catering, recycling, flags and banners, knitting, car care, laundry service and industrial clothing production. These enterprises have emerged from Traveller organisations and Traveller training centres. Many remain tightly linked with the organisation or centre from which they emerged.

5.2.3 Initially, Traveller community enterprises were managed by 'Settled' people along with a significant management input from the founding organisations. More recently such enterprises have been managed by Travellers with founding organisations playing an ongoing support role. This represents an important advance by and for Travellers - both for those directly involved and for the broader community in terms of new role models.

5.2.4 In common with others, Traveller community enterprises have faced a number of difficulties. These include:

– short life span;
– fragmented support from a broad range of agencies;
– limited interpretations of the demands of job creation which have hampered the emergence of part-time work, home-based work, and Traveller managed enterprises;
– access to premises and start-up capital;
– grant aid limited to the initial year or two of the enterprise;
– absence of grant aid for organisational supports to the enterprise after an initial start-up period;
– an absence of grant aid for post start-up training requirements.

5.2.5 A primary difficulty facing Traveller community enterprises, again in common with other similar initiatives, is the lack of economic resources in the community they serve due to the impact of social exclusion. This leads to the difficulty that, while the raw material costs which these enterprises bear are determined nationally, having regard to market forces, the price of their output, namely services and products, is determined by local economic conditions. As such even with good management and high demand the enterprise is unable to cover its costs. A specific and additional difficulty facing Traveller community enterprise is that of the general lack of acceptance of Travellers. Existing initiatives report problems in relation to both suppliers and customers.

5.2.6 There is a need for a new approach to support strategies for Traveller and other community enterprise particularly where it is based within communities experiencing social exclusion. A different range of supports are required for these enterprises. These would be:

– funding pre-training initiatives run by organisations committed to the emergence of Traveller community enterprises;
– developing and resourcing, in conjunction with the relevant Traveller organisations linked to the enterprise, appropriate post start-up training experiences for the Travellers involved;
– funding mechanisms for the ongoing support role provided by organisations setting up Traveller community enterprises;
– long term subsidy mechanisms to offset the impact of a depressed local market for existing and future Traveller community enterprises, e.g. price support mechanisms could be considered;
– access for Traveller community enterprises to existing incubator units and an increase in the number of such units;
– better facilities within training centres for developing enterprise initiatives.
– encouragement to the private sector to purchase goods and services from Traveller community enterprises in their area.

5.2.7 Community enterprise brings both economic and social gain for the Traveller community. Its benefits include:

– job creation for members of a community without any significant presence in the mainstream labour force;
– promotion of the circulation of local wealth within the local economy;
– service gaps experienced in the community being identified and resolved;
– releasing local talent and ideas and supporting new role models;
– the emergence of a local enterprise culture.

5.2.8 The development of new supports for Traveller community enterprise is in line with the European Union White Paper "Growth, Competitiveness, Employment", (op. cit, 4). This White Paper states that:

"Member States have to ensure that additional jobs are most effectively made available to those in a disadvantaged position in the labour market".

It also identifies that this will involve:

"examining ways in which the social economy can be encouraged through tax-exemptions, public/private partnerships, part work and part income support models, to engage unemployed people, voluntarily, in actions which close the gap between people wishing to work and unmet social needs".

The White Paper identifies local services, improvements in the quality of life, and environmental protection as important sources of new jobs. These are the activities it identifies as making up the social economy. It states that:

"several estimates agree that some three million new jobs could be created in the Community, covering local services, improvements in the quality of life and environmental protection".

5.3 Public Service Employment

5.3.1 The 1983 Report of the Travelling People Review Body, (op. cit, 2) recommended that:

"Public service agencies should identify suitable employment opportunities for Travellers and offer employment to any Travellers who are available for regular work".

The Task Force endorses the thrust if not the scope of this recommendation. Public sector employment strategies should have a particular commitment to recruitment from groups at present excluded from the mainstream labour force. This commitment is already evident in relation to people with disabilities.

The recruitment of Travellers into the public sector should embrace all services. However, particular attention should be paid to the recruitment of Travellers into those parts of the public sector providing services to the Traveller community or in contact with the Traveller community. This would bring benefits by providing jobs for Travellers, increasing the sensitivity of public service provision to the particular needs of Travellers, increasing Travellers' sense of their own autonomy and providing valuable role models (Ref. 21).

Although the Review Body reported in 1983 there has been little progress made in relation to the above recommendation. There is clearly a need for a specific strategy to be identified and implemented for change to take place.

5.3.2 The voluntary community sector has made some progress in creating jobs for Travellers. This is particularly evident in the field of youth and community work where a range of organisations employ Travellers as youth workers and as community workers. A pilot project is also being developed in Pavee Point with Eastern Health Board assistance employing Traveller women as primary health care workers.

There are a number of relevant lessons identified from this experience:

– the recognition of a need for pre-training prior to taking up the job to build on existing knowledge and experience and to offset any educational disadvantage;
– the need for in-service training and appropriate supports within the work environment;
– the importance of jobs created offering clear routes for career advancement.

5.3.3 Strategies implemented in Australia by the Aboriginal and Torres Strait Islanders Commission (ASTIC), (Ref. 22) in relation to the employment of Aboriginal and Torres Strait Islanders provide a relevant starting point for securing employment of Travellers in the Irish Public Sector.

These strategies are based on the nomination of certain positions as "identified positions". Identified positions are those:

"where a significant part of the duties of a job involve the development of policy or the delivery of services and programmes to Aboriginal and Torres Strait Islander people and related support positions".

While it is expected that the selection process for these identified positions will result in the employment of Aboriginal and Torres Strait Islander People, the process is still based on open competition and selection on merit.

The positive action mechanism lies within the selection criteria for an identified position. These will always include:

"A demonstrated knowledge and understanding of Aboriginal and Torres Strait Islander societies and cultures and an understanding of the issues affecting Aboriginal and Torres Strait Islanders in contemporary Australian society and the diversity of circumstances of Aboriginal and Torres Trait Islander people" and *"A demonstrated ability to communicate sensitively and effectively, including the requirement for proper negotiation and consultation, with Aboriginal and Torres Strait Islanders on matters relevant to the delivery of the Government's Aboriginal and Torres Strait Islander development policies"*.

5.3.4 FÁS has defined apprenticeships as a method whereby a person works for an employer in a chosen occupation and learns the necessary skills, knowledge and attitudes to become a qualified craftsperson (Ref. 23). Traditionally, apprenticeships have been in industry and the various trades. However, FÁS has also stated that:

"Many of the provisions proposed for designated apprenticeships could usefully be applied to other areas of youth training" and *"the concept of apprenticeship could be broadened to include non-designated trades or occupations"*.

The new standards-based apprenticeship schemes aim to facilitate modular development and assessment over a four year period with off and on-the-job modules.

Entry to apprenticeships is not easy. However, special access measures exist in relation to women with pre-apprenticeship courses. A programme of Traveller apprenticeships allied to identified positions within the public sector would be an effective strategy for the employment of Travellers in the public sector within those sections that are in contact with or provide services to Travellers.

5.3.5 The policy of identified position should be allied to a more general policy facilitating recruitment in the public sector for Travellers. The identified position and apprenticeship strategy should be initially piloted within the health care, education, training and local authority sectors.

The following are examples of such posts:

Health:

- *Child care service*
- *Home help service*
- *Carer for the Aged*
- *Health Promoter*

Education:

- *Pre-schools*
- *Classroom Assistants*
- *Visiting Teacher Assistants*

Training:

- *Training Instructor Assistants*

Local Authorities:

- *Site Caretaker*

5.3.6   It is considered that the setting of specific targets would prove an effective means of encouraging the recruitment of Travellers into the public service. Precedents exist already in this regard, such as the three per cent quota for those with a physical or other disability and the Government policy that there should be a minimum of forty per cent of both men and women among the members on State boards. In those instances, however, the target population forms a large proportion of the overall population. As this is not the case with the Traveller community, a modified approach is proposed, as follows:

- a rolling programme of targets for recruitment to identified posts over the next five years: ten per cent in year one rising in equal steps to fifty per cent in year five;
- a target of 100 for employment in non-identified posts in the public service over the next five years.

The Department of Finance which has charge of public service recruitment policies, should have overall responsibility for monitoring the implementation of these targets and should review them after five years in consultation with the Equality Authority/Commission recommended in section C, "Discrimination" and relevant Traveller organisations. The Department should also prepare an annual report on the achievement of recruitment targets in respect of Travellers.

5.4   Recommendations

GR.21   The Departments of Education and of Enterprise and Employment, in conjunction with the relevant third-level institutions, should develop special access measures for Traveller entry into third-level education and into mainstream training. These measures should include preparation courses, adequate grants, and special tutorial assistance.

GR.22   The Department of Enterprise and Employment, in conjunction with FÁS and Traveller organisations involved in enterprise development, should develop a new funding strategy to support community enterprise, whose primary market is local supply, within communities such as the Traveller community which experience social exclusion. This funding strategy should be of a long term nature and should take account of special needs in relation to access to start-up capital and premises, and in relation to training requirements.

260

GR.23 The local partnership companies in the designated areas of disadvantage should be supported and encouraged to develop programmes of private sector purchasing from local community enterprise, including Traveller community enterprise.

GR.24 The public service should take a lead role in the recruitment of Travellers into the mainstream labour force. This role should be played in three ways:

- setting targets for Traveller inclusion in general recruitment strategies. These would include a rolling programme for recruitment to identified posts over the next five years as outlined in paragraph 5.3.6. above and a target of 100 for the employment in non-identified posts during the same period;

- the nomination of existing posts as identified positions with specific Traveller sensitive selection criteria, particularly in education, health and local authority recruitment;

- the development of new posts as identified positions, particularly in education, training, health and local authorities;

- the Department of Finance should have overall responsibility for monitoring the implementation of these targets. It should review them after five years in consultation with the Equality Authority/Commission and relevant Traveller organisations. The Department of Finance should also prepare an annual report on the achievement of recruitment targets in respect of Travellers.

GR.25 The Department of Enterprise and Employment, in conjunction with FÁS and Traveller organisations with experience in this field, should develop a Traveller apprenticeship scheme within the broader apprenticeship model. The Traveller apprenticeship should be designed around the skills, knowledge and attitude required for particular identified positions, as described in paragraph 5.3.4.

GR.26 The Department of Education, in conjunction with relevant funding agencies and Traveller organisations, should develop the special additional funding supports required to promote and support the further employment of Travellers as youth workers.

GR.27 The proposed Equality Authority/Commission should have a role in reviewing, evaluating and making recommendations in relation to these and future affirmative action measures to promote greater access for Travellers to the mainstream labour force. This role should be played in conjunction with the relevant government departments and Traveller organisations.

6.   Traveller Inclusion in Education and Training Schemes and the Local Development Programme

6.1   Training and Employment Schemes

6.1.1   Background

6.1.1.1 There is a range of employment and training schemes available through the Departments of Enterprise and Employment, Education and Social Welfare that individuals and groups can access. Voluntary and community groups have used some of these employment and training schemes to run development, training and employment programmes for Traveller women and young Travellers. The importance of these schemes and the opportunities they provide in a Traveller orientated environment need to be viewed in the light of low Traveller participation in mainstream education and training. Groups also use these schemes to undertake and develop the work of the group in the absence of other sources of funding and support.

6.1.1.2 Amongst the schemes available are:

(i)   the *Community Employment Programme* which replaces the Community Employment Development Programme and the Social Employment Scheme;

(ii)   the *Community Response Programme* which is part of the Community Training Programme and supports projects in the cultural, heritage, genealogical or archaeological area;

(iii)   the *Community Youth Training Programme* which is also part of the Community Training Programme and supports projects restoring buildings and machinery;

(iv)   the *Women's Programmes* undertaken are Traveller women's equivalent of courses run for 'Settled' women, called "Return to Work", with the programmes appropriately designed to meet Traveller women's distinct needs and funded under the FÁS external training budget;

(v)   the *Employment Incentive Scheme* is a scheme whereby the employer is paid a subsidy to employ someone who has been unemployed. Travellers are named as one of the groups who are not obliged to meet the entry requirements;

(vi)   the *Job Training Scheme* is a scheme designed to give the participants training on the job in a structured way;

(vii)   *YOUTHREACH* is a programme designed especially for early school leavers who have no formal qualifications and few chances of getting employment in the mainstream labour market;

(viii) *Vocational Training Opportunities Scheme (VTOS)* offers people who are over twenty-one years of age and who are unemployed for a year or more an opportunity to re-enter the education system in a more accessible way.

(ix)   *Linked Work Experience* is a six month training programme for people over sixteen years of age who are progressing from a basic training programme. The trainee is placed with an employer who agrees to provide an on the job training programme, which has been drawn up in consultation between the employer, FÁS and the trainee. There is a specified period of off the job training in the programme. It is monitored by a mentor, nominated by the employer and FÁS. The duration of the programme may be extended.

Schemes (i) to (vi) and (ix) are run under the auspices of FÁS. YOUTHREACH is organised jointly by FÁS and the VEC. VTOS is run by the VEC.

6.1.2 Community Employment Programme

"Given the high levels of unemployment in Ireland, it is important that those who are long-term unemployed or otherwise disadvantaged are given special assistance to improve their labour market performance. Without such assistance these groups will become ever more removed from the labour market and increasingly socially excluded." (Ref. 24).

The Community Employment Programme is emerging as the main scheme. Its features include:

*   Participants should be over twenty-one years of age IF they are receiving Unemployment Assistance. There is no age limit for potential participants if they are receiving Unemployment Benefit or Lone Parent's Allowance;

*   Participants should be on the Live Register for six months or else be in receipt of a Lone Parent's Allowance;

*   Participants retain their secondary benefits: provided they had claimed them and were receiving them prior to joining the course;

*   Participants can stay on the programme for a year. If the group can illustrate that it is both beneficial for a participant and for the group it may be possible for participants to stay for up to two years;

*   Groups can avail of the programme for up to two years to undertake a wide variety of community and socially useful work. Groups in areas designated for local development may be able to access the programme for up to three years for social projects;

*   There is a training element included for both the supervisors and the workers on the programme. The workers can, as one part of their training, pursue a course of their own choice.

The Community Employment Programme with its longer time frame and more flexible approach to continued participation of interested participants could be, and should be, of great use for Traveller groups in the pursuit of their capacity building and community development work.

6.1.3 Issues

6.1.3.1 *"The regular employment schemes and services of the National Manpower Service (FÁS) and other agencies should be adapted to provide for the particular employment needs of the Travelling people." (op. cit, 2)*

Very few Travellers gain access to mainstream training provision, which is regarded as the main follow-on to the training opportunities identified above. Entry requirements are now very competitive and Travellers do not have the required qualifications. Barriers to access also exist where mainstream provision does not recognise and resource the distinct needs of Travellers, including those related to Traveller mobility.

6.1.3.2 The issue of low Traveller participation relates, not only to mainstream training and employment schemes but also, to many of the schemes designed to address the needs of groups experiencing disadvantage named in paragraph 6.1.1.2 above such as YOUTHREACH and VTOS.

6.1.3.3 *"Traveller women suffer from a double burden of discrimination both as Travellers and women. So they need to be facilitated and encouraged to participate in schemes which will give them an opportunity to develop themselves, explore their lives and gain new skills ... They require a programme which will not exclude them because they did not meet a particular educational standard ... six months is too short a time in which to address these issues."* (Ref. 25)

The requirement in the Community Employment Programme for participants to be signing on the Live Register in practice excludes many married women. Traveller women tend to marry young which exacerbates this situation for them in relation not only to the Community Employment Programme but also to similar schemes. This means there is now no employment scheme the vast majority of Traveller women can access. This has particular implications for Traveller women as there has been no appropriate increase in the number of places being made available through the Women's Training Programmes sponsored by FÁS under their external training budget.

6.1.3.4 There is no employment scheme for those young people between the age of eighteen and twenty-one years, since the abolition of the Teamwork scheme, which catered for this group. While the age for receipt of Unemployment Assistance is eighteen years, potential participants of the Community Employment Programmes must be twenty-one years. The underlying logic appears to be the belief that people in this age group should be involved in education and/or training only. However, this does not recognise or cater for the specific needs of Travellers where employment schemes can have a particular relevance for this earlier age group, especially in a situation of low mainstream labour force participation.

6.1.3.5 *"Participants experience a loss of secondary benefits and incur day-to-day costs. The latter appear to give rise to higher levels of additional expenditure. For non-participants, the loss of security attached to certain secondary benefits can be as significant a disincentive to participation as the economic value of the benefit."* (Ref. 26).

There are costs for the potential trainee in participating on a scheme. Allowances that are the equivalent of or marginally better than the participant's social welfare benefits on most of the schemes further add to their situation. Allowances are often designed in a manner more appropriate to young single people without dependants. However, many Travellers marry young and the level of allowances effectively bars their entry to schemes targeted on disadvantaged people.

6.1.3.6 An issue for groups running schemes is the need for core funding. Core funding facilitates groups to maintain staff, premises and administrative back-up in the

264

transition between schemes and to cover additional expenses and cash flow problems that may arise. Lack of core funding can reduce the options considerably.

6.1.3.7 Groups can apply for a further scheme after completing one. However, the re-application process can be characterised by delay and by a lack of recognition of the groups' past record. This situation makes long term planning and development for the groups and the participants extremely difficult.

6.1.3.8 The length of time schemes run for is often inadequate. They can be too short to complete work projects or give participants adequate time to gain skills and knowledge. This is particularly true for groups such as Travellers who lack mainstream employment opportunities and therefore experience. A start has been made in addressing this within the Community Employment Programme.

6.1.3.9 The NESF has stated that:

"Acknowledgement of Culture Diversity: the distinct culture of Travellers and other minority ethnic groups are acknowledged in national and EU discussions and in some policies designed to meet their needs. But such acknowledgement is meaningless unless it is reflected in the practice and procedures for policy delivery in a variety of areas including that of social policy." (Ref. 27)

and the following recommendations reflect the spirit of this statement.

6.1.4 Recommendations

GR.28 The FÁS Employment Incentive Scheme sets an important precedent in specifically facilitating Traveller access, by naming them as a special category and waiving entry requirements. The same flexibility in relation to Travellers in the structure of and regulations governing other schemes, in particular the Community Employment Programme, should be implemented to enhance access for Travellers and Traveller organisations.

GR.29 In view of the difficulty of access to mainstream training, education and employment, the lifespan of all schemes for Travellers should be extended to a three year programme to facilitate skills development, planning and progression into mainstream provision.

GR.30 To encourage greater participation the level of allowances should be increased to cover the full costs associated with participation and to ensure an appropriate increase in comparison with social welfare payments.

GR.31 The number of programmes and places available through the Women's Training Programme for Traveller women and Traveller groups, sponsored by FÁS through the External Training budget, should be increased.

GR.32 Traveller groups should have access to schemes on a multi-annual basis, with guaranteed funding for core staff and facilities.

GR.33 Partnerships between funding agencies and Traveller groups should be developed at national level so that Traveller groups have an input into policy and procedures relating to training and employment schemes.

GR.34   Pilot programmes for Travellers using YOUTHREACH and VTOS should be designed and implemented in partnership with Traveller organisations. This would facilitate greater Traveller participation on these programmes.

GR.35   In-service training, focusing on anti-discriminatory practices and Traveller culture, should be made available for people providing training and employment scheme opportunities for Travellers.

GR.36   A number of strategies including links with the private sector should be developed to ensure progression for Travellers on schemes both into the mainstream labour force and within the Traveller economy.

6.2   Local Development Programme

6.2.1   Background

6.2.1.1   Chapter 7 of the National Development Plan 1994 - 1999 (op.cit 24) describes the Local Development Operational Programme which aims to address long term unemployment and support local development. The Programme will consist of four parts:

(i)   the Local Development Initiative - this is the extension of the area based response to long-term unemployment initiated under the Programme for Economic and Social Progress (PESP). The PESP established partnership companies in twelve areas experiencing high levels of unemployment. There will be thirty-three partnerships in all when the Local Development Operational Programme is fully operational;

(ii)   the County Enterprise Boards which were established to encourage *"a local economy of real strength and permanence which will give jobs and wealth sufficient to its needs"* (Ref. 28) through supporting locally based enterprises;

(iii)   the Community Employment Programme which is described in paragraph 6.1.2 above;

(iv)   the Urban Renewal Programme which will focus primarily on environmental improvements.

6.2.1.2   *"The Government recognises both the general role which local initiatives can play as a catalyst for local economic development throughout the country and the particular importance of locally based measures in ensuring that areas and communities characterised by long-term unemployment and severe disadvantage, which might otherwise not participate fully in mainstream programmes, are specifically targeted". (op. cit, 24)*

Through the Local Development Operational Programme an initiative called the Traveller Economy Programme is funded. This promotes the integration of Travellers into the developments taking place. The three principal objectives of the Programme are:

(i)   to support local Traveller groups throughout the country in developing and implementing new agendas and in accessing local development resources for this;

(ii)   to resource area based structures in including Travellers appropriately into their plans and actions;

(iii) to generate new information, debate and understanding of the Traveller economy at national and local level.

The Traveller Economy Programme is a good example of a mechanism of affirmative action for the appropriate integration of Travellers.

6.2.1.3   There will also be resources available through the Local Development Operational Programme for groups in non-designated areas, but of a more limited nature.

6.2.2   Issues

6.2.2.1   Under existing arrangements, if Travellers are not in one of the Local Partnership Company areas, they and other long-term unemployed are unable to avail of the resources and opportunities opening up through these initiatives. This is an issue for Traveller groups and others experiencing disadvantage living in non-designated areas. Mainstream resources targeted on these groups are threatened as they are withdrawn to provide resources for designated areas. The inclusion of non-designated areas in the new operational programme should begin to address this situation.

6.2.2.2   The narrow commercial enterprise focus of the County Enterprise Boards is unlikely to facilitate the inclusion of Travellers or other groups experiencing disadvantage. The parameters the County Enterprise Boards are required to operate within indirectly discriminate against Travellers who are mobile.

6.3   The Local Development Initiative

Recommendations

GR.37   Within the Local Development Programme for non designated areas, particular attention should be given to the inclusion of Travellers.

GR.38   In drawing up the Local Action Plan, Travellers and Traveller organisations should be consulted by the Local Development Partnership Company.

GR.39   Local Development Partnership Companies should be supported and encouraged to develop strategies in support of the social economy in their area. This would include local purchasing strategies as referred to in GR.23.

The County Enterprise Boards

Recommendations

GR.40   County Enterprise Boards are focused on job creation. Supports appropriate to a range of different forms of economic activity, including that of the Traveller

Economy with its income focus rather than a job creation focus, should be developed.

GR.41 The Boards should provide resources for job creation in the social economy particularly in the area of local services. This should also include funding strategies of a long-term nature for service enterprises located within disadvantaged communities and serving primarily a local market.

References

1.   Report of the Commission on Itinerancy, Stationery Office, Dublin, 1963.

2.   Report of the Travelling People Review Body, Stationery Office, Dublin, 1983.

3.   Liégeois Jean-Pierre, Gypsies and Travellers, Dossiers for the Intercultural Training for Teachers, Council of Europe, Strasbourg, 1987.

4.   Growth, Competitiveness, Employment - The Challenges and Ways Forward into the 21st Century, White Paper, Commission of the European Union, 1993.

5.   Ryan, Lorna. Policies and Strategies targeting indigenous Australians. Paper commissioned by the Task Force, Task Force Report, 1995.

6.   Annual Housing Statistics Bulletin, 1994 Stationery Office, Dublin, 1995.

7.   The Casual Trading Act, 1980 and Explanatory Memorandum. Stationery Office, Dublin, 1980.

8.   The Casual Trading Bill, 1994. Stationery Office, Dublin, 1994.

9.   A European Community Programme Policy and Action in relation to the Environment and Sustainable Development (The Fifth Environmental Action Programme). Official Journal of the European Communities C138 17th May, 1993.

10.   Amended Proposal for a Council Directive on the Land Fill of Waste. Official Journal of the European Communities C212 5th August, 1993.

11.   European Parliament and Council Directive on Packaging and Package Waste 94/62/EC of 20/12/94. Official Journal L365, 31st December, 1994.

12.   "Towards a Recycling Strategy for Ireland", Report commissioned by the Department of the Environment, 1993.

13.   Recycling and the Traveller Economy: Income, Jobs and Wealth Creation, Pavee Point Publications, Dublin, 1993.

14.   Recycling for Ireland: A Strategy for Recycling Domestic and Commercial Waste: Department of the Environment, 1994.

15.   Smith, Julia, Traveller participation in the Horse Trade, Paper commissioned by the Task Force, Task Force Report, 1995.

16.   Survey of Traveller Employment. National Association of Traveller Training Centres, June, 1994. (unpublished)

17.   Cantillon S., Curtis J., Fitzgerald J., Medium Term Review, ESRI, 1994.

18. "Ending Long-Term Unemployment", Report No. 4, National Economic and Social Forum, June, 1994.

19. In from the Cold - Support for Small Businesses in Disadvantaged Areas: Ballymun Community Action Project, 1994.

20. Redefining the concept of "Commercial Viability" in Partnership Areas, Paper by Ciaran Byrne (Industrial Development Manager with Ballymun Partnership) at Ballymun Community Action Project Conference, 1994.

21. "Traveller Inclusion in the Mainstream Labour Force - New Strategies for New Choices", Pavee Point Publications, 1995.

22. "Guidelines on Identified Positions". Aboriginal and Torres Strait Islander Commission (ASTIC). Australia.

23. "Apprenticeship: A New Approach", FÁS, Dublin, 1989.

24. Ireland: National Development Plan, 1994 - 1999. Stationery Office, Dublin, 1993.

25. "ARE YOU SCHEMING?" Pavee Point Publications, Dublin, 1993.

26. Duggan, Carmel and Cosgrove, Majella, Participation Costs on Labour Market Provision for the Long-Term Unemployed, PAUL Partnership Limerick, 1994.

27. Income Maintenance Strategies, Report No. 5, National Economic and Social Forum, July, 1994.

28. County Enterprise Boards, Department of Enterprise & Employment, 1993.

Section H: Traveller Women

1.   Introduction

1.1   Traveller women have played particular and significant leadership roles within their own community and representing their own community. A Traveller woman stood for election to the Dáil in response to anti-Traveller campaigns in Dublin in the early 80's and secured a considerable vote. In 1994 a Traveller woman was elected town commissioner in a west of Ireland town. A number of Traveller women have been accorded various national awards and commendations. Traveller women have produced widely acclaimed poetry, art and crafts. However, the central contribution which women make to the well-being of the Traveller community is largely unrecognised.

1.2   Traveller women, like 'Settled' women, are not a homogenous group and do not all share the same needs. Differences in age, status or income also lead to differences in the way issues are perceived and addressed by different Traveller women.

1.3   Traveller women through the years have had primary responsibility for rearing, often large families, except that they had to endure conditions unheard of by most 'Settled' women. Traveller women have played crucial roles in maintaining Traveller culture and identity.

1.4   Today, Traveller women are attempting to make the most of possible avenues for progress that are opening up for all women. Traveller women who have always played significant roles in the Traveller economy are exploring new ways of developing these roles. Much, however, needs to be done to achieve equality and to have this contribution fully acknowledged.

1.5   The establishment of the First and Second Commissions on the Status of Women represent an acknowledgement by the Government of the need to pay particular attention to the role, status and contribution of women to our society. They are also an acknowledgement that women are not automatically included, but in fact are more likely to be excluded from, general policies and programmes. The Task Force acknowledges a similar requirement and position with regard to Traveller women.

2.   Traveller Women and the Task Force Report

2.1   The Task Force recognises the need to examine the way in which each of the areas discussed in this Report affects Traveller women and to specify the gender impact of the various recommendations in preparation for their implementation. This is in line with the Government decision of 9th February 1993 that all proposals by Departments for change in existing Government policies should give an indication of the probable impact on women of such proposals.

2.2   The Task Force also acknowledges the commitment to gender proofing in the National Development Plan (Ref.1), the Structural Funds Regulations (Ref.2), as reinforced by the Council of Ministers' resolution, (Ref.3) on promotion of equal opportunities for men and women through action by the European Structural Funds, and consequential monitoring procedures now being adopted. All of these have implications for

Travellers, Traveller women and policies and programmes that support them which may emerge as a consequence of the Task Force's recommendations.

2.3 As stated in paragraph 2.1 above, there should be a gender impact statement accompanying policy changes implemented as a result of this Report. This section does not constitute such a statement but rather provides an overall context and framework within which it might be done. The overall aim, in line with current approaches to addressing equality issues, is to focus directly on Traveller women's needs, and to ensure that these needs are addressed in each of the areas of concern for the Task Force. The approach in this regard is similar to the methods which the Second Commission on the Status of Women (Ref.4) and the National Report of Ireland to the UN Fourth World Conference on Women (Ref.5) began to develop.

2.4 The task of describing, analysing and attempting to set out possible ways forward regarding Traveller women's needs is made particularly difficult by the lack of information regarding the various aspects of Traveller women's lives. The Task Force acknowledges the work of voluntary groups who, with Traveller women, have produced books of photographs, crafts, stories and viewpoints. However, there is an urgent need for further specific research on Traveller women to ensure that measures for Travellers meet the needs of Traveller women.

3. Discrimination and Women in Minority Groups

3.1 Any examination of the needs and concerns of Traveller women must take account of current analyses of and responses to the needs of women from other minority groups. There are important parallels and lessons to be drawn from other experiences.

3.2 Women from minority groups are recognised globally as having specific needs and concerns and as being particularly vulnerable to discrimination. The Forward Looking Strategies Document agreed at the third UN Global Summit on Women in Nairobi (Ref.6) by all Member States, including Ireland, states that: *"some women are oppressed as a result of belonging to minority groups or populations which have historically been subjected to domination..."* and goes on to call for full human rights for women from minority groups and respect for their economic and cultural rights. The Document emphasises *"the distinctive role of women in sustaining the identity of their people"*. It also states that women belonging to minority groups should be fully consulted and should participate in the development and implementation of programmes affecting them. The double burden of oppression experienced by minority group women is underlined.

3.3 Black and minority group women have extensively documented the interplay between, and contradictions of addressing, gender oppression and racism in their lives. This can involve these women in invidious choices between raising the issue of sexism within their own community and being in solidarity with their own community in resisting external oppression.

4. Discrimination and Traveller Women

4.1 The inequalities experienced by women generally are also experienced by Traveller women. In addition, Traveller women suffer from discrimination experienced by

Travellers as a group in Irish society. For Traveller women this discrimination which very forcibly affects their daily lives, has to take priority. A Traveller woman followed around a supermarket by suspicious staff, or refused service altogether has to find ways of dealing with that discrimination if she is to feed her family.

4.2 Much of the discrimination experienced by Travellers in Irish society has a particular impact on the lives of Traveller women due to their primary roles as home-makers in their own communities. Such practices in these areas are not only discriminatory towards Travellers as a whole group, they also contribute to shaping Traveller women's particular experiences of inequality as women.

4.3.1 One of the primary indicators of the status of a group of people is average life expectancy. A study carried out by the Health Research Board in 1987, (Ref.7) pointed out that *"at birth male Travellers can expect to live 9.9 years less than Settled males, whereas life expectancy at birth is 11.9 years less for female Travellers than Settled females"*. Thus while the status of all Travellers is low, Traveller women are even further marginalised.

4.3.2 Many Travellers experience difficulty gaining access to places of entertainment and public houses. In some instances however, even when men are given access, women are barred, or men are not allowed in when they are accompanied by women. Again the women are further marginalised and the external discrimination actively promotes an internal parallel.

4.4 'Settled' people's responses to Traveller women's difficulties are often to blame them for their own situation. A Traveller woman writing in 1989, (Ref. 8) said: *"Settled women look down on Traveller women and give out about them for the oppression they suffer. But what a lot of Settled women don't see is that Travelling and Settled women are in the same boat when it comes to the way they are looked down on and treated in society by men"*.

4.5 This process of blaming can often be a feature of Traveller women's experience in dealing with the various social services - medical, social work, accommodation, social welfare or schools. Some of those they deal with promote and support their right to their Traveller identity. Others, often unconsciously, undermine it. Traveller women can be left with the message that their problems can best be solved if they cease to be Travellers. This leaves Traveller women in an impossible and unenviable situation, effectively being blamed for being Travellers.

4.6 Traveller women, on the other hand, like so many other women from minority groups experiencing oppression, may be left with little opportunity to address their own situation as women. Challenging this oppression is often seen as attacking the culture, which is already under threat from the outside, and therefore must be supported internally by all members. This ignores the fact that cultures are not stagnant, but are dynamic relationships which change with time as the lives and experiences of their members change.

4.7 It is widely recognised that young women from minority groups can experience particular discrimination, especially at times of major changes in their culture. The

UN placed a particular focus within this Year of Tolerance on promoting their rights. The current tension between traditional approaches and modern developments evident in Traveller culture (and in Irish society as a whole over the past twenty years) has particular implications for young Traveller women. It is essential that young Traveller women have their particular education and developmental needs met in ways that do not blame them for being Traveller women, but which acknowledge the changing dynamic of Traveller culture and the crucial importance of equality for Traveller women in the future.

5. Responding to Discrimination Against Traveller Women

5.1.1 Both the internal and external discrimination experienced by Traveller women need urgent responses. For this to begin to happen such discrimination must be named in ways which do not further marginalise Traveller women. This requires that key areas are examined in terms of how these issues affect Traveller women including the often hidden gender dimension; how policies and practices in each area contribute to or block progress for Traveller women; what steps might be put in place to ensure equality for Traveller women in each area; and how these will be monitored.

5.1.2 It is recognised that there are issues other than those touched on below. The intention in the remainder of this section is to focus on a limited number of areas to which responses are required as an essential pre-requisite to any progress.

5.2 Childcare

5.2.1 The need for child care provision is included in EU Directives and in the Report of the Second Commission on the Status of Women (op.cit,4) as a fundamental prerequisite to creating the conditions for progress for women. Last year the Department of Equality and Law Reform made available £1m for developing childcare facilities in disadvantaged areas. Although the availability of child care and social care is crucial for women's progress, childcare should not be designated as only a women's issue. It is of particular importance to all members of the community and should be focused on the needs of the children being cared for. This means that the area of childcare for Traveller children needs review and analysis in its own right.

5.2.2 As regards Traveller women, the absence of childcare is obviously a barrier to participation in social and economic activity. The assumption however, that Traveller women require the same child and social care support as 'Settled' women may not always be accurate. Traveller women's childcare needs have to be identified and addressed in terms that acknowledge their culture and lifestyle.

5.2.3 Traveller women also need opportunities to access training and resources which might make them providers as well as recipients of such services.

5.3 Reports

5.3.1 The Second Commission on the Status of Women (op.cit,4) and the Irish Government's report to the United Nations for the Fourth Global Conference on

Women (op.cit,5) explicitly name and address some Traveller women's concerns. All research and reports to promote progress for women should explicitly include Traveller women in their deliberations.

5.3.2 Traveller women should not be discussed only under the heading of poverty, which, while an issue, can fail to acknowledge many other concerns. Traveller women's rights to sustain their identity as per the Nairobi Declaration (op.cit 6) must be a starting point of all such work.

5.3.3 Research and reports on Travellers must acknowledge the particular needs of Traveller women in ways that respect their culture and do not blame them for being Travellers. Traveller women must be subjects rather than objects of such research.

5.4 Violence

5.4.1 Some Traveller women, as with 'Settled' women, experience male violence that is used to dominate, control and demean through the abuse of power. Measures must be taken to develop consciousness, address this violence and provide means of redress for those experiencing it.

5.4.2 Traveller women also experience coercion and violence from 'Settled' people and their institutions in many areas of their lives. More recently a particular concern for women has been illegal attacks on Travellers. Such violence is a clear violation of the human rights of Traveller women as outlined in the UN CEDAW Declaration (Ref.9) to which Ireland is a signatory, and should be responded to urgently.

5.5 The Law

5.5.1 Many Traveller women feel that the fact that they are women is ignored in their interaction with the law and have particular feelings of vulnerability when pregnant or accompanied by small children. This has been a particular concern when evictions are taking place. New initiatives to deepen understanding of Travellers' way of life by the relevant statutory authorities, and in particular by the Gardaí, must explicitly focus on Traveller women in this regard.

5.6 Traveller Economy

Traveller women have always played active roles in the Traveller economy and are now trying to find ways to develop and diversify those roles in a rapidly changing environment. Women in Third World countries traditionally also play significant and active roles in their economies. A number of development programmes however tended to designate key roles in "projects for progress and modernisation" to men and/or to exclude women from such projects. It is essential that interventions in the Traveller economy acknowledge, support and resource the key roles of women in that economy.

6. Training and Employment Programmes and Traveller Women

6.1 A decade ago Traveller women's formal training and education opportunities were confined to opportunities for younger women through Traveller Training Centres.

Considerable progress has been made but much remains to be done if Traveller women are to achieve their full potential. For example, while State schemes are open to accepting Travellers they are often culturally inappropriate for Travellers, especially Traveller women. Integrated, 'Settled' and Traveller women's programmes are not designed to sustain and support the particular needs, potential and identity of Traveller women. Recruitment policies for such courses do not often target Traveller women.

6.2 There are no particular national initiatives targeted for Traveller women. The NOW Programme (EU Community Initiative) 1989 - 1994 in Ireland has provided positive opportunities, which need to be further resourced and developed. As far as can be ascertained the two Traveller women NOW projects in Ireland were the only ones focusing exclusively on Traveller and Gypsy women in the NOW programme throughout the Member States in the period 1989-1994.

7. Voluntary Sector and Traveller Women

7.1 Particular progress has been made in the last decade through the development of a number of Traveller women's groups and leadership and personal development programmes for Traveller women. These were piloted initially through Pavee Point in the Dublin area. These have been run by voluntary groups sometimes with assistance from various grant giving bodies, including FÁS, throughout the country. There are no particular national training initiatives targeted on Traveller women, but voluntary groups have been able to secure resources from various agencies and to build programmes to meet the women's needs.

7.2 The women's groups are now co-ordinated nationally through the National Traveller Women's Forum, which organises national and regional days for Traveller women, focuses on policy and issues of concern, and is playing a significant role in ensuring Traveller women's 'visibility'.

7.3 Traveller women's groups participate in exchanges with 'Settled' women's groups, in local networks of women's groups, and in the Council for the Status of Women and contribute to national discussions regarding issues for all women.

8.1 Recommendations

HR.1 In implementing each of the recommendations addressed in this Report the gender dimension should be examined in order to ascertain how policies and practices in each area contribute to or block progress for Traveller women. Proposals for future initiatives in each area must be monitored in terms of their impact on equality for Traveller women. Each must outline its objectives, targets and likely outcomes for Traveller women.

HR.2 The Government should make resources available for the collection and collation of data on Traveller women through specific research projects. In these projects Traveller women and Traveller women's groups should be subjects rather than objects of the research. The research should build on local profiles and accounts already produced and on other research underway so that any study complements rather than repeats, and addresses gaps not heretofore the subject of detailed scrutiny.

HR.3 In line with the recommendations of the Second Commission on the Status of Women, Government policies on this matter and EU Directives, progress for Traveller women is recognised as a priority in the move towards equality for all women. It is also recognised as essential if progress is to be made for all Travellers. This necessitates a particular focus on Traveller women by any body set up as a consequence of the Task Force Report and in all Government Departments concerned with its implementation. It also requires a particular focus on Traveller women in procedures and legislation adopted towards the implementation of the Report of the Second Commission on the Status of Women.

HR.4 The special needs of different groups of Traveller women should be looked at separately acknowledging that not all Traveller women are the same, for example, the specific situation of young Traveller women referred to at paragraph 4.7 above.

HR.5 **(i)** Particular issues which affect the human rights of Traveller women must be urgently addressed. Institutionalised violence towards Traveller women requires detailed examination and responses. Culturally appropriate ways to support Traveller women who experience violence within their community, and to respond to the issue of male violence, need to be worked on with Traveller women. Such work should take into account the responses already being made by voluntary groups, refuges and Women's Aid. The Department of Health should provide resources for pilot projects in this area.

(ii) There should be no discrimination or exclusion of Traveller women wishing to access these services.

(iii) Resources should be made available by the Department of Health to expand and improve existing facilities in these areas. This should ensure provision for family units of different sizes.

(iv) Those working in this area should have access to training in order to ensure their understanding of Travellers and their way of life.

(v) The childcare needs of Traveller women should be researched and addressed.

HR.6 Traveller women's economic roles in their community should be acknowledged and resourced so that any economic progress for Travellers is supportive of, rather than at the expense of, Traveller women.

HR.7 **(i)** Targeted responses to Traveller women's needs in a variety of areas such as health, education, training and personal development are required as a prerequisite towards progress and equality. These should be designed and delivered in partnership with Traveller women's organisations. They should be flexible and capable of integrating local work already underway and building on the knowledge of existing groups.

(ii) Ongoing targeted initiatives for Traveller women, as outlined above, should be built into maintream programmes of FÁS and other State agencies. Staff on such programmes should be selected and managed by Traveller women's organisations.

References

1. Ireland: National Development Plan, 1994 - 1999, Stationery Office, Dublin 1993.

2. European Structural Fund Regulations, Regulations 2081/93, OJ No. 4193, 31st July, 1993.

3. Council of Ministers Resolution 22nd June, 1994, OJ No. C 231, 20th August, 1994.

4. Second Commission on the Status of Women, Report to Government, Stationery Office, Dublin, 1993.

5. National Report of Ireland, United Nations Fourth World Conference on Women, Stationery Office, Dublin, 1994.

6. The Forward Looking Strategies Document, Third UN Global Conference on Women, Nairobi, 1985.

7. Barry, Joseph, Herity, Bernadette, Solan, Joseph, The Traveller Health Status Study: Vital Statistics of Travelling People (1987): Health Research Board, Dublin, 1989.

8. Maughan, Margaret. Co-options. Journal of the Community Workers Co-Operative, May, 1989.

9. CEDAW - Convention on the Elimination of All Forms of Discrimination Against Women acceded to by Ireland, December, 1985.

Section J: Travellers with a Disability

1. Concerns

1.1   Travellers with a disability share the concerns of the broader community of people with a disability. These include:

–   offensive language and imagery that reinforces perceptions of people with a disability as passive victims;

–   discrimination in the provision of goods and services through lack of physical access, segregation and inappropriate services; and

–   lack of control over their own lives and lack of access to financial resources.

1.2   Equally, Travellers with a disability stand to benefit from the new political commitment to the rights of people with a disability and a growing demand for new approaches. This demand seeks to ensure an accessible environment so that people with a disability can be integrated within mainstream society while being facilitated in terms of their specific needs. However, new understandings and new initiatives will not fully respond to the needs of Travellers with a disability unless they specifically name Travellers. Travellers with a disability live out of a twofold identity and this should be recognised and respected.

1.3   Research carried out by Pavee Point under the title "Travellers with a Disability" (Ref. 1) :

–   identified a number of issues of concern to Travellers with a disability such as the experience of isolation from their own community, a lack of recognition of their Traveller identity from care service providers, inaccessible Traveller accommodation facilities and a lack of contact with Traveller groups;

–   explored a range of issues in relation to service provision including a lack of data on Traveller take-up of services, little appreciation of the importance of cultural difference, the absence of in-service training on interculturalism, and a range of negative stereotypes of Travellers expressed by service providers.

2. Access

Recommendation

JR.1   The relevant Government Departments and State agencies should make resources available:

–   to ensure that the premises of Traveller groups in their area are accessible to people with a disability;

–   to develop a programme for care service providers, Traveller groups or organisations of people with a disability, to train and employ personnel as

Traveller advocates. These advocates would play a role in ensuring that the buildings and resources of Traveller groups are accessible, ensuring that the policies and practices of care service providers are sensitive and appropriate to cultural difference, and are supportive of Travellers with a disability, enabling them to express their double identity with confidence. It is envisaged that funding this work would be the responsibility of the Department of Health and local health boards as appropriate;

–   to further research the particular experience and needs of Travellers with a disability.

3. Identity

Recommendation

JR.2   Those responsible for the provision of care services to people with a disability should be required by the various health boards and the Department of Health, as appropriate, to develop appropriate responses to the particular needs of Travellers with a disability including initiatives to reduce their isolation, and programmes to assist those who wish to affirm their Traveller identity and to challenge any discrimination experienced.

4. Training

Recommendation

JR.3   The various health boards and the Department of Health, as appropriate, should support and resource care service providers to develop in-service training on intercultural work practices in co-operation with Traveller groups.

5. Policy

Recommendation

JR.4   (a)   The Commission on the Status of People with Disabilities should make specific reference in its work and reporting to the distinct needs of Travellers with a disability.

(b)   In the implementation of the National Health Strategy, the Health Development Sectors should provide resources and opportunities for Travellers and Traveller groups and, within this, specific mention should be made of the needs of Travellers with a disability.

References

1.   McDonagh, Rosaleen, Travellers with a Disability: A Submission to the Commission on the Status of People with Disabilities, Pavee Point Publications, Dublin, 1994.

Section K: Co-ordination of Services by Statutory Bodies and Implementation and Monitoring of Task Force's Report

1.   **The Need for a Co-ordinated Approach**

1.1   As illustrated throughout this Report, the Traveller community comes into contact with various statutory agencies, such as local authorities, health boards and government departments, at national and local levels, for a wide variety of reasons. In particular, this contact takes place on a regular basis at local level with local authorities, health boards and with the providers of education and social welfare services.

1.2   At a central level, issues which impact on the Traveller community, particularly in the policy area, are dealt with by Government Departments such as the Departments of Social Welfare, Environment, Health, Education and Equality and Law Reform.

1.3   The Task Force places particular importance in this Report on ensuring that suitable mechanisms are put in place, or where necessary strengthened, in all relevant statutory agencies whose functions impact on Travellers, so that appropriate co-ordination and planning is undertaken in relation to the formulation of policy and the administration and delivery of services.

1.4   A co-ordinated approach by statutory agencies at national and local levels in relation to the services which they provide for the Traveller community is essential for a number of reasons including:

- At a policy level, it is important that the views of service providers on the ground such as local authority social workers, public health nurses, visiting teachers and housing welfare officers are taken into account in the framing of policies which may impact on Travellers through the administration and delivery of services.

- In all statutory agencies it is essential that information and feedback on Travellers' needs is available to all relevant sections in those agencies.

1.5   The adoption of adequate mechanisms for co-ordination should ensure that resources being directed towards the Traveller community are utilised to their maximum potential, particularly in the area of service provision so that duplication is avoided. Such mechanisms should also assist in ensuring that services to Travellers are provided in a consistent and uniform manner in all parts of the country and that Travellers' needs are catered for in an efficient and effective manner.

2.   **Present Co-ordination Arrangements**

2.1   At present, a variety of co-ordination arrangements are in place within and between statutory agencies and at national and local levels in respect of the formulation of policy and the administration and delivery of services to members of the Traveller community. While the following paragraphs provide a general outline of the present arrangements which exist, it is not intended to comment on the position in individual statutory agencies.

2.2   Research carried out for the Task Force by the Social Policy Research Unit, Department of Applied Social Studies, University College Cork, (Ref. 1) indicates that planning and co-ordination mechanisms differ greatly between statutory agencies.

2.3   With regard to policy formulation on Traveller issues in the social policy area, few formal mechanisms are in place for co-ordination between statutory agencies. However, informal arrangements for co-ordination do exist, particularly in the area of health policy between, for example, health boards and the Department of Health. Consultation also takes place on an ad-hoc basis between the health boards and the Departments of Education, Environment and Justice and between local authorities and Government Departments in the area of policy development. The Minister for Equality and Law Reform has overall responsibility for the co-ordination of Government policy in respect of the Traveller community.

2.4   Within the relevant statutory agencies a number of mechanisms exist to ensure a co-ordinated approach to the delivery of services to members of the Traveller community. Examples include the following:

    (i)   **Health and Community Care Services:** Three broad trends can be identified. Firstly, an important role is played by the public health nurse (PHN) in co-ordinating services to members of the Traveller community. The PHN reports back to, and seeks operational support from, colleagues in the health board as the need arises. Secondly, most co-ordination is carried out on an ad-hoc basis and finally designated staff are not generally provided for co-ordination purposes. More comprehensive arrangements do, however, exist for co-ordination purposes, for example, in the Eastern Health Board.

    (ii)   **Accommodation and Environmental Services:** Local authorities generally have some framework in place for the co-ordination of service delivery. Again broadly three types of mechanism may be identified. In most cases, the local authority social worker plays a vital role. Some local authorities have a special section or committee which oversees co-ordination arrangements. Finally, in some instances, the housing welfare officer co-ordinates accommodation services for Travellers.

    (iii)   **Education Services:** At a national level, the function of the National Education Officer for Travellers includes some co-ordination responsibilities. At a local level, the Visiting Teacher Service, where it is in place, co-ordinates the service on the ground at primary school level. The VTS is co-ordinated at regional level by divisional inspectors in the Department of Education and ultimately by the Special Education Section of the Department.

    (iv)   **Social Welfare Services:** Under new procedures recently introduced to co-ordinate social welfare services for Travellers, the Regional Director's Office in the Department of Social Welfare is responsible for co-ordination arrangements between the different social welfare regions and between the different sections of that Department. Co-ordination applies in particular to signing arrangements for members of the Traveller community and the Department of Social Welfare is in the process of establishing structures to co-ordinate its funding arrangements for voluntary groups.

2.5.1   In relation to inter-agency co-ordination of services, the research carried out for the Task Force indicates that few mechanisms are in place for this purpose between the different statutory agencies whose services impact on the Traveller community.

2.5.2   In the case of the health boards, informal arrangements for inter-agency co-ordination are in place. For example, under the aegis of most health boards, representatives of other statutory agencies most notably the local authority social worker, the visiting teacher, representatives of the Probation and Welfare Service and the Gardaí attend multi-disciplinary case conferences if cases involving members of the Traveller community are being discussed.

2.5.3   In the majority of health boards, staff on the ground such as public health nurses and environmental health officers liaise in the course of their everyday work with the staff of other statutory agencies dealing with the needs of Travellers.

2.5.4   In those local authorities which employ the services of a social worker for Travellers, these usually take responsibility for the co-ordination of services with other outside agencies.

3.   Summary of Task Force Recommendations on Co-ordination

3.1   Throughout this Report, the Task Force makes a number of recommendations with a view to introducing and/or strengthening co-ordination arrangements within and between the various statutory agencies whose work impacts on the Traveller community particularly in the areas of accommodation, health and education.

3.2   For ease of reference these recommendations are summarised in a co-ordinated manner in this section. The full text of the recommendations together with the relevant section of this Report in which further background information can be found, are also listed below:

Section A: Relationships with Settled Community

AR.5   The Department of Equality and Law Reform in conjunction with other relevant departments and Non-Governmental Organisations, and taking account of previous work in this field, should play a role in exploring and devising a framework for mediation.

Section C: Discrimination

CR.6.1 and CR.8.1: That an Equality Authority/Commission be established based on a re-structured Employment Equality Agency. The Equality Authority/Commission be comprised of an Employment Board and a non-Employment Board. The non-Employment Board in turn would establish a distinct Traveller Unit which would ensure cohesive action on Traveller issues, which would encompass officers in the following areas; legal, enforcement, information, legislation, positive action and research, and which would have adequate clerical and financial support. The research officer would initiate in-house research, co-ordinate with research commissioned in other sections of the Equality Authority/Commission and make an input into such research.

CR.11.1: That the Department of Equality and Law Reform, or its successor, in its work of co-ordination in relation to services to Travellers, would promote and support the introduction of an Equal Status policy within the various public sector institutions providing services of an essential nature to the Traveller community, as a matter of priority.

Section D: Accommodation

DR.22: An independent statutory body, to be known as the Traveller Accommodation Agency, should be established to draw up, in consultation with local authorities, a National Programme for the provision of Traveller specific accommodation in order to achieve the Government objective of provision of such accommodation by the year 2000.

(Full details of the co-ordination role of the proposed Traveller Accommodation Agency are included in Section D).

DR.18: Co-ordinated strategies for the accommodation of Travellers over the Greater Dublin area are required between the four local authorities concerned. A Strategic Planning Unit should be established drawing together relevant officials from the four councils chaired by a representative from the Traveller Accommodation Agency to ensure co-ordination and best use of resources. This Unit should also meet on a regular basis with relevant Traveller organisations.

Section E: Health

ER.3: A Traveller Health Advisory Committee should be appointed by the Minister for Health, its brief to include a co-ordination role in relation to a number of aspects of the health status of the Traveller community.

ER.4: Each health board should establish a Traveller Health Unit, its brief to include a co-ordination role in relation to a number of aspects of the health status of Travellers.

ER.7: An improved system of transferring records, within and between health board regions, should be introduced. The application of information technology systems such as those used in the field of banking should be explored to establish data bases of Traveller health records that would ensure this transfer of records between community care, hospital services and pharmacies within and between health board regions. The process should be approved by the Data Protection Commissioner.

Section F: Education and Training

FR.28: In order to facilitate a more co-ordinated, structured and comprehensive approach to Traveller education, the Task Force recommends the establishment without delay of a Traveller Education Service (TES) under the aegis of the Department of Education. The TES would include a Traveller Education Unit in the Department of Education and an Advisory Committee to be appointed by the Minister for Education.

(Full details of the co-ordination role and proposed terms of reference of this Service are included in Section F).

FR.133: The Department of Education with the other relevant departments should ensure that an integrated inter-departmental approach is achieved between youth work, childcare, sports and recreation, home/school links, the Juvenile Liaison Scheme, literacy and other adult education schemes. This integrated approach should be reflected in structures at national and local level.

FR.142: The Department of Education should appoint a National Co-ordinator to promote the development and monitor the performance of Senior Traveller Training Centres. The person appointed should have a clear commitment to Travellers' development, a knowledge of the development of Traveller Training Centres and proven management and facilitation skills.

Section G: Traveller Economy

GR.27: The proposed Equality Authority/Commission should have a role in reviewing, evaluating and making recommendations in relation to......future affirmative action measures to promote greater access for Travellers to the mainstream labour force. This role should be played in conjunction with the relevant government departments and Travellers' organisations.

4.   Implementation and Monitoring of Task Force's Report

KR.1   In order to oversee the implementation and monitoring of this Report, the Task Force recommends that the following arrangements be put in place by the Minister for Equality and Law Reform or his successor:

(a)   The Minister for Equality and Law Reform as part of his/her responsibility for co-ordinating Government policy in relation to Traveller issues should monitor and co-ordinate the implementation of the recommendations contained in this Report.

(b)   A Traveller Unit with adequate resources should be established within the Department of Equality and Law Reform to assist the Minister in regard to (a).

(c)   An annual progress report should be published on the implementation of the Task Force's Report and a formal mechanism should be established for discussion of that progress report with all relevant interests.

References

1.   Norris Michelle, The co-ordination of statutory services for the Travelling Community in the Republic of Ireland: A report for the Task Force on the Travelling Community, Social Policy Research Unit, Department of Applied Social Studies, UCC, 1995.

Section L: Sport and Other Recreations, Culture and the Arts

1.   Introduction

1.1   Participation by Travellers in sport and other recreational activities, cultural initiatives and the arts, as well as being a fundamental right which should be promoted and encouraged, is another way in which mutual understanding and respect can be developed between the Traveller and 'Settled' communities thereby contributing positively to the process of reconciliation referred to in section A: Relationships between the Traveller and 'Settled' Communities.

1.2   This section deals with Traveller involvement in sport and other recreational activities, Culture and the Arts, from the point of view of participation in such activities, and in respect of access to the venues or locations in which such activities take place.

2.   Access to Sport, Community, Cultural and Recreational Facilities

2.1   The Traveller community should enjoy the same level of access to and use of sport, community and recreational facilities as every other individual. Unfortunately, particularly at local level, this is not the case at present with Travellers' access to such facilities being denied either on the basis of a prohibition on entry or by means of some artificial limitation or restriction on access.

2.2   In addition to an equal right of access to recreational facilities, the Traveller community must enjoy equal rights to participate in recreational activities with particular reference to participation in sport.

2.3   The effective denial of access and of the right to participate in recreational activities may often happen through poor levels of contact between Travellers and 'Settled' people within a particular recreational or cultural facility, or, in some instances, through a failure to acknowledge cultural difference in terms of the activities provided.

2.3.1   Recommendations

LR.1   In relation to all forms of recreational activity and access to the venues in which these activities take place, the Task Force recommends that discriminatory practices of a direct and indirect nature, should be prohibited against any group particularly vulnerable to discrimination, including Travellers. The Task Force notes, in particular, that legislative proposals in this regard are being drawn up by the Minister for Equality and Law Reform.

LR.2   The Task Force welcomes the provisions of the European Sports Charter (Ref.1) adopted by Member States of the Council of Europe in 1993 and recommends that in line with that Charter, special emphasis should be placed on encouraging greater involvement by those who are disadvantaged, including members of the Traveller community, in sporting activities at all levels.

2.4   In addition, the Task Force recommends that as a means of encouraging such increased participation the following initiatives be undertaken:

2.4.1   Recommendations

LR.3 The Department of Education should draw up a statement of practice in relation to access to and participation in sporting activities by all members of the Traveller community.

LR.4 There should be an increased commitment on the part of the Department of Education and Vocational Education Committees in relation to the provision of funding, including funds from the National Lottery, to enable Traveller groups to participate in sporting activities.

LR.5 Present arrangements operated by the Department of Education for the allocation of grant-in-aid approvals in respect of sports facilities should include a reference to Travellers' right of access to such facilities.

LR.6 National sports organisations should issue statements of practice to their members on the same lines as recommended at LR.3 above.

LR.7 In making grant allocations, sporting organisations including VEC sports committees, should assist less well known sports pursued by Travellers, such as, road bowling and trotting, to ensure greater standards of safety in appropriate locations.

2.5   Culture and the Arts

2.5.1 The Task Force welcomes the commitment included in the mission statement of The Arts Council (Ref.2) that *"everyone in Ireland has an entitlement to meaningful access to and participation in the arts"*. It also welcomes the Council's concern (Ref.3) about the development of the arts in the regions, which stems from the twin beliefs that *"all people, wherever they might live, are entitled to broadly equal services from Government"* and *"all people have a right to cultural self-determination"*.

2.5.2 The Task Force also endorses the statement contained in the White Paper on Cultural Policy "Access and Opportunity" (Ref.4) published in 1987, to the effect that the role of the Government in relation to culture might be expressed by the following objective among others:

"to provide for every individual, from the earliest age, conditions conducive to the full achievement of his or her creative potential and to develop opportunities for creative activity and self expression".

2.5.3   Recommendations

LR.8 The Task Force recmmends, in relation to Traveller involvement in and the development and administration of cultural policy, including participation in the arts and access to cultural facilities such as museums and theatres that:

    –   The statements quoted above should act as fundamental principles to be implemented, developed and built upon as necessary in relation to the Arts;

– The Arts Council should publish a Code of Practice for access by Travellers to the Arts along the lines of that published in 1985 for people with a disability;

– Increased funding should be provided, at national and local levels, by the relevant statutory agencies, including The Arts Council, in order to assist and encourage Travellers to develop their artistic and cultural potential and to participate fully in the cultural and artistic life of the State particularly at community level;

– Museums, galleries and other institutions in which artistic work is displayed, should accommodate the work of the Traveller community.

References

1. European Sports Charter, Council of Europe, 1993.

2. Art Matters. The Arts Council, No. 17, Dublin, 1994.

3. Art Matters. The Arts Council, No. 16, Dublin, 1993.

4. White Paper on Cultural Policy "Access and Opportunity" Stationery Office, 1987.

Addendum

The recommendations in the Report represent the deliberations of the Task Force in response to the Terms of Reference given to it. The approach taken was dictated by the urgent needs of the traveller community and, in particular, the Government's target of providing permanent serviced caravan site accommodation for all traveller families who require it by the year 2000. However, the undersigned members of the Task Force, while endorsing the recommendations in the Report, are of the view that the emphasis which has been given to the element of nomadism in the lives of the traveller community begs the assumption that there will be no significant change in the nomadic way of life for the foreseeable future. They also feel that the formulation of Government policy to the year 2000 and beyond should include consideration of alternatives to the nomadic way of life in view of:-

- the disadvantages of the current life-style of the traveller community.

- the changing pattern of work opportunities available to the traveller community.

- the increasing conflict with the settled community which arises mainly from the consequences of the nomadic lifestyle.

- the inordinate cost to the exchequer of catering for this way of life.

Nomadism in the context of today's traveller lifestyle is a contentious and emotive issue but any lifestyle which places that community at a significant disadvantage in virtually every walk of life and which is inordinately expensive on the taxpaying community to maintain for the questionable benefit of a small section of the population must be regularly reviewed in the interests of society as a whole and particularly in the interests of that community.

Such a lifestyle will always place those who participate in it at a disadvantage in terms of accessibility to health and educational services, job opportunities and general services like insurances, loans, mortgages etc. and these facts must be acknowledged by those who espouse it for themselves and for their children. A permanent base for young families would give the children opportunities in life very similar to those enjoyed by most settled children. The caravan has long been recognised as totally unsuitable for all year round habitation in the Irish climate and makes personal privacy in the home impossible particularly for large families. The 1983 Review Body Report also commented on this factor.

The traditional economic reasons for constant travelling have largely disappeared and there is significant evidence of less mobility by the traveller community. It is clear that as educational and health facilities are improved and better accommodation is provided, this trend will increase. Research carried out by the Task Force and verbal evidence from individual travellers confirm that such change is already underway. Further change will require co-operation from those travellers who up to now have resisted any change from their traditional practices, even to importing their rural economic activities into highly urbanised residential areas. It will mean allowing their culture and patterns of behaviour to adapt to new ways, but change is not a new phenomenon in Traveller culture for, by their very nature, they are a highly adaptable and resourceful people who have coped with many changes throughout the centuries.

It is not so many years ago since travellers were seen by most people as a skilful and colourful group of people travelling the roads of Ireland admired for their skills, services and trades who were of service to the settled community and who in this way, eked out a living without serious conflict with the general community. This picture is very different from the traveller way of life that we know today; travellers having been forced to change their ways in a rapidly changing society and coming more and more into conflict with the settled community. Thirty years ago nobody would have suggested that this change would take place in such a short space of time and to do so would have been seen as an attempt to undermine traveller culture. It should be possible to build on this change, which took place over such a relatively short period of time, to encourage further change to a different and better standard of accommodation for future generations of the traveller community. The change may be painful for some but many have already made the transition. In particular, there are many groups of traveller families in different locations around the country for whom group housing would provide this opportunity.

The vast majority of the settled community are appalled at the prospect of a traveller halting site next to them and the arrival of a group of travellers in an area usually provokes panic and fear among the settled community. There are a number of reasons for this reaction not least the investment made by individuals in their homes and the sacrifices that have to be made to support the investment and to give their families a better start in life. If the present desire of the majority of travellers to live apart continues into the future it is difficult to see how any local authority area can continue to meet the need for caravan sites. A decision to explore alternatives to the nomadic way of life would demonstrate to the settled community that future strategies will not be confined solely to the provision of caravan accommodation and ancillary services but will look also to creating an environment that will encourage travellers to assume their rightful place in society and to accept their responsibilities to their locality. In this way, current conflicts, tensions and opposition to travellers accommodation proposals might be reduced which could be helpful to more speedy implementation of accommodation programmes.

Part of the conflict is also due to the failure of travellers and traveller organisations to recognise that today's society finds it difficult to accept a lower standard of conduct from a section of the community who consciously pursue a way of life which sets its members apart from ordinary citizens, appear to expect that their way of life takes precedence over that of settled persons, and which carries no responsibility towards the area in which they happen to reside.

Excluding the area of housing, the costs of implementing the recommendations in the Report have not been estimated. It is, however, clear that major additional funding will be required to finance the implementation of the majority of the recommendations. As required by the Terms of Reference an estimate of cost has been calculated in relation to the cost of providing accommodation for the traveller community by the year 2000. This cost is estimated at £218m. If this figure is to be provided over a 5 year period 1996 - 2000, the requirement is £43.6m per annum, i.e. an annual increase of £28.6m over the expenditure incurred in 1994.

Included in the estimated cost is the proposal to develop a network of transient sites around the country (estimated cost £20m). This requirement is ancillary to the cost of providing permanent accommodation and is aimed at providing the traveller community with the option to continue to travel. As already stated, the traditional movement of travellers has been steadily declining over the last decade and for the majority of families this movement is now mainly confined to events like fairs, weddings and funerals. Nevertheless, the investment in transient sites is essential if the recurring scenes of conflict when a group of travellers arrive in an area are to be avoided.

This level of investment (£218m) in the provision and maintenance of accommodation will place a significant additional financial cost on the taxpaying community. The recommendations in the other areas of the Task Force's Report will add substantially to this cost. Everybody agrees that proper living conditions must be provided for all traveller families who require it as a matter of urgency and this objective must be pursued vigorously. However, the cost of the investment to meet the projected demand beyond the existing requirement must be a consideration in determining future Government policy. The level and cost of the public service is constantly being reviewed to improve standards and reduce costs. The service to the traveller community should be subjected to the same scrutiny.

All sections of the population have to adapt to the changing patterns of society. The publication of this Report is an opportune time to start a process of exploring ways and initiatives to accelerate the change away from a mainly nomadic existence. However, it must be recognised that the traveller community, in common with any marginalised minority, cannot make the transition to full citizenship unless the majority population, whose values society reflects, makes the space available for that transition to take place.

CLLR. GABRIEL CRIBBEN   DAN O'SULLIVAN
CLLR. JOAN MAHER   CLLR. CATHERINE QUINN

Appendix 1

List of Persons/Organisations Which
Forwarded Submissions to the Task Force

Area Committee for Travellers - Rowlagh
Association of Municipal Authorities of Ireland
Association of Teachers of Travelling People
A.S.T.I.
Athy Friends of the Travelling People

Barnardo's
Dr. Moosajee Bhamjee, T.D.
Mr. Robert Black
Mr. Hugh Byrne

Mr. Dermot Canning
Catholic Social Service Conference
Catholic Youth Council
Churchtown West Residents Association
Clarecare
Clondalkin Alliance of Residents and Tenants Associations
Clondalkin Travellers Development Group
Clonskeagh Residents Association
Ms. Madeline Connolly
Cork Co. Council (Southern Committee)
County and City Managers' Association

Dalkey Community Council
Mr. Paul Daly
Ms. Celia De Fréine
Mr. Jim Desmond
Dodder Residents Association

Ms. Mary Teresa English
Enniscorthy Urban District Council
Exchange House Family Support Service
Exchange House Horizon 1 & 2, Programmes 1994 (Participants in the)

Dr. Michael Fitzgerald
Mr. Michael P. Flynn
Ms. Sally Flynn
Focus Point
Mr. James Forbes
Mr. Maurice Wm. Foster

Mr. Michael Galvin
Galway Youth At Risk Project
General Council of County Councils

Mr. Patrick Hayes

I.N.T.O.
Irish Association of Social Workers (Special Interest Group on Travellers)

Mr. Michael Jeffares

Ms. Una Kavanagh
Kerry Diocesan Youth Service
Rev. Tomás King SSC and Sr. Rose Kelly RJM
Ms. Sara Kinsella

Ms. Joan Lahiff
Labour Party - Galway West
Longford Travellers Committee
Mr. A.C. Louwrens

Mr. Seamus Macken
Máire MacAongusa, Uas.
Mr. Michael McCullagh PC MIAVI
Rev. J. McGuinness SPS
Mount Merrion Residents' Association

National Parents Council - Primary
Teachers of Navan Travellers Training Centre
Newbridge Travellers Support Group
Sinéad Ní Shuinéar, Uas.

Ms Margaret Phelan
Progressive Democrats - Laois/Offaly

Sgt. Tim O'Leary
Seán O Riain, Uas.

Residents' Group, Westport, Co. Mayo.
Respect
Ms. Jocelyne Rigal
Roscrea Chamber of Commerce

Mr Duncan Sloan
Social Workers Group - Fingal Co. Council; South Co.Dublin
Society of St. Vincent de Paul - Dublin Regional Council
South Dublin Co. Council
St Colmcille's Travellers Workshop
St. Joseph's Training Centre

Tallaght Travellers Support Group
Tralee Horizon Partnership
Travellers and Speech and Language Therapy Working Party
Traveller Resource Centre - New Ross
Tullamore Travellers Movement

Appendix 2

List of Visits made by and of People/Organisations who met with the Task Force

Chairperson

CEO's, Health Boards
Clondalkin Residents' Association
Clondalkin Travellers Support Group
Dr. Tim Collins, Department of Health, Special Advisor to Minister for Health
Cork Corporation
County & City Managers' Association - Housing and Infrastructure Sub-Committee
Exchange House Horizon 1 & 2 Programmes, 1994 (Participants in)
Irish College of General Practitioners
Tallaght Travellers Support Group

Plenary Task Force
Ballinasloe Horse Fair
County and City Managers Association
Traveller Specific Accommodation in the Dublin area
Egan House and Traveller Specific Accommodation in Tuam
Limerick Co. Council
Ms. Lee MacCurtain, Psychological Service, Department of Education
Rathkeale (Representatives of Traveller and 'Settled' Communities)

Sub-Committee on Accommodation

Cork County Council Sub-Committee on Traveller Accommodation
Cork Traveller Visibility Group
Traveller Specific Accommodation in the Cork area

Sub-Committee on Education and Training

Ad Hoc Group of CEO's of VEC's
The Association of Teachers of Travelling People
Ms. Maugie Francis, National Education Officer for Travellers
ITM - Sub-Committee on Education
Representatives of staff of Junior Training Centres

Dublin   Pre-school, c/o St. Francis Junior National School, Priorswood, Coolock;
                 St. Joseph's Junior National School, Balcurris, Ballymun;
                 St. Francis Junior National School, Priorswood, Coolock;

Bray   St. Kieran's Special National School, Old Connaught Road;

Galway City   Holy Trinity Girls' National School;
                 Pre-School Hillside Community Centre;

Young Travellers' Training Centre Ltd., Sandy Road;
St. Brigid's Special School;
School Attendance Committee Mill Street Garda Station

Letterkenny   St. Fiachra's Senior Training Centre, Kilmacrennan Road
St. Gabriel's Pre-School for Traveller Children
St. Colmcille's Primary School

Sub-Committee on Health

Dr. Joe Barry, Eastern Health Board

Appendix 3

List of Researchers/Consultants*

Research Project: Paul Butler, Analysis and Operations Research Section, Department of Finance: "Accommodation Needs of Travellers in Galway, 1994 to 2000".

Paper: Brian J. Chesser and Co., Solicitors: "The Electoral Acts and Votes for Travellers".

Research Papers: Shaun Elder & Co., Solicitors: (a) "Perspectives and Recommendations on legislation relation to Accommodation, as relevant to the Travelling Community" (b) "How the system of "zoning" under the Planning Acts may be standardised; whether amendment to legislation is required."

Research Paper: Essex University: "Paper on International and United Kingdom Law relevant to the Protection of the Rights and Cultural Identity of the Travelling Community in Ireland".

Survey: Liam Keane (Member of Task Force): "Surveys of Local Authorities".

Paper: Mary Moriarty (Member of Task Force): "Traveller Education in Tuam".

Research Project: Nexus Research Co-Operative: "Report of National Study on the Travelling Community".

Paper: John O'Connell: "The Rights of the Traveller Child".

Research Paper: Lorna Ryan: "Policies and Strategies Targetting Indigenous Australians".

Paper: Julia Smith: "Traveller Participation in the Horse Trade".

Research Project: Social Policy Research Unit (UCC): "Co-ordination of Services by Statutory Bodies".

Research Project: Department of Health Promotion, (UCG) & Patricia McCarthy & Associates: "Health Service Provision for the Travelling Community in Ireland".

*The texts of these research projects/papers are published separately.

Appendix 4

Conferences and Lectures Attended by
Task Force Members/Secretariat

NESF - Plenary meeting of January '95 on "Equality Proofing Issues".

National Education Convention (facilitated by the National Parents Council - Primary)

DTEDG Health Conference, All Hallows, Drumcondra

Seminar: Resolving Public Disputes Through Mediation (Irish Times/Commercial Dispute Resolution Ltd.)

ATTP's Conference - 1993

ATTP's 21st Anniversary Conference - 1994 "Travellers and Education - Towards the 21st Century"

DTEDG Public Lecture by Prof. Alex J. Bittles - Consanguinity

Seminar on the Report of the Special Education Review Committee